By His Hands

A COLLECTION OF RECIPES AND INSPIRATION

First Presbyterian Day School
Macon, Georgia

The recipes in this book were submitted from the personal collections
of friends and family of First Presbyterian Day School. The Cookbook Committee
cannot attest to the origin or originality of any recipe printed herin.

Copies of *By His Hands* may be obtained by sending
$25.00 plus $5.00 shipping and handling to the address below or
by contacting First Presbyterian Day School.

First Presbyterian Day School
5671 Calvin Drive
Macon, Georgia   31210
478-477-6505
fpdcookbook@fpdmacon.org

Find us on f at:
By His Hands - FPD Cookbook

First Printing   October 2011

ISBN: 978-0-615-47737-4

Artwork by
Steve Penley

WIMMER
COOKBOOKS

A CONSOLIDATED GRAPHICS COMPANY

800.548.2537 wimmerco.com

 Printed in the USA

Table of Contents

About the School

First Presbyterian Day School has offered a Christ-centered college preparatory education since its inception in 1970.

Founded by a small group of church and community leaders and visionaries, the school has grown exponentially and now serves as a beacon of Christian education whose alumni now number more than 2,400. Our graduates are leaders in politics, medicine, law, education, the military, the arts and beyond.

One of the goals of the FPD faculty and staff is to impact the world by preparing our students for our nation's finest universities. We believe tomorrow's leaders should possess not only bright minds but also sound character.

Our faculty and staff are committed to these ideals as we seek to live out our mission statement: "To educate and equip students to change the world for God's glory."

We are grateful for the work of countless volunteers who gave of their time and talents to produce this cookbook.

About the Artist

Steve Penley is a world-renowned artist whose work graces the Federal Reserve Board, Washington, D.C., the World of Coca-Cola, the Georgia State Capitol, the 2004 G8 Summit Host Committee, Sea Island, Georgia and other prominent corporate and private collectors around the world.

Though his work includes landscapes and other still-life subjects, Penley is best known for painting iconic figures from history such as George Washington, Abraham Lincoln, Winston Churchill and Ronald Reagan.

Penley also has published three books of his work, *Penley* (Longstreet Press), *The Reconstruction of America* (Mercer Press) and his latest, *Ronald Reagan and the American Ideal* (Looking Glass Books).

He also illustrated *Vince Dooley's Garden* (John F. Blair Press), a book about the legendary football coach's passion for horticulture.

He is a 1983 graduate of First Presbyterian Day School in Macon.

For a more extensive biography on Steve Penley, visit www.penleyartco.com.

oreword

Jesus never refused an invitation to dinner. *By His Hands* is an invitation for you to enjoy the Lord's bountiful gifts of nourishment. In addition to a wonderful collection of recipes to nourish the body and satisfy the palate, thoughts, reflections and scriptures for your spiritual nourishment are included as well.

Everyday God invites us to spend time with Him through His Word and He also intends for us to enjoy the abundance of blessings that He has bestowed upon us here on Earth.

Food is a source of pleasure in many ways and is normally associated with fellowship and hospitality. The Bible describes the fellowship enjoyed by the first Christ followers in Acts 2:46 by saying, "Everyday they continued to meet together in the temple courts. They broke bread in their homes and ate together with glad and sincere hearts, praising God and enjoying the favor of all the people. And the Lord added to their number daily those who were being saved." We shouldn't be surprised that it was at a meal, His last, that Christ revealed, "I am the way, and the truth and the life. No one comes to the Father except through me." John 14:6

Our prayer in offering this cookbook to you is that you will not only enjoy and relish the time spent preparing the wonderful recipes, but that you will also receive blessings, pleasure and refreshment from the scripture and inspirations as well.

We can vouch for the goodness of each recipe and know that you will be delighted with every one that you try. Each recipe has been tested twice for clarity, accuracy and "deliciousness." Our recipe collections provide something for everyone, from the very sophisticated to the very simple for today's busy family. We know that *By His Hands* will become your new favorite cookbook and we hope you will challenge yourself to try every recipe included.

Jan Barry
Cookbook Chairman

Committee

Chairman

Jan Barry

Co-Chairmen

Lea Lisenby

Traci Johnson

Testing Chairman

Willa Ham

Design Coordinator

Ravonda Bargeron

Proofing

Deborah Combs, Chairman

Jan Barry

Art Barry

Lea Lisenby

Side Bar Editor

Beth Simmons

Business Manager

Leah Lee

Recipe Collection

Jan Barry

Marketing Chairperson

Carol Sawyer

Computer Input

Jan Barry

Lea Lisenby

Mary Boddy

Ravonda Bargeron

Traci Johnson

ontributors

We offer many heartfelt thanks to the countless volunteers who helped to make *By His Hands* a reality. A cookbook is only as good as its recipes, and thanks to all of the recipe contributions, we are confident that we have some of the best. Our only regret is that we were unable to use every recipe received due to space limitations and duplications. Please know that your submission was extremely appreciated and contributed greatly to the overall quality of our cookbook.

To the countless people who spent many hours testing and evaluating the recipes, writing, editing, compiling, proofing, marketing, and selling, we extend a very big thank you. Thanks as well to those whose efforts are yet to come as this book continues to be read and enjoyed for many years to come. To anyone whose name was inadvertently omitted, please accept our sincere apologies. To Lance and Cindy Souther, thank you for allowing us to use your house as a recipe drop point. Lastly, an extra special thank you goes to our families who have waited so patiently with us for this book to become a reality.

RECIPE CONTRIBUTORS AND TESTERS

Carol Souther Adams
Kathy Adams
Carol Albright
Cindy Allen
David Anderson
Penny Ballard
Robin Barfield
Ravonda Bargeron
Sally Barron
Mr. and Mrs. A.P. Barry, Sr.
Art Barry
Carolyn Barry
Jan Barry
Patrick Barry
Reid Barry
Russ Barry
Thayer Bates
David Battson
Donna Battson
Meg Adams Baxter
Tyler Beach
Katie Bird
Cissy Black
Donna Blizzard
Mary Boddy
Dana Bolles
Ruby Braswell
Deidre Bridges
Tammy Brittain
Tammie Brooks
Melissa Brown
Stella Patterson Brown
Penny Buckland

Kelly Bullington
Heather Burns
Kellie Burns
Laura Carlton
Stacy Carr
Sabrina Carter
April Cassel
Susan Causey
Michelle Chapman
Loray Childs
Jenny Clausen
Edward Cloaninger
Anne Cole
Betty Vann Collins
Jim Collins
Kathleen Collins
Laurie Colter
Debbie Combs
Amanda Cook
Beth Coon
Salita Cooper
Cassandra Cox
Teresa Crumpton
Jeanna Cundiff
Tammy Curtis
Kris Cutright
Amiee Dasher
Amy Davis
Jeanette Davis
Elaine Deckbar
Abby Deckbar
Natalie Deckbar
Kimbrough Donner

Susan Douglas
Margaret DuBose
Leigh Durham
Dr. Linda Brennan Easter
Karen Ennis
Renita Eversole
Scarlett Farr
Nancy Faulk
Michael Ferguson
Lagina Fillingim
Nina Fleming
Lorrie Floyd
Gina Foil
Saynor Foshee
Kellie Foster
Cheri Frame
Lisette Funk
Stephanie Gaither
Emily Garnett
Tee George
Kathleen Gettman
Kay Gilbert
Cheryl Goldin
Elise Goodson
Dr. William H. Goodson, Jr.
Lydia Gray
Connie Greene
Memorie Grice
Carol Griffin
Miranda Griggs
Kelley Hague
Carol Hall
Betty Ham

Rachel Ham
Sara S. Ham
Willa Ham
Jennie Hash
Dianne Hattaway
Kelli Heard
Barbara Henley
Bobbie Hester
Fred Hester
Margaret Hester
Tabitha Hinson
Kelli Hoffman
Kristy Holcomb
Melissa Hollingsworth
Holly Howard
Joy Howell
Paige Howell
Cynthia Huggins
Marilyn Hudgins
Emily Hulsey
Traci Humphries
Kim Hunnicutt
Donna Hyatt
Stacy Ingram
Ruby Jackson
Jill Amos Jauregui
Haviland Amos Jauregui
Lee Jimenez
Robert Jimenez
Amber Johnson
Traci Johnson
Heather Jones
Kaitlynn Jones
Sandra Jones
Tammy Jones
April Kitchell
Matt Kitchell
Flo Keys
Laura Kostovetsky
Jenny Kortrey
Cathy Knight
Susan Lack
Amy Lako
Judith Lamb
Brenda Lambert
Margaret Layton
Stephanie Leaptrot
Angela Leigh
Laura Lengel
Caroline Lisenby
Dr. Clay Lisenby
Elizabeth Lisenby
Lea Lisenby
Nancy Lisenby

Kathy Little
Connie Lockerman
Margaret Lyles
Ann McClure
Keene McClure
Beverley McCoy
Hazle McCraine
Gail McFarling
Judy McDonald
Kara McMickle
Jill McSwain
Courtney Markel
Debbie Markel
Cindy Martin
Patti C. Martin
Traci Martin
Irene Marxsen
Lori Mealor
Kim Meyer
Dawnita Moore
Susan Morgan
Johnny Morton
Amy Motorman
Lori Mullis
Kim Murray
Carole Myers
Nicki Leigh Neufeld
Terri Newberry
Dawn Newsome
Stephanie Neyman
Jean O'Dillon
Dave Osborne
Peggy Overman
Monni Parrish
Mary Parmater
Wanda Patrick
Lisa Patterson
Lynne Patterson
Betsy Peake
Molly Pearson
Shelly Pearson
Cindy Phillips
Gayle Putnal
Kay F. Putnal
Elizabeth Cloaninger Putnam
Terry Rabun
Kerry Reeves
Julie Renfroe
Robyn Robertson
Jeanne Roddenberry
Carrie Rogers
Ellen Royal
Pam Rule
Nate Rupp

Michelle Ryle
Lisa Saitow
Robin Sanders
Carol Sawyer
Ann Schultz
Holly Scott
Jeanne Scurry
Annie Ola Seagler
Scott Seman
Kay Sexton
Laurie Shealy
Beth Simmons
Marilyn Lisenby Skene
Gigi Slagle
Dorena Smith
Kelly Smith
Miriam Smith
Terri Smith
Lisa Spear
Cindy Souther
Lance Souther
Jacki Spivey
Sara Spivey
Christy Whitfield Spurlin
Joy Stanley
Caroline Stewart
Kristen Stone
Lucia Strickland
Nancy Stroud
Julie Suttles
Katelyn Sutton
Linda Sutton
Ruth Tate
Brigitte Terrell
Rana Thigpin
Vickie Thomas
Jessica Tillman
Judi Tillman
Stephanie Tinkey
Christy Trieste
Dorothy Turner
Kim Tyson
Bob Veazey
Nora Veazey
Victoria Vanhuss
Betty Wade
Jean Watkins
Lally Weaver
Julie Wheeler
Melissa White
Nancy White
Nan Williams
Tonya Wilson
Elaine Wright
Bobbye Wynne

APPETIZERS & BEVERAGES

"This is the day the Lord has made;
let us rejoice and be glad in it."

Psalm 118:24

APPETIZERS

Asiago Dip with Crostini, 11

Bacon Chestnuts, 11

Baked Corn Dip, 11

Black-Eyed Susans, 12

Cheese Fondue, 12

Buffalo Chicken Dip, 12

Cheese Dip in a Loaf, 13

Fried Asparagus with Creole Mustard Sauce, 13

Creole Mustard Sauce, 13

Green Olive Cheese Bites, 14

Stuffed Mushrooms, 14

Jalapeño Popper Spread, 14

Hot Crab and Artichoke Dip, 15

Mushroom Pâté, 15

Layered Pizza Dip, 15

Mushroom Croustades, 16

Peppy Party Appetizers, 16

Roasted Baby Potatoes, 17

Sausage and Cheese Pinwheels, 17

Spinach and Artichoke Dip, 18

Sea Island Dip, 18

Spinach and Bacon Dip, 18

Spinach Squares, 18

Sun-Dried Tomato and Pesto Torta, 19

Yummy, Yummy Cocktail Weenies, 19

Vidalia Onion Dip, 19

Tex-Mex Egg Rolls with Cilantro Dipping Sauce, 20

Creamy Cilantro Dipping Sauce, 20

Bleu Cheese Ball, 21

Daddy Bill's Cheese Straws, 21

Pineapple and Cream Cheese Ball, 21

Tabbouleh, 22

Pimento Cheese, 22

Chocolate Chip Ball, 23

Tomato Sandwiches, 23

Chunky Guacamole, 23

Homemade Tomato Salsa, 24

Peach Salsa, 24

Mango Salsa, 24

Sassy Bean Salsa, 25

Apple Dip, 25

Ultimate Salsa, 25

Feta Dip, 26

Cucumber Dip, 26

Enchilada Dip, 26

Grilled Pita Triangles, 26

BEVERAGES

Frosted Orange Slush, 27

Frosty Basil Lemonade, 27

Glorious Punch, 27

Sherbet Ring, 27

Nanee's Boiled Custard, 28

Tangerine Spritzers, 28

White Grape and Orange Cooler, 28

Honey and Ginger Green Tea, 29

Hot Chocolate Mix, 29

Hot Wassail, 30

Hot Winter Spiced Tea, 30

Mocha Coffee Punch, 30

Asiago Dip with Crostini

¾   cup mayonnaise
½   cup thinly sliced green onions
½   cup plus 2 tablespoons grated Asiago cheese, divided

¼   cup sun-dried tomatoes, chopped
1   (8 ounce) carton sour cream
¼   cup chopped mushrooms (optional)

Preheat oven to 350°. Mix mayonnaise, onion, ½ cup cheese, tomatoes and sour cream in a bowl. Spoon into a 1 quart baking dish. Sprinkle with remainder of cheese. Bake 30 minutes or until bubbly.

Serve warm with toasted slices of French bread or crackers.

Bacon Chestnuts

2   (8 ounce) cans water chestnuts, whole
2   pounds bacon, slices cut in half

½   cup sugar
¾   cup ketchup
½   cup light brown sugar

Preheat oven to 350°. Wrap bacon around water chestnut. Secure with toothpick. Place on cookie sheet lined with foil. Bake 30 to 40 minutes or until bacon becomes brown. Transfer to baking dish. Mix sugar, ketchup and brown sugar. Pour over water chestnuts. Bake 25 minutes.

"*I* know that nothing is better for them than to rejoice, and to do good in their lives, and also that every man should eat and drink and enjoy the good of all his labor–it is the gift of God."

Ecclesiastes 3:12

Baked Corn Dip

1   (14½ ounce) can fiesta style Mexican corn
1   cup mayonnaise
1   cup Monterey Jack cheese

½   cup shredded Parmesan cheese
    Chopped jalapeño peppers to taste

Preheat oven to 350°. Mix all ingredients together and bake 30 minutes.

Serve warm with tortilla or pita chips.

Black-Eyed Susans

2 sticks unsalted butter, softened	½ teaspoon cayenne pepper
1 pound grated extra sharp Cheddar cheese	2 (8 ounce) boxes pitted dates, halved lengthwise
2 cups all-purpose flour	Sugar

Preheat oven to 300°. Blend butter and cheese. Add flour and pepper to form dough. Chill if sticky. Roll ½ tablespoon dough around date half. Place on nonstick baking sheet. Bake 25 to 30 minutes. Sprinkle with sugar while hot. Serve warm or at room temperature.

To freeze, place unbaked dates on cookie sheet. Freeze and place in zip-top plastic bag in freezer until ready to serve.

BUFFALO CHICKEN DIP

3 cups cooked chicken, shredded (about 4 breasts)

1 (8 ounce) package cream cheese, softened

½ cup ranch dressing

1½ cups shredded Cheddar cheese

¾ cup hot wing sauce

Preheat oven to 350°. Cook and shred chicken. Mix cream cheese and ranch dressing. Combine with chicken and Cheddar cheese. Add hot wing sauce to taste. Bake until bubbly.

Serve with taco chips.

Cheese Fondue

1 large clove garlic	Dash ground mustard
1 (12 ounce) can flat beer	1 pound Cheddar cheese (or ½ Swiss and ½ Gouda)
3 tablespoons all-purpose flour	
¾ teaspoon pepper	1 loaf French bread
Splash of Tabasco sauce	Cubed carrots
Pinch of salt	Broccoli florets

Rub garlic inside of fondue pot. Mince garlic. Stir together a small amount of beer and all the flour to make a paste in a heavy pan on stove. Add garlic. Add rest of beer, pepper, Tabasco, salt and mustard. Heat over medium heat and slowly add cheese until it is melted. Transfer to the fondue pot and serve with bread and vegetables.

Cheese Dip in a Loaf

4   cups grated sharp Cheddar cheese
2   (8 ounce) packages cream cheese
3   packages corned beef, chopped
1   tomato, chopped
¾   cup chopped bell pepper, (optional)
1   tablespoon Tabasco sauce
1   teaspoon chili powder
½   teaspoon black pepper
1   round French bread or Boule

Preheat oven to 350°. Combine all ingredients in a bowl. Hollow out a French bread loaf or Boule. Fill with mixture. Bake 40 minutes.

Fried Asparagus with Creole Mustard Sauce

1   pound fresh asparagus
1   cup all-purpose flour
1   cup whole buttermilk
1   tablespoon hot sauce
1   large egg
1½ cups self-rising cornmeal mix
1   tablespoon Cajun seasoning
    Peanut oil for frying
    Creole Mustard Sauce (recipe in sidebar)

Snap off tough ends of asparagus. Rinse asparagus with water and leave damp. Place flour in a large zip-top plastic bag. Add asparagus, seal and shake to coat. In a shallow dish whisk together buttermilk, hot sauce and egg.

In another shallow dish combine cornmeal and Cajun seasoning. Dip asparagus in buttermilk mixture then dredge in cornmeal mixture.

In a large Dutch oven, pour oil to a depth of 2 inches. Heat oil over medium heat to 365°. Fry asparagus in batches for 4 to 5 minutes or until golden brown. Drain on paper towels. Serve immediately with Creole Mustard Sauce.

Makes 12 to 15 servings

CREOLE MUSTARD SAUCE

⅔ cup sour cream

3 tablespoons Creole mustard

1½ teaspoons dry ranch dressing mix

1 teaspoon fresh lemon juice

¼ teaspoon Creole seasoning

¼ teaspoon onion powder

¼ teaspoon garlic powder

Garnish: parsley leaf

In a small bowl, combine sour cream, Creole mustard, dressing mix, lemon juice, Creole seasoning, onion powder and garlic powder. Cover and chill up to three days. Garnish with parsley, if desired.

Green Olive Cheese Bites

48	small pimento stuffed green olives	1	cup flour
½	pound sharp Cheddar cheese, grated	½	teaspoon salt
		1	teaspoon paprika
½	cup butter, softened		Cayenne to taste

Preheat oven to 400°. Drain olives and dry thoroughly. Blend cheese and butter. Sift together salt, flour, paprika and cayenne. Combine with cheese and butter mixture. Wrap teaspoon size amounts of dough around each olive. Bake on an ungreased cookie sheet 15 minutes.

Yields 4 dozen

Stuffed Mushrooms

3	(8 ounce) packages fresh baby bella mushrooms, wiped clean	2	tablespoons Dijon mustard
		1	tablespoon lemon zest
2	tablespoons butter	1	teaspoon dried tarragon
1	(5 ounce) package prosciutto, chopped	1	teaspoon freshly ground black pepper
⅓	cup minced fresh chives		Garnish with chopped fresh parsley
2	(8 ounce) packages cream cheese, softened		

Preheat oven to 350°. Remove stems from mushrooms. Finely chop enough mushroom stems to equal ⅓ cup. Discard remaining mushroom stems.

In a large skillet, melt butter over medium heat. Add prosciutto, chives and chopped mushroom stems.

Cook, stirring frequently, for 6 minutes or until prosciutto is crisp and mushrooms are tender. Reduce heat to low. Add cream cheese, mustard, lemon zest, tarragon and pepper. Stirring until mixture is combined. Remove from heat.

Spoon cream cheese mixture into mushroom caps. Place on a rimmed baking sheet. Bake 20 minutes. Garnish with chopped fresh parsley, if desired. Serve immediately.

Mushrooms can be stuffed up to two days ahead and stored in the refrigerator. Bake before serving.

Makes about 3 dozen mushrooms

JALAPEÑO POPPER SPREAD

2 (8 ounce) packages cream cheese, softened

1 cup mayonnaise

1 (4 ounce) can chopped green chilies, drained

1 (2 ounce) can diced jalapeño peppers, drained

1 cup grated Parmesan cheese

Mix cream cheese and mayonnaise in a large bowl until smooth. Stir in green chilies and jalapeño peppers. Pour mixture into a microwave-safe serving dish and sprinkle with Parmesan cheese. Microwave on high 3 minutes or until hot.

OR

Bake 20 minutes at 325°.

Serve with tortilla chips.

Hot Crab and Artichoke Dip

1 (8 ounce) package cream cheese, softened
2 cups mayonnaise
1 package imitation crab
1 (8½ ounce) can artichoke hearts, drained and chopped
1 medium onion, chopped
¾ cup grated Parmesan cheese

Preheat oven to 350°. Mix cream cheese and mayonnaise until smooth. Shred crabmeat. Add artichoke hearts, onion and Parmesan cheese. Pour mixture into a lightly greased baking dish. Bake 20 to 30 minutes, until bubbly.

May use crab and shrimp.

Serve with toasted party bread or Parmesan toast.

Mushroom Pâté

2½ tablespoons butter
1 pound white mushrooms, sliced
1 medium onion, chopped
2 large cloves garlic, pressed
2 tablespoons white wine
1 (8 ounce) package cream cheese, softened
½ teaspoon salt
¼ teaspoon freshly ground black pepper
1-2 teaspoons dried thyme to taste

Melt butter in a large skillet over medium-high heat. Add mushrooms, onions and garlic. Sauté for about 10 minutes until liquid is evaporated. Add wine and cook, stirring occasionally until evaporated. Let cool slightly.

Place in food processor. Add cream cheese, salt and pepper and pulse until blended. Put thyme in mixture and pulse a few times. Pack into small crocks or ramekins. Cover and refrigerate until chilled, up to five days.

To serve, let pâté sit at room temperature for about 15 minutes. Serve with plain crackers.

LAYERED PIZZA DIP

1 (8 ounce) package cream cheese, softened

½ cup sour cream

½ cup freshly grated Parmesan cheese

½ teaspoon garlic salt

¾ cup prepared pizza sauce

¾ cup shredded mozzarella cheese

1 (3½ ounce) package pepperoni, finely chopped

Preheat oven to 350°. Beat cream cheese until fluffy. Stir in sour cream, Parmesan cheese and garlic salt. Spread into lightly greased (9 inch) pie plate. Spread pizza sauce over cheese. Sprinkle with mozzarella cheese and top with pepperoni. Bake 20 minutes.

Serve with toasted pita bread wedges or tortilla chips.

Mushroom Croustades

2	tablespoons butter, softened	1	cup heavy cream
24	thin slices fresh bread (*Sunbeam)	½	teaspoon salt
3	tablespoons finely chopped red onion	⅛	teaspoon cayenne pepper
½	pound mushrooms, finely chopped	1	tablespoon chopped fresh parsley
4	tablespoons butter	1½	tablespoons chopped fresh chives
2	tablespoons flour	½	teaspoon fresh lemon juice
		¼	cup grated Parmesan cheese

Preheat oven to 400°. With a pastry brush, coat the inside of 24 muffin tins with 2 tablespoons butter. Using a 3 inch round or fluted cookie cutter, cut center out of bread. Carefully fit the bread into the muffin tins, pushing the center of the bread into the well and gently molding it around the bottom of the tin. Bake croustades 6 to 10 minutes until lightly brown on the rims. Remove from tins and allow to cool on rack. At this point the croustades will freeze well if preparing for a later date.

For the filling, melt 4 tablespoons of butter in a frying pan, add onions and sauté for about 4 minutes. Do not brown. Stir in mushrooms and cook until all moisture is evaporated, about 10 minutes. Remove the pan from the heat. Sprinkle flour evenly over mixture and mix well. Pour cream into mixture and bring to a boil, stirring continuously until thickened. Remove from heat and add salt, cayenne, parsley, chives and lemon juice. Arrange croustades on a cookie sheet and pack with filling. Sprinkle with Parmesan cheese and bake at 350° 8 to 10 minutes, until heated through.

Peppy Party Appetizers

1	pound sage sausage	1	loaf small square party rye bread
1	pound lean ground beef		
1	pound processed cheese loaf		

Preheat oven to 400°. Brown sausage. Drain and pat dry. Brown ground beef; drain and pat dry. Cut cheese into cubes and melt in small pan over low heat. Mix well. Place rye bread on baking sheet and spread about 1 tablespoon of mixture onto each piece. Bake until bubbly.

Roasted Baby Potatoes

16 tiny red thin-skinned potatoes (about 2 inches in diameter), scrubbed

Preheat oven to 375°. Pierce each potato in several places and place on lined baking sheet. Bake about 30 to 40 minutes, until tender, let cool. Cut each potato in half and slice off the bottoms so potato can stand upright. Scoop small cavity in each half about ½ inch deep. Place on rimmed baking sheet.

TOPPING
½ cup grated Parmesan cheese or Asiago

½ cup mayonnaise

2 tablespoons diced green onions

Paprika

Mix together cheese, mayonnaise and onions. Spoon or pipe into each potato cavity. Return to oven until warm. Sprinkle with paprika.

Sausage and Cheese Pinwheels

1 (8 ounce) can refrigerated crescent roll dough

1 pound hot sausage, room temperature

2 cups grated sharp Cheddar cheese

Place dough on wax paper, being careful not to separate. Smooth out seams to form a large rectangle, gently pulling dough as needed (about 18x4 inches). Carefully spread the sausage in an even layer over the dough. Sprinkle cheese evenly over the sausage. Roll the dough lengthwise to form a long roll. Wrap in wax paper and place in freezer at least 15 minutes. Preheat oven to 350°. Cut dough into ½ inch slices, using a serrated knife. Place on ungreased baking sheet. Bake 15 to 20 minutes or until sausage is cooked through. Drain off any juices. Serve hot. Refrigerate leftovers.

SPINACH SQUARES

1 (10 ounce) package
frozen chopped
spinach

2 eggs

1 (8 ounce) carton
sour cream

1 tablespoon
grated onion

½ cup Parmesan
cheese

1 tablespoon flour

2 tablespoons butter

1 teaspoon salt

⅛ teaspoon pepper

Preheat oven to 350°.
Cook spinach according
to directions. Drain
well. Beat eggs and add
to spinach. Blend in
sour cream, onion,
Parmesan cheese, flour,
butter, salt and pepper.
Pour mixture into
a lightly greased
9x9 inch baking dish.
Bake uncovered for
23 to 30 minutes. Cut
in squares to serve.

Spinach and Artichoke Dip

10	ounces frozen spinach, thawed and squeezed	½	cup sour cream
1	(14 ounce) can artichoke hearts, drained and chopped	¾	cup mayonnaise
1	pound pepper jack cheese, grated	⅛	teaspoon salt
		⅛	teaspoon garlic powder
		⅛	teaspoon white pepper

Preheat oven to 350°. Mix all ingredients. Pour into a greased ovenproof glass baking dish and bake until bubbly, about 20 to 30 minutes.

Sea Island Dip

1   (8½ ounce) can artichokes

1   cup mayonnaise

1   cup grated Parmesan cheese

4   teaspoons lemon juice

½   onion, chopped (or less)

Garlic salt (optional)

Preheat oven to 375°. Mix artichokes, mayonnaise, cheese, lemon juice, onion and a dash of garlic salt. Bake 15 to 20 minutes.

Serve with crackers.

Spinach and Bacon Dip

3   (8 ounce) packages cream cheese, softened

1   pound bacon, cooked and crumbled

1   (10 ounce) package frozen chopped spinach, thawed and squeezed dry

1   medium onion, chopped

1   (5 ounce) package shredded Parmesan cheese

1   cup shredded mozzarella cheese

½   cup mayonnaise

Preheat oven to 350°. In a medium bowl, combine cream cheese, bacon, spinach, onions, cheeses and mayonnaise. Spoon mixture into a 2 quart baking dish. Bake 30 minutes or until hot and bubbly.

Serve with corn chips.

Sun-Dried Tomato and Pesto Torta

20 ounces cream cheese
1½ sticks butter
5 ounces goat cheese
6 large fresh basil leaves
16 ounces provolone cheese, sliced thinly

¾-1 cup pesto
12 sun-dried tomatoes, packed in oil and drained
⅓ cup pine nuts, lightly toasted

Line a loaf pan with double thickness cheesecloth or spray pan with cooking spray. Line with plastic wrap and spray again. Beat softened cream cheese, butter and goat cheese until smooth.

To assemble: Place basil leaves on bottom. Put a thin layer of provolone slices on top of basil. Spread layer of cheese mixture, then pesto. Continue layering until all ingredients are gone. Top with sun-dried tomatoes and pine nuts.

Cover last layer with plastic wrap and press with the palm of hand to compress layers. Refrigerate overnight. When ready to serve, remove the cheesecloth or plastic wrap from the top and unmold onto a serving platter. Arrange crackers or freshly sliced French bread around the torta.

Prepare 24 hours in advance.

Can keep a week in refrigerator.

Nice to slice and wrap to give as a gift with a spreader.

Yummy, Yummy Cocktail Weenies

3 packages original bacon
3 packages cocktail weenies

Wooden toothpicks
2 boxes dark brown sugar

Preheat oven to 350°. Cut the bacon into thirds and discard the fatty parts of the bacon. Wrap the cocktail weenies in bacon and secure with a toothpick. Divide the weenies between two disposable aluminum pans. Pour 1 box dark brown sugar over weenies in each pan. Cover with aluminum foil and cook for 30 minutes and then uncover and cook 30 to 40 more minutes.

Using disposable aluminum pans helps with the clean up; however, you may use glass casserole dishes.

This recipe may be halved for less weenies.

5 Vidalia onions, chopped

3 (8 ounce) packages cream cheese, softened

3 cups shredded Parmesan cheese

½ cup mayonnaise

Preheat oven to 350°. Mix onions, cream cheese, Parmesan cheese and mayonnaise. Bake 15 to 25 minutes, until bubbly. Serve hot.

Recipe may be cut in half for smaller quantity.

Serve with corn chips, crackers or pita chips.

Tex-Mex Egg Rolls
with Cilantro Dipping Sauce

1   (5 ounce) package yellow rice

1   teaspoon salt

1   pound ground hot pork sausage, cooked and drained

1   (14½ ounce) can black beans, rinsed and drained

1   (14½ ounce) can Mexican-style diced tomatoes, undrained

2   cups shredded Monterey Jack cheese

6   green onions, finely chopped

1   package taco seasoning

28 egg roll wrappers

1   large egg, lightly beaten

4   cups peanut oil
    Garnish with fresh cilantro sprigs
    Creamy Cilantro Dipping Sauce

Cook rice according to package directions, using 1 teaspoon salt. Cool completely. Stir together rice, sausage, black beans, tomatoes, cheese, onions and taco seasoning in a large bowl. Spoon ⅓ cup rice mixture into center of each egg roll wrapper. Fold top corner of wrapper over filling, tucking tip of corner under filling. Fold left and right corners over filling. Lightly brush remaining corner with egg. Tightly roll filled end toward the remaining corner, and gently press to seal. Pour oil into a heavy Dutch oven, heat to 375°. Fry egg rolls in batches 2 to 3 minutes or until golden. Drain on wire rack over paper towels. Serve with Creamy Cilantro Dipping Sauce. Garnish with fresh cilantro, if desired.

These are just as good as the ones at California Pizza Kitchen.

Makes 28 egg rolls

Creamy Cilantro Dipping Sauce

2   (10 ounce) cans Mexican-style diced tomatoes, undrained

1   (8 ounce) package cream cheese, softened

2   cups loosely packed fresh cilantro leaves (1 bunch)

1   cup sour cream

3   garlic cloves, minced

Place tomatoes, cream cheese, cilantro, sour cream and garlic in food processor and blend until smooth.

Makes 3 cups

"Awake, late and harp. I will awaken the dawn."

Psalm 108:2

APPETIZERS

Bleu Cheese Ball

1	(8 ounce) carton cream cheese, softened	1	tablespoon Worcestershire sauce
5	ounces grated sharp Cheddar cheese	1	small clove garlic, pressed
3	ounces bleu cheese or Roquefort	½	cup chopped parsley
		½	cup chopped pecans

Mix cream cheese, Cheddar, Roquefort, Worcestershire sauce, garlic, and 2 tablespoons parsley. Chill until firm. Shape into a ball. Roll in nuts and parsley. Chill overnight.

Serve with crackers or thinly sliced cucumbers.

Daddy Bill's Cheese Straws

¾	stick margarine	2	cups all-purpose flour
1	pound extra sharp Cheddar cheese	1	teaspoon salt
		¾	teaspoon cayenne pepper

Preheat oven to 375°. Leave margarine and cheese out for 8 hours to soften. Mix margarine, cheese, flour, salt and cayenne pepper. Push through small star shaped cookie press onto ungreased cookie sheet. Cut into desired lengths. Bake 16 to 22 minutes, until slightly brown. Watch closely. Cool on wire rack. Store in airtight container.

May increase cayenne pepper to 1 teaspoon for hot cheese straws.

May sprinkle with paprika, if desired.

Freezes well.

PINEAPPLE AND CREAM CHEESE BALL

2 (8 ounce) packages cream cheese, softened

2 tablespoons chopped onion

1 (8 ounce) can crushed pineapple, drained

1 large bell pepper, chopped

1½ cups chopped pecans

Mix cream cheese, onion, pineapple and bell pepper. Shape mixture into a ball. Roll in pecans. Chill until firm.

Tabbouleh

1	cup boiling water	1-2	large tomatoes, diced
½	cup cracked wheat (bulgur)	½	cup lemon juice
2	large bunches parsley, finely chopped	½	cup olive oil
2	bunches spring onions, chopped	2	cloves pressed garlic (optional)
1	large cucumber, diced		Salt and pepper

Pour boiling water over bulgur, let stand. Pick parsley leaves from stalks. Wash and squeeze in paper towels to remove all water. Chop finely. Add onions, cucumber, tomatoes, lemon juice, oil, garlic, salt and pepper to taste. Strain water from bulgur and add to mixture, toss well. Refrigerate at least 1 hour before serving.

Store leftovers in tightly sealed jar.

"*My* father was from Lebanon and prepared Tabbouleh often. The garlic adds a Mediterranean flavor. The dish is most delightful with homegrown tomatoes in midsummer!"

~Laura Lengal

Pimento Cheese

1	(8 ounce) package grated sharp Cheddar cheese	1	heaping tablespoon finely diced pickled jalapeños
1	(8 ounce) package grated medium Cheddar cheese	1	teaspoon curry powder
1	(8 ounce) package cream cheese, softened	½	teaspoon salt
1	(4 ounce) jar pimentos, reserve 1 teaspoon juice	¼	teaspoon pepper
		½-¾	cup mayonnaise

Mix cheeses, pimentos, reserved juice, jalapeños, curry powder, salt, pepper and mayonnaise until very spreadable.

May use more mayonnaise for creamier pimento cheese. Just keep adding mayonnaise until it is very spreadable.

Buy a good cheese and grate it yourself.

Chocolate Chip Ball

1 (8 ounce) package cream cheese, softened
½ cup butter, softened
¾-1 cup powdered sugar
2 tablespoons brown sugar
¼ teaspoon vanilla
6 ounces mini semisweet chocolate chips
½ cup chopped pecans

Blend cream cheese and butter. Mix sugars, vanilla and chocolate chips into cheese and butter. Chill until firm. Shape mixture into a ball. Chill again and roll in chopped pecans.

Serve with graham cracker sticks.

Tomato Sandwiches

1 (8 ounce) package cream cheese, softened
½ teaspoon mayonnaise
½ teaspoon seasoning salt
Juice of one lemon
1 cup coarsely chopped pecans
Freshly ground black pepper to taste
1 loaf Roman Meal Bread, or any whole wheat bread
6 small tomatoes, thinly sliced
Dried parsley

Mix cream cheese with ½ teaspoon mayonnaise or enough for cream cheese to be spreading consistency. Add seasoning salt, lemon juice and pecans. Add a dash of freshly ground black pepper.

Cut bread into 2 inch rounds using a cookie cutter or small juice glass. Cut a corresponding number of crescent shapes using the same cookie cutter or glass. Spread rounds with cream cheese mixture and sprinkle with a little more seasoning salt and dried parsley. Place tomato on top of mixture, then top with crescent shapes, allowing part of the tomato to show. Refrigerate prior to serving.

CHUNKY GUACAMOLE

1 medium tomato, diced

2 ripe avocados

2 tablespoons lemon juice

1 teaspoon salt

½ small onion, minced

1 small clove garlic, minced

1 (4 ounce) can chopped mild green chilies, drained

Peel and dice tomato. Cut avocado lengthwise. Peel and remove pit. Mash avocado. Mix in lemon juice, stir. Add tomatoes, salt, onion, garlic and chilies.

Serve with chips.

Homemade Tomato Salsa

1   (14½ ounce) can diced
    tomatoes
1   (10 ounce) can original
    tomatoes with chilies
1   small onion, coarsely chopped

1   large bunch cilantro, coarsely
    chopped
    Dash garlic salt
    Juice of one lemon or lime
    Salt and pepper to taste
    Sour cream (optional)

Combine tomatoes, onion, cilantro, garlic salt, pepper and lemon juice into a blender. Pulse 4 or 5 times until mixed well, not creamy.

Serve with chips.

Goes well with a bowl of sour cream on the side.

For a kick, may substitute hot tomatoes with chilies for original tomatoes with chilies. Beware, this is really hot, but oh so good!

MANGO SALSA

3 ripe mangoes,
peeled and chopped

2 tablespoons diced
red onion

¼ cup red
bell pepper

¼ cup chopped
cilantro

3 tablespoons
lime juice

1 tablespoon
chopped jalapeño

Combine mangoes,
onion, bell pepper,
cilantro, lime juice and
jalapeño in bowl. Mix
well. Refrigerate
until chilled.

Serve with corn chips.

Peach Salsa

1   large sweet onion, chopped
1   jalapeño pepper, seeded and
    minced
¼   cup sugar
2   tablespoons grated fresh
    ginger
2   tablespoons olive oil

6   large firm peaches, peeled
    and chopped
¼   cup fresh lemon juice
¼   teaspoon salt
2   tablespoons chopped fresh
    cilantro

Sauté onion, pepper, sugar and ginger in hot oil in a large skillet over medium heat for 5 minutes or until onions are tender. Stir in peaches and remaining ingredients, and cook, stirring gently for 5 minutes. Serve warm or at room temperature. Store leftovers in an airtight container in the refrigerator up to 2 days.

Sassy Bean Salsa

1 (14½ ounce) can black beans, drained
1 (14½ ounce) can shoepeg corn, drained
1 bunch spring onions, chopped
¼ cup sugar
¼ cup balsamic vinegar
¼ cup olive oil
Garlic salt to taste
1 (6 ounce) container feta cheese

Combine beans, corn and chopped onions. Set aside. Mix together sugar, vinegar, olive oil and garlic salt. Pour marinade over bean mixture and top with feta cheese. Serve immediately.

On New Year's Eve, double the recipe and substitute a can of black-eyed peas for good luck! This is a crowd pleaser!

Apple Dip

2 (8 ounce) packages cream cheese, softened
1 bag Heath Bits 'O Brickle
1 cup granulated sugar
½ cup light brown sugar
1 teaspoon vanilla flavoring
2 large cans pineapple juice
5 pounds apples, sliced ⅛ inch thick

Add brickle, sugars and vanilla flavoring to cream cheese and mix well. Stir well. Keep refrigerated. Place apple slices in pineapple juice to keep apples from discoloring until serving.

1 (28 ounce) can whole peeled tomatoes, drained

1 (14½ ounce) can stewed tomatoes, drained

1 tablespoon freshly chopped parsley

3-4 green onions, chopped

2 tablespoons red wine vinegar

Salt and pepper to taste

Lime juice to taste

2-4 jalapeños from a jar

Diced cilantro (optional)

Combine all ingredients in a food processor. Blend well.

Serve with tortilla chips.

Feta Dip

1 (8 ounce) container feta cheese
1 (8 ounce) container cream cheese, softened

1 teaspoon dill
1 teaspoon garlic powder
1 teaspoon onion salt

In medium bowl, blend feta and cream cheese. It will be lumpy. Add dill, garlic powder and onion salt. Mix well.

May serve cold or room temperature.

Great as a cold dip and also very good on meat.

Cucumber Dip

5 small cucumbers, unpeeled
½ cup rice vinegar
1 teaspoon kosher salt
1 teaspoon garlic salt, divided

2 (8 ounce) packages cream cheese, softened
½ cup mayonnaise
2 teaspoons chopped fresh chives

Grate cucumbers into a medium bowl. Toss with rice vinegar, salt and ½ teaspoon garlic salt. Cover and chill 8 hours. Drain well, pressing between two paper towels. Beat cream cheese, mayonnaise and remaining ½ teaspoon garlic salt at medium speed with an electric mixer until smooth. Stir in cucumber mixture and chives. Cover and chill 1 hour.

Serve with pita chips. Also great as a sandwich spread.

Enchilada Dip

1 pound ground beef
1 (8 ounce) processed cheese loaf

1 (8 ounce) container cream cheese
1 can enchilada sauce

Brown beef and drain. Add cheeses and enchilada sauce. Heat until cheese melts.

Serve hot with corn chips.

GRILLED PITA TRIANGLES

4 (6 inch) pita bread rounds, cut into quarters

1 tablespoon vegetable oil

Preheat grill to medium-high heat. Brush each side of bread with vegetable oil. Grill bread, covered with grill lid, for 2 to 3 minutes per side or until grill marks begin to form on bread.

Makes 8 servings

Frosted Orange Slush

1   (6 ounce) can frozen orange   1   cup water
     juice concentrate   1   cup milk
½   cup sugar   1   teaspoon vanilla extract

Pour all ingredients into a blender and fill remainder of blender with ice. Blend until smooth.

Makes 4 to 5 cups

Frosty Basil Lemonade

3   cups water   ½   cup fresh basil leaves
1½   lemons, peeled, halved seeded   1   cup ice cubes
¼   cup sugar or sweetener of
     choice (may use honey)

Place all ingredients into a blender. Blend on high for 1 minute.

May garnish with a fresh basil sprig or lemon wedge, if desired.

Glorious Punch

1   (46 ounce) can pineapple   1   (8 ounce) jar maraschino
     juice   cherries, undrained
2   (6 ounce) cans lemonade   2   oranges, sliced
     concentrate   1   quart ginger ale, chilled
4   cups cranapple juice

Combine pineapple juice, lemonade, cranapple juice, cherries and orange slices in large bowl; chill. Add ginger ale just before serving.

Red food coloring may be added for color.

SHERBET RING

1 pint raspberry
sherbet

1 pint lemon sherbet

2 cups cranberry juice

Place scoops of sherbet
in bottom of ring mold.
Pour cranberry juice
over sherbet and freeze.

*1 quart of mixed fruit
may be added, if desired.*

This glorious punch is a refreshing treat on a hot summer afternoon. The raspberry sherbet mold is pretty and refreshing. Edible flowers add a beautiful touch to the frozen ice ring.

White Grape and Orange Cooler

⅓ cup sugar

1 cup water

1 cup
white grape juice

½ cup orange juice

1 (1 liter) bottle
ginger ale, chilled

Ice

Garnish with
orange slices

Bring sugar and 1 cup water to a boil over medium-high heat and cook, stirring often 3 minutes or longer or until sugar dissolves. Remove from heat, cool. Stir in grape and orange juice. Chill 2 hours. Stir in ginger ale just before serving. Serve over ice. Garnish, if desired, with orange slices.

Tangerine Spritzers

1	quart tangerine juice	Sliced oranges or maraschino cherries for garnish, optional
1	liter grapefruit juice or lemon-lime flavored carbonated soda	

Chill tangerine juice and soda. Combine in 2 quart pitcher. Garnish with orange slices or cherries if desired.

Makes 8 to 10 servings

Nanee's Boiled Custard

1	scant teaspoon flour		1	quart whole milk
⅓	cup sugar		1	tablespoon vanilla or
4	eggs			4 teaspoons almond extract
	Pinch of salt			

Mix flour and sugar together. Mix eggs, sugar/flour mixture and salt in a bowl. Beat together well.

Scald milk. (Let milk turn barely to skim on top and bubbles on side, not to a boil.) Add to egg mixture and stir. Strain mixture through a sieve and return to boiler (after washing boiler). Stir constantly on medium heat until custard thickens (no more than 5 minutes). Remove from heat. Add vanilla or almond extract. Pour into container and cool.

This boiled custard is meant to be served cold.

As soon as thickening begins, remove from heat. It can be as little as two minutes. Don't be afraid to try this recipe using almond or rum flavoring instead of the traditional vanilla extract.

> "This is a wonderful winter beverage that is part custard and part heaven. What beautiful, wonderful memories this custard brings, as we remember our sweet Nanee, who served this with lots of love."
>
> *~Jan and Art Barry*

Honey and Ginger Green Tea

1 (1 inch) piece fresh ginger, peeled
1 regular-sized green tea bag
1 tablespoon fresh lemon juice
2 tablespoons honey
1 cup boiling water

Grate ginger, using the large holes of a box grater, to equal 1 tablespoon. Squeeze juice from ginger into a teacup, discard solids. Place tea bag, lemon juice and honey in teacup. Add boiling water. Cover, steep 3 minutes. Remove and discard tea bag, squeezing gently.

Makes 1 cup

Hot Chocolate Mix

5 (1 quart) envelopes instant dry milk powder
1 (16 ounce) box powdered sugar
1 (22 ounce) container non-dairy powdered coffee creamer
1 (32 ounce) powdered chocolate drink mix
1 small bag marshmallows (optional)
Whipped cream (optional)

In a very large bowl, combine dry milk powder, powdered sugar, powdered coffee creamer and powdered chocolate drink mix. Stir until blended well. Store in covered containers.

Brand name ingredients work best.

To make 1 cup, use ½ cup mixture and 8 ounces very hot water. Stir well and top with whipped cream and marshmallows.

A decorative container of this hot chocolate mix makes a lovely Christmas gift.

"*And* let the beauty of the Lord our God be upon us, and establish the work of our hands for us; yes, establish the work of our hands."

Psalm 90:17

Hot Wassail

1	gallon apple cider	1	cup lemon juice
1	gallon orange juice	24	cloves
1	cup sugar	4	cinnamon sticks

Mix all ingredients together. Heat and serve.

Hot Winter Spiced Tea

3	quarts water	1½	cups sugar
3-4	cinnamon sticks	1	(6 ounce) can concentrated orange juice
1	teaspoon whole cloves		
7	regular tea bags (or 3 family size)	1	(6 ounce) can concentrated lemonade

Bring water to a boil. Add cinnamon and cloves. Remove from stove, add tea bags. Cover and steep for 15 minutes. Remove spices and tea bags. Add sugar, orange juice and lemonade. Stir well, serve hot.

May reheat, but do not boil. Keep in refrigerator.

Mocha Coffee Punch

½	cup instant coffee	2	gallons vanilla ice cream, softened
1	gallon milk		
1	large can chocolate syrup	½	gallon frozen vanilla ice cream

Dissolve instant coffee in milk, add chocolate syrup and softened ice cream and mix. Float additional ½ gallon ice cream in punch.

May double recipe for a larger crowd.

"*But let those who love Him be like the sun when it comes out in full strength.*"

Judges 5:31

BREAKFAST, BRUNCH AND BREADS

"Then Jesus declared, 'I am the bread of life. He who comes to me will never grow hungry, and he who believes in me will never be thirsty."

John 6:35

BREAKFAST AND BRUNCH

Banana Pecan Pancakes, 33

Dorothy's Homemade Granola, 33

French Toast Casserole, 34

Christmas Morning Cheese Grits, 34

Sausage and Cheese Grits Casserole, 34

Breakfast Burritos, 35

Best Ever Breakfast Casserole, 35

Summer Strata, 36

Sausage and Egg Casserole, 36

Ultimate Breakfast Casserole, 37

Bacon Broccoli Quiche, 37

Ham and Swiss Quiche, 38

Sausage and Mushroom Quiche, 38

Scrumptious Cheese Quiche, 39

BREADS

Zucchini Bread, 39

Broccoli Cornbread, 40

White Cheddar Cheese Cornbread, 40

Company Cornbread, 40

Cheese Biscuits with Garlic Butter, 41

"Quiet Dogs" (Hush Puppies), 41

Sour Dough Bread Starter, 42

Sour Dough Bread, 43

Smoked Paprika Butter, 43

Yeast Dinner Rolls, 44

Three Seed Pan Rolls, 44

Buttermilk Biscuits, 45

Irish Soda Bread, 45

Apple Muffins, 46

Rise and Shine Muffins, 46

Banana Crunch Muffins, 47

Orange Poppy Seed Bread, 47

Banana Bread, 47

White Cheddar Muffins, 48

Peach Bread, 48

Pumpkin Cranberry Bread, 49

Blueberry Squares, 50

Cinnamon Coffeecake, 50

Cream Cheese Braid, 51

L. L. Bean Blueberry Coffee Cake, 52

Christmas Morning Sticky Buns, 52

Bread Machine Cinnamon Rolls, 53

Ninety Minute Cinnamon Rolls, 54

Banana Pecan Pancakes

1 ripe banana
⅔ cup white wheat flour or all-purpose flour
1 tablespoon baking powder
2 tablespoons granulated white sugar
½ teaspoon salt
⅓ cup yellow cornmeal
¾ cup milk
1 large egg
3 tablespoons oil
⅓ cup chopped pecans, lightly toasted

Chop banana. Mix dry ingredients. Add pecans to dry ingredients. Mix milk, egg, oil and banana; add to dry ingredients. Heat griddle. Drop by quarter cup measures on hot griddle. Cook until bubbles appear on surface and undersides are golden brown, about 1 minute.

Serve with warm maple syrup.

Dorothy's Homemade Granola

3 cups old-fashioned oats
1 cup shredded coconut
1 cup chopped nuts (almonds or pecans)
1 teaspoon cinnamon
4 tablespoons melted butter
⅓ cup honey, melted with butter
1 teaspoon vanilla
1 cup raisins, dried cherries, etc. (optional)

Preheat oven to 350°. Mix oats, coconut, nuts and cinnamon in a large bowl. Combine butter, honey and vanilla. Pour over dry mixture and mix well. Spread evenly on a cookie sheet and bake 20 minutes, mixing every 5 minutes to prevent burning. Watch carefully. Cool and store in airtight container for a few weeks.

May be used with vanilla yogurt and fruit or to top ice cream.

"My voice you shall hear in the morning. Oh Lord, in the morning I will direct it to you, and I will look up."

Psalm 5:3

French Toast Casserole

1	(10 ounce) loaf French bread, cut into 1 inch cubes, about 10 cups	3	cups milk
		4	teaspoons sugar
		1	teaspoon vanilla extract
8	eggs	¾	teaspoon salt

Place bread cubes in greased 9x13 inch baking dish. In a large bowl, whisk the eggs, milk, sugar, vanilla and salt. Pour over bread. Cover and refrigerate for 8 hours or overnight.

TOPPING

2	tablespoons butter	2	teaspoons ground cinnamon
3	tablespoons sugar		

Remove from refrigerator 30 minutes before baking. Preheat oven to 350°. Dot with butter. Combine sugar and cinnamon, sprinkle over top. Cover and bake 45 to 50 minutes or until a knife inserted near the center comes out clean. Let stand for 5 minutes. Add syrup to individual servings.

Makes 12 servings

Christmas Morning Cheese Grits

1	quart milk	1	egg, beaten
½	cup butter	⅓	cup butter
1	cup uncooked grits	4	ounces Gruyère cheese, grated
1	teaspoon salt		
½	teaspoon pepper	½	cup Parmesan cheese, grated

Preheat oven to 350°. Boil milk, stirring often; add ½ cup butter and grits, stir often for 5 minutes. Remove from stove and add salt, pepper and egg. Stir until mixed. Add ⅓ cup butter and Gruyère cheese. Mix well. Pour into 9x13 inch greased pan, sprinkle with Parmesan cheese. Bake for 1 hour.

SAUSAGE AND CHEESE GRITS CASSEROLE

1 pound hot sausage

1 cup quick grits

4 cups boiling water

½ teaspoon salt

½ teaspoon garlic salt

1 stick butter

1 cup sharp cheese, grated

½ cup milk

4 eggs, slightly beaten

Paprika

Preheat oven to 350°. Cook and drain sausage. Cooks grits for 5 minutes in boiling salted water. Add garlic salt, butter and cheese. Stir until melted. Remove from heat; add milk, eggs and sausage. Pour into 9x13 inch pan sprayed with nonstick spray. Sprinkle Paprika on top. Bake 35 to 45 minutes.

Breakfast Burritos

¾ cup sour cream
2 tablespoons taco seasoning mix
6 eggs
2 tablespoons water

6 (8 inch) flour tortillas, warmed
¾ cup shredded Cheddar cheese
1 cup shredded romaine lettuce
1 medium tomato, seeded, chopped

Blend the sour cream and taco seasoning mix in a small bowl. Set aside. Beat the eggs with the water in a small bowl until well blended. Preheat a large skillet sprayed with nonstick cooking spray over medium-low heat. Add the beaten eggs. Cook until set, stirring occasionally. Spread the tortillas with the sour cream mixture. Divide the eggs, cheese, romaine lettuce and tomato among the tortillas and roll up tightly. Serve immediately.

Serve 6

Best Ever Breakfast Casserole

6 eggs, slightly beaten
2⅔ cups milk
1 tablespoon brown sugar
¼ teaspoon paprika
1 tablespoon minced onion
½ teaspoon dry mustard
½ teaspoon salt

½ teaspoon black pepper
⅛ teaspoon white pepper
⅛ teaspoon red pepper
2 pounds sausage (1 mild and 1 hot), cooked, drained
8 slices bread, crust removed
½ pound grated sharp cheese

Mix eggs, milk, brown sugar, paprika, minced onion, dry mustard, salt and peppers. Spray 9x13 inch dish with cooking spray. Layer bread, sausage and then cheese. Pour liquid on top. Refrigerate overnight. Let sit at room temperature for 2 hours before cooking. Bake 1 hour at 350°.

"The Sovereign Lord has given me an instructed tongue, to know the word that sustains the weary. He wakens me morning by morning, wakens my ear to listen like one being taught. The Sovereign Lord has opened my ears, and I have not been rebellious; I have not drawn back."

Isaiah 50:4-5

Summer Strata

½ cup diced fresh baby bella mushrooms

½ cup chopped green bell peppers

½ cup chopped onion

1 bunch of fresh asparagus tips

2 cups cooked cubed ham

2 tablespoons olive oil

9 slices of bread, torn into bite size pieces

16 ounces shredded sharp Cheddar cheese

8 eggs

2 cups half-and-half

1 teaspoon Worcestershire sauce

Salt and pepper to taste

Garlic powder to taste

Preheat oven to 350°. Grease a 9x13 inch baking dish. Sauté mushrooms, peppers, onion, asparagus, and ham in a sauté pan with 2 tablespoons of olive oil. Layer half of the torn bread in the bottom of the dish. Layer half sautéed veggies and ham and sprinkle with half of shredded cheese. Repeat layers.

Whisk together the eggs, half-and-half, Worcestershire, salt, pepper and garlic powder to taste. Pour over the entire pan. Cover with aluminum foil and refrigerate for 12 to 24 hours. Bake covered for 35 minutes. Remove foil and bake for an additional 15 minutes until it is evenly browned.

Can adjust amount of veggies and ham to personal taste.

Sausage and Egg Casserole

1 pound sausage

8 ounces sharp Cheddar cheese, grated

6 large eggs

1 cup milk

Salt and pepper to taste

Preheat oven to 350°. Spray 9x13 inch casserole dish with nonstick cooking spray. Cook and drain sausage. Spread sausage on the bottom of the dish. Mix eggs, milk, cheese, salt and pepper together. Pour over sausage. Do not mix. Bake until brown.

Makes 6 to 8 servings

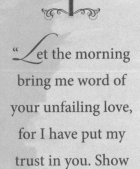

"*Let the morning bring me word of your unfailing love, for I have put my trust in you. Show me the way I should go, for to you I lift up my soul.*"

Psalm 143:8

Ultimate Breakfast Casserole

1 pound bulk pork sausage	¼ teaspoon salt
2½ cups frozen hash brown potatoes, thawed	⅛ teaspoon pepper
1 cup shredded Cheddar cheese	½ cup chopped red or green bell pepper
1¾ cups milk	¼ cup shredded Cheddar cheese
1 cup baking mix	
4 eggs	

Preheat oven to 400°. Grease a 10x10 inch casserole dish. Cook sausage well and drain. Mix sausage, potatoes and cheese. Place into dish and spread evenly. Beat milk, baking mix, eggs, salt and pepper; stir in bell pepper. Pour over sausage mixture. Bake 40 minutes. The last 3 to 5 minutes, sprinkle with cheese and bake until it melts.

This recipe can be doubled, using a 9x13 inch dish and bake at 425° for 1 hour.

Bacon Broccoli Quiche

1 pound bacon, cut into ½ inch pieces	1 (10 ounce) package frozen chopped broccoli, thawed
3 tablespoons melted butter	1 small onion, chopped
1¼ cups rye cracker crumbs	Nutmeg to taste
1½ cups shredded Swiss cheese	2 tablespoons grated Parmesan cheese
15 ounces ricotta cheese	
4 eggs	

Preheat oven to 350°. Cook the bacon in a skillet until crisp and drain on paper towels. Combine the butter and cracker crumbs in a bowl and mix well. Press over the bottom of an 8 inch springform pan. Combine the Swiss cheese and ricotta cheese in a bowl and mix well. Add the eggs one at a time, mixing well after each addition. Add the bacon, broccoli and onion and mix well. Pour in to the prepared pan. Sprinkle with nutmeg. Bake 1 hour or until the center is set. Sprinkle with the Parmesan cheese. Let stand for 10 minutes before serving.

Makes 6 servings

"*It is good to praise the Lord and make music to your name, O Most High, to proclaim your love in the morning and your faithfulness at night.*"

Psalm 92:1-2

Ham and Swiss Quiche

1 (9 inch) unbaked deep-dish pie shell	1 cup shredded Swiss cheese
1 (12 ounce) can evaporated milk	½ cup cubed cooked ham
3 large eggs	¼ cup chopped green onions
¼ cup all-purpose flour	½ teaspoon dried thyme
	¼ teaspoon salt
	⅛ teaspoon black pepper

Preheat oven to 350°. Whisk together evaporated milk, eggs and flour in large bowl. Stir in ½ cup cheese, ham, green onions, thyme, salt and pepper. Pour mixture into pie shell. Sprinkle with remaining cheese. Bake 45 to 50 minutes or until knife inserted near center comes out clean. Cool on wire rack for 5 to 7 minutes before serving.

"She rises while it is yet night, and provides food for her household."

Proverbs 31:15

Sausage and Mushroom Quiche

1 (9 inch) unbaked pie crust	8 ounces bulk pork sausage, browned and drained
½ cup milk	1 small carton baby Portobello mushrooms, chopped
2 eggs	¾ cup Cheddar cheese, grated
½ cup mayonnaise	¾ cup Swiss cheese, grated
1 tablespoon cornstarch	

Preheat oven to 350°. Prepare pie crust in a 9 inch pie pan. In a large bowl, whisk together milk, eggs, mayonnaise and cornstarch until smooth. Add sausage, mushrooms and cheese; combine thoroughly. Pour mixture into pie crust and bake 45 minutes or until golden.

This is delicious for breakfast or for dinner.

Use the Pie Crust recipe (page 206) or opt for a prepared refrigerated pie crust.

Scrumptious Cheese Quiche

1	cup grated Swiss cheese	¼	teaspoon salt	
1	cup grated mozzarella cheese	⅛	teaspoon red pepper	
6	slices of cooked, crumbled bacon	1	teaspoon dried basil	
1	(9 inch) pastry pie shell	1	tablespoon melted butter	
¾	cup half-and-half cream	1	tablespoon grated Parmesan cheese	
2	eggs, beaten			

Preheat oven to 375°. Place Swiss and mozzarella cheeses and bacon in pie shell. In a mixing bowl, combine cream, eggs, salt, pepper, and basil. Blend well and pour over cheeses and bacon. Drizzle with melted butter and then sprinkle Parmesan cheese on top. Bake for 30 minutes.

Makes 4 to 6 servings

Zucchini Bread

3	cups sifted all-purpose flour	1¾	cups sugar	
1	teaspoon salt	1	cup vegetable oil	
1	teaspoon baking powder	2	cups shredded zucchini	
1	teaspoon baking soda	1	tablespoon grated lemon rind	
1	tablespoon ground cinnamon	2	teaspoons vanilla	
3	eggs	½	cup coarsely chopped walnuts	

Preheat oven to 350°. Sift flour, salt, baking powder, baking soda and cinnamon onto wax paper.

Beat eggs lightly in a large bowl. Stir in sugar, oil, zucchini, lemon rind and vanilla. Add flour mixture, blending thoroughly. Stir in walnuts. Spoon batter into 2 well-greased 8x4 inch loaf pans.

Bake 50 minutes or until centers spring back when lightly pressed with fingertips. Cool in pans on wire rack for 10 minutes. Remove from pans and cool completely.

"But may they who love you be like the sun when it rises in its strength."

Judges 5:31

Broccoli Cornbread

1	stick butter	4	eggs
1	package chopped broccoli, thawed	1	(8½ ounce) box cornbread mix
1	small onion, chopped	1	teaspoon salt

Preheat oven to 425°. Melt butter. Mix all other ingredients with melted butter. Spray an 8x12 inch dish and pour in batter. Bake 40 to 50 minutes.

May need to cover with foil near the end of baking time to prevent overbrowning.

White Cheddar Cheese Cornbread

1½	cups cornmeal	1½	cups milk
1½	cups all-purpose flour	⅔	cup vegetable oil
1	cup sugar	1	cup yellow corn
2	eggs	1	cup white Cheddar cheese, shredded
1½	teaspoons salt		
5	teaspoons baking powder		

Preheat oven to 400°. Generously spray a 10 inch cast iron skillet with cooking spray. In a large bowl, combine cornmeal, flour, sugar, salt and baking powder. Form a well in the center of the dry ingredients and add the eggs, milk and vegetable oil. Combine the wet ingredients and then gradually incorporate the dry ingredients. Add the corn and mix well.

Pour the batter into a greased skillet or baking pan. Bake 20 to 25 minutes or until a toothpick inserted in the center comes out clean. Remove from the oven and immediately sprinkle with cheese.

Makes 8 to 10 servings

COMPANY CORNBREAD

1 cup self-rising flour

2 teaspoons baking powder

2 eggs, beaten

1 cup sour cream

½ cup salad oil

8 ounces cream style corn

Preheat oven to 400°. Mix all ingredients together. Pour into a 9x9 inch pan sprayed with vegetable cooking spray. Cook 30 minutes.

Cheese Biscuits with Garlic Butter

2	cups self-rising flour	⅓	cup shortening
1	teaspoon baking powder	¾	cup grated Cheddar cheese
1	teaspoon sugar	1	cup buttermilk

Preheat oven to 350°. Mix flour, baking powder and sugar in a bowl with a fork. Cut in shortening until mixture resembles cornmeal. Add cheese and buttermilk and mix until dry ingredients are just moistened. Do not over mix. Drop batter by tablespoonfuls or with an ice cream scoop onto a well-greased baking sheet. Bake 12 to 15 minutes.

GARLIC BUTTER

½	cup butter, melted	2	cloves garlic, crushed

Combine butter and garlic in a saucepan. Cook over medium heat until butter absorbs garlic. Brush garlic butter over the top of warm biscuits.

"Quiet Dogs" (Hush Puppies)

1½	cups self-rising white cornmeal mix	1	large egg, lightly beaten
½	cup all-purpose flour	2	tablespoons vegetable oil
1	teaspoon salt	½	cup minced onion or 2 green onion tops, minced
1	teaspoon baking powder		Vegetable oil for frying
½-¾	cup milk		

Sift cornmeal, flour, salt and baking powder together in a large bowl. Combine milk, egg, oil and minced onion in a separate bowl. Mix milk mixture with dry ingredients, adding up to ¼ cup more milk if needed. Should be able to drop batter from a spoon.

Heat 2 to 3 inches of oil in a skillet or deep fryer to 375°. Drop rounded teaspoonfuls of batter into hot oil. Fry 3 minutes or until golden brown. Remove from oil with a slotted spoon and drain on paper towels. Be sure oil returns to cooking temperature between batches.

Add 1 seeded, diced jalapeño to batter. Proceed with recipe as directed.

"Go, eat your bread with joy."

Ecclesiastes 9:7

Sour Dough Bread Starter

1	package dry yeast	2	tablespoons instant potato flakes
1	cup warm water		
¾	cup sugar		

Select a container that your "pet" will live in; a wide-mouth jar works well. Punch a couple of holes in the lid. (No metal containers.)

MORNING: Dissolve yeast in ½ cup of water; combine remaining ingredients. Pour into jar and let stand in a warm place all day (70 to 85 degrees is perfect for 10 to 12 hours).

EVENING: Refrigerate for 3 days. (Your starter should be frothy and bubbly on top.)

MORNING of the 4th day, take starter out of the refrigerator and "feed" with the following recipe:

¾	cup sugar	1	cup warm water
3	tablespoons instant potato flakes		

Mix well and let stand in warm place all day.

EVENING: Stir and remove 1 cup to use in bread making and return the remaining 1 cup to the refrigerator. REPEAT FEEDING PROCESS EVERY 3 to 5 DAYS (or more often if the need or want to bake arises). If you are not making bread after feeding, throw away 1 cup and return remaining starter to refrigerator.

If the starter is not frothy and bubbly by the evening, you may need to do the "feeding process" 2 or 3 times before it is ready to make bread.

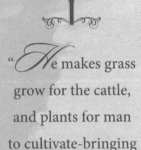

"He makes grass grow for the cattle, and plants for man to cultivate-bringing forth food from the earth; and bread which strengthens man's heart."

Psalm 104:14-5

Sour Dough Bread

6 cups bread flour	½ cup canola oil
½ cup sugar	1 cup starter
2 teaspoons salt	1½ cups warm water

Mix bread flour, sugar and salt in a large bowl. In another bowl, add oil. Stir in 1 cup of starter that you have had out all day, add water and stir well. Add wet mixture to dry mixture and gently mix all together with hands. Place dough in a greased bowl, cover with dishcloth and let rise about 8 hours (or overnight) in a warm place.

Divide dough into 3 sections. Roll out each section onto a floured surface to make a rectangle, then roll up like a jellyroll and place in greased bread pans on a cookie sheet. Cover pans with a dishcloth and let rise in a warm place for about 8 hours (or overnight).

Preheat oven to 350°. Be very careful not to move the pans too much or the bread will "fall." When preheated, gently remove the dishcloth and place cookie sheet with bread pans on it in the oven for 25 to 35 minutes or until slightly golden brown on top. Let cool in pans for about 10 minutes, then turn out onto a cooling rack to completely cool. Wrap in plastic wrap and bread bags to keep fresh.

Freezes well. Can make cinnamon rolls from this recipe.

"Then Jesus declared, 'I am the bread of life. He who comes to me will never go hungry, and he who believes in me will never be thirsty.'"

John 6:35

Smoked Paprika Butter

2 sticks butter (not margarine), softened	1 small clove of garlic
2 teaspoons smoked paprika	½ teaspoon sugar
	Pinch of salt

Blend all ingredients together in a food processor or mash with fork until smooth. Put this mixture on plastic wrap and work into a "log." Refrigerate for several hours. Great on grilled corn on the cob or as butter for French bread.

Yeast Dinner Rolls

1	package active dry yeast	1¼	teaspoons salt
¼	cup warm water	1	egg, beaten
¾	cup hot milk	4	cups all-purpose flour or
3	tablespoons shortening		enough to make dough stiff
3	tablespoons sugar		Melted butter

Dissolve yeast in warm water. Mix hot milk, shortening, sugar and salt in large mixing bowl. Cool to lukewarm. Stir in yeast and beaten egg. Add 2 cups flour and beat until smooth. Gradually stir in more flour until dough leaves sides of bowl. Turn dough out onto lightly floured surface and knead until smooth and elastic, about 8 to 10 minutes. Place in a large buttered bowl. Turn over once to grease upper side of dough. Cover dough and let rise in warm draft-free place until almost double in bulk, about 1 hour. Press dough down into bowl to remove the big air bubbles.

Put a small amount of shortening or butter on hands. Divide dough into small pieces. Roll into balls and place in shallow greased baking pan with sides touching. Cover loosely with cloth. Let rise in warm place until double in bulk, about 45 to 60 minutes. Bake in preheated 400° oven 15 to 20 minutes or less time if rolls are small. Remove from oven and brush with melted butter while hot.

Makes 2 to 3 dozen, depending on size

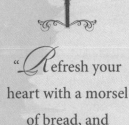

Three Seed Pan Rolls

4	teaspoons fennel seeds	9	frozen bread dough rolls
4	teaspoons poppy seeds	1	egg white, beaten
4	teaspoons sesame seeds		Melted butter

Combine seeds in a small bowl. Dip dough rolls one at a time in egg white, roll in seed mixture. Arrange rolls 1 inch apart in a lightly greased 8 inch pan. Cover with lightly greased plastic wrap, and let rise in a warm place (85°), free from drafts, 3 to 4 hours or until doubled in bulk. Preheat oven to 350°. Uncover rolls, and bake 15 minutes or until golden. Brush with melted butter.

May substitute 1 (11 ounce) can refrigerated French bread dough for frozen bread dough rolls.

Irish Soda Bread

4	cups sifted all-purpose flour	1	cup raisins
¾	cup sugar	¾	stick butter
¼	teaspoon salt	2	cups buttermilk
3	teaspoons baking powder	1	egg, beaten
2	tablespoons caraway seeds (optional)	¾	teaspoon baking soda

Preheat oven to 350°. In a large bowl, sift together flour, sugar, salt and baking powder. Mix in caraway seeds and raisins. Crumble in butter.

In another bowl, combine buttermilk, beaten egg and baking soda. Quickly stir into dry ingredients. Combine everything by hand. Place into a 9x5 inch greased loaf pan and bake for 1 hour.

This version is more like a sweet bread or cake and may be used as a dessert or breakfast bread served with coffee or tea.

Buttermilk Biscuits

3½	cups self-rising flour	¼	cup butter, chilled and cut into pieces
2¼	teaspoons baking powder		
2¼	teaspoons sugar	1½	cups buttermilk
¼	cup shortening	½-1	cup self-rising flour
		1	tablespoon butter, melted

Preheat oven to 450°. Combine flour, baking powder and sugar until well blended. Cut in shortening and chilled butter pieces with a pastry blender or a fork until crumbly. Add buttermilk, stirring just until dry ingredients are wet. Turn dough out onto a well-floured surface; sprinkle with ½ cup flour. Knead about 25 times, adding up to ½ cup additional flour until dough is smooth and springy. Pat dough into a ¾-inch-thick circle (about 8½ inches round). Cut dough with a well-floured 2 inch round cutter, making 12 biscuits.

Place on ungreased baking sheets. Knead remaining dough together 3 or 4 times; repeat procedure, making 6 more biscuits. Lightly brush tops with melted butter. Bake about 9 minutes or until biscuits are golden brown.

"*Just before dawn Paul urged them all to eat.*" Saying "*you need it to survive. And when he had said these things, he took bread and gave thanks to God in the presence of them all. And when he had broken it, he began to eat. Then they were all encouraged, and also took food themselves.*"

Acts 27:33-36

Apple Muffins

¾	cup vegetable oil	¾	teaspoon cinnamon
1	cup sugar	½	teaspoon salt
2	eggs	1½	cups diced apples
1	teaspoon vanilla extract	½	cup raisins
2	cups all-purpose flour	½	cup walnuts or pecans
¾	teaspoon baking soda		

Preheat oven to 400°. Grease 12 cup muffin tin. Combine oil and sugar in large mixing bowl, beat 2 minutes. Add eggs and vanilla, beat 1 minute. Sift together flour, baking soda, cinnamon and salt. Stir dry ingredients into wet ingredients. Add apples, raisins and walnuts. Stir into batter. Fill muffin cups ¾ full. Bake 20 minutes. Cool for 5 minutes in the pan. Transfer to cooling rack.

"I am the bread of life."

John 6:48

Rise and Shine Muffins

2	cups all-purpose flour	2	cups grated carrots
½	teaspoon salt	1	Granny Smith apple, peeled and chopped small
2	teaspoons baking soda	½	cup raisins
2	teaspoons cinnamon	½	cup shredded sweetened coconut
3	eggs, slightly beaten	½	cup chopped pecans
1	cup vegetable oil		
1¼	cups sugar		
2	teaspoons vanilla		

Preheat oven to 350°. Mix the flour, salt, baking soda and cinnamon together. Combine the eggs, vegetable oil, sugar, vanilla, carrots, apple, raisins, coconut and pecans; mix well. Stir in the dry ingredients just until moistened.

Fill greased and floured or paper-lined muffin cups ⅔ full. Bake 15 to 20 minutes or until the muffins are done.

Makes 24 regular muffins or 72 mini muffins

Banana Crunch Muffins

3	cups all-purpose flour	1	cup mashed ripe bananas (2 bananas)
2	cups sugar	1	cup medium-diced ripe bananas (1 banana)
2	teaspoons baking powder	1	cup walnuts, diced small
1	teaspoon baking soda	1	cup granola
½	teaspoon salt	¾	cup sweetened shredded coconut
2	sticks unsalted butter, melted and cooled		Dried banana chips, granola, or shredded coconut (optional)
2	large eggs		
¾	cup whole milk		
2	teaspoons pure vanilla extract		

Preheat oven to 350°. Line 18 muffin cups with paper liners. Sift the flour, sugar, baking powder, baking soda and salt into the bowl of an electric mixer fitted with a paddle attachment. Add the melted butter and blend. Combine the eggs, milk, vanilla and mashed bananas, and add them to the flour and butter mixture. Scrape the bowl and blend well. Do not overmix. Fold the diced bananas, walnuts, granola and coconut into the batter.

Spoon the batter into the paper liners, filling each one to the top. Top each muffin with dried banana chips, granola or coconut if desired. Bake 25 to 30 minutes or until the tops are brown and a toothpick comes out clean. Cool slightly, remove from the pan and serve.

BANANA BREAD

⅔ cup margarine

1½ cups sugar

2 eggs

1½ cups plain flour

2 teaspoons baking powder

¼ teaspoon salt

4 tablespoons milk

1 cup mashed bananas

½ cup chopped pecans

1 teaspoon vanilla

Preheat oven to 350°. Cream margarine and sugar, add eggs. Sift flour, baking powder and salt together. Add flour mixture and milk to the creamed ingredients. Add mashed bananas, nuts and vanilla. Pour in greased loaf pan or Bundt pan. Bake 45 minutes for loaf pan, 55 minutes for Bundt pan. Cool for 30 minutes. Invert pans.

Orange Poppy Seed Bread

3	cups all-purpose flour	1	tablespoon grated orange rind
2½	cups sugar	1½	teaspoons baking powder
1½	cups milk	1½	teaspoons salt
1½	cups vegetable oil	1	teaspoon vanilla extract
3	eggs	1	teaspoon lemon extract
1½	tablespoons poppy seeds		

Preheat oven to 350°. Mix all ingredients together at the same time at medium speed until well blended. Pour batter into two greased and floured 8x4 inch loaf pans. Bake for 1 hour. Cool completely in pans and then remove on serving platter.

Freezes well.

White Cheddar Muffins

⅓ cup butter
¼ cup chopped fresh chives
1 teaspoon minced garlic
1¾ cups whole buttermilk

3 cups all-purpose baking mix
1½ cups shredded sharp white Cheddar cheese

Preheat oven to 350°. Spray 16 muffin cups with nonstick cooking spray.

In a small saucepan, melt butter over medium heat. Add chives and garlic, and cook for 2 minutes. Whisk in buttermilk.

In a medium bowl, combine baking mix and cheese. Add buttermilk mixture, stirring just until dry ingredients are moistened. Spoon batter into prepared muffin cups. Bake 25 to 30 minutes or until golden brown. Cool in pans for 5 minutes.

Makes 16 muffins

"I, Jesus, have sent my angel to give you this testimony for the churches. I am the root and the offspring of David, and the bright and morning star."

Revelation 22:16

Peach Bread

1½ cups sugar
½ cup shortening
2 eggs
2¼ cups fresh peach purée (6-8 peaches)
2 cups flour

1 teaspoon cinnamon
1 teaspoon baking soda
1 teaspoon baking powder
¼ teaspoon salt
1 teaspoon vanilla extract
1 cup finely chopped pecans

Preheat oven to 325°. Cream sugar and shortening together. Add eggs and mix thoroughly. Add peach purée. (Peach purée is made by blending peaches finely in a blender.)

In a separate bowl, combine flour, cinnamon, baking soda, baking powder and salt. Fold into peach mixture. Mix thoroughly. Add vanilla extract and chopped pecans and stir until blended. Pour into two 5x9 inch loaf pans that have been greased and floured. Bake for 55 minutes to 1 hour. Let bread cool for 20 minutes before removing from pan.

Pumpkin Cranberry Bread

3	cups flour	1	(15 ounce) can pumpkin
1	tablespoon plus 2 teaspoons pumpkin pie spice	4	eggs
2	teaspoons baking soda	1	cup vegetable oil
1½	teaspoons salt	½	cup orange juice
3	cups sugar	1	cup fresh or frozen cranberries

Preheat oven to 350°. Combine flour, pumpkin spice, baking soda and salt in a large bowl. Combine sugar, pumpkin, eggs, oil and juice in a small mixer bowl; beat until just blended. Add pumpkin mixture to flour mixture; stir just until moistened. Fold in cranberries.

Spoon batter into 5 or 6 greased mini loaf pans or 3 greased 8x4 inch regular loaf pans. Bake for 50 to 55 minutes or until a toothpick inserted in center comes out clean. Cool for 10 minutes in pan, remove to wire racks. When completely cool, frost with Cream Cheese Frosting.

CREAM CHEESE FROSTING

1	(8 ounce) package cream cheese, softened	1	cup marshmallow cream

Mix ingredients together and frost loaves of bread.

"Once more the Heavenly Power makes all things new."

(Alfred Lord Tennyson)

Blueberry Squares

2	cups all-purpose flour		1	cup granulated sugar
2	teaspoons baking powder		2	eggs
½	teaspoon salt		2	teaspoons vanilla
½	teaspoon cinnamon		1	cup blueberries
1	stick margarine		1	cup chopped pecans
1	cup firmly packed light brown sugar			

Preheat oven to 350°. Sift flour, baking powder, salt and cinnamon together. Melt margarine in saucepan and remove from heat. Add sugars, eggs and vanilla to margarine. Stir with wooden spoon until smooth. Stir in flour mixture until smooth. Stir in blueberries and pecans. Spread into a greased 9x13 inch pan. Bake 30 minutes.

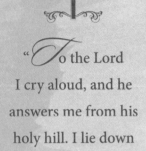

"To the Lord I cry aloud, and he answers me from his holy hill. I lie down and sleep; I wake again, because the Lord sustains me."

Psalm 3:4-5

Cinnamon Coffeecake

1	cup sour cream		2	eggs
½	teaspoon baking soda		1	teaspoon vanilla
1	cup butter		1½	cups flour
1	cup sugar		1½	teaspoons baking powder

Mix together the sour cream and baking soda and let sit for 1 hour. Cream together the butter and sugar; add eggs and vanilla, beat well. Add sour cream mixture to the egg mixture. Stir in flour and baking powder, beat well.

TOPPING

½	cup brown sugar		½	cup chopped pecans
1	teaspoon cinnamon			

Combine topping ingredients. Preheat oven to 350°. Pour half the batter into a greased 9 inch pan. Spread half the topping on batter. Add the remaining batter, then the remaining topping. Bake for 40 minutes.

Cream Cheese Braid

1 cup sour cream	2 packages yeast
½ cup sugar	½ cup warm water
½ cup margarine, softened	4 cups all-purpose flour
2 eggs	1 teaspoon salt

Mix sour cream, sugar, margarine and eggs together. Dissolve yeast in warm water. Sift flour and salt. Mix all together and form a dough roll. (May have to add a little more flour to make into dough-like consistency.) Refrigerate overnight.

FILLING

2 teaspoons vanilla	⅛ teaspoon salt
2 (8 ounce) packages cream cheese, softened	¾ cup sugar

Make filling by mixing vanilla, cream cheese, salt and sugar. Set aside.

Cut dough into fourths and roll each into balls. Roll each ball flat. Spread filling on top of each. Close rolls and braid two together. Do the same for the other two rolls. Let rise until they double in size. Bake at 375° for 10 to 14 minutes.

TOPPING

Powdered sugar	Lemon juice
Water	Red maraschino cherries

Mix topping ingredients together to desired consistency. Put cherries in each braid.

This is absolutely delicious and so much fun to make.

"*Refresh your heart with a morsel of bread, and afterwards go your way.*"

Judges 19:5

CHRISTMAS MORNING STICKY BUNS

1 package frozen roll dough (18 to 20 pieces)

1 (3 ounce) package butterscotch pudding (not instant)

½ cup sugar

2 tablespoons cinnamon

1 cup pecans, whole

1 stick butter, melted

The night before, place frozen roll dough in greased Bundt pan. Mix dry pudding mix, sugar, cinnamon and nuts. Sprinkle over frozen dough. Pour melted butter over top as evenly as possible. Cover with a towel and leave on the counter overnight. In the morning, bake at 350° for 30 minutes or until lightly browned on top.

To serve, invert Bundt pan on serving dish and lift carefully. Sticky sauce will run.

L.L.Bean Blueberry Coffee Cake

½	cup butter	1	cup milk
1	cup sugar	1	egg
2	cups all-purpose flour	1	cup blueberries, fresh or frozen
3	teaspoons baking powder		
1	teaspoon salt		

Preheat oven to 350°. Cream butter and sugar. Combine dry ingredients and mix with butter. Slowly add milk and egg and mix for 2 minutes. Lightly grease a 9x13 inch pan and spread half the batter in the pan. Add blueberries and top with the rest of the batter. Add streusel topping and bake 40 minutes.

STREUSEL TOPPING

½ cup chopped pecans		½	teaspoon cinnamon
⅓	cup brown sugar	3	teaspoons butter
¼	cup flour		

Mix all ingredients together.

GLAZE

1	cup powdered sugar	¼	teaspoon vanilla extract
2	tablespoons milk		

Mix all together and drizzle over warm cake.

May want to add more blueberries.

Bread Machine Cinnamon Rolls

4 tablespoons butter, melted	1 cup brown sugar

DOUGH

¼ cup warm water	1 egg, room temperature
¼ cup butter, melted	1 tablespoon white sugar
½ (3.4 ounce) package instant vanilla pudding mix	½ teaspoon salt
	4 cups bread flour
1 cup warm milk (room temperature)	1 (.25 ounce) package active dry yeast

Combine melted butter and brown sugar. Spread some over the bottom of pan. Reserve the rest to pour over the top of rolls after they have risen.

Dough: Grease 9x13 inch pan. In bread machine bowl, combine in order: water, melted butter, pudding, warm milk, egg, sugar, salt, flour and yeast. Set machine to dough cycle, press start. When dough has finished, turn dough out onto lightly floured surface and roll into 17x10 inch rectangle.

FILLING

¼ cup butter, softened	4 teaspoons cinnamon
1 cup brown sugar	¾ cup chopped pecans

Preheat oven to 350°. For the filling, spread softened butter on dough. In a small bowl, stir together brown sugar, cinnamon and pecans. Sprinkle brown sugar mix over dough. Roll up dough, starting with long side. Slice into 16 (1 inch) slices and place in pan. Let rise until doubled, about 45 minutes, in a warm place. Pour remaining extra over rolls. Bake 15 to 20 minutes. Make icing while baking rolls.

ICING

4 ounces cream cheese, softened	½ teaspoon vanilla extract
¼ cup butter, softened	1½ teaspoons milk
1 cup powdered sugar	

For icing, stir together cream cheese, soft butter, powdered sugar, vanilla and milk. Remove rolls from the oven and top with frosting.

Melted caramel can be added to filling.

If in a hurry, let dough rise in a warm oven until dough has doubled.

Icing may be mixed with a mixer.

Good frozen and reheated.

Ninety Minute Cinnamon Rolls

¾ cup milk	¼ cup water
¼ cup margarine, softened	1 egg
3¼ cups all-purpose flour	1 cup brown sugar, packed
1 (.25 ounce) package instant yeast	1 tablespoon ground cinnamon
¼ cup white sugar	½ cup margarine, softened
½ teaspoon salt	½ cup raisins, optional

Heat the milk in a small saucepan until it bubbles, remove from heat. Mix in margarine, stir until melted. Let cool until lukewarm. In a large mixing bowl, combine 2¼ cups flour, yeast, sugar and salt; mix well. Add water, egg and the milk mixture; beat well. Add the remaining flour, ½ cup at the time, stirring well after each addition.

When the dough has just pulled together, turn it out onto a lightly floured surface and knead until smooth, about 5 minutes. Cover the dough with a clean, damp cloth and let rest for 10 minutes.

In a small bowl, mix together brown sugar, cinnamon, softened margarine. Roll out dough into a 12x9 inch rectangle. Spread dough with margarine-sugar mixture. Sprinkle with raisins if desired. Roll up dough and pinch seam to seal. Cut into 12 equal size rolls and place cut side up in 12 lightly greased muffin cups. Cover and let rise until doubled, about 20 minutes. Preheat oven to 375°. Bake 20 minutes or until brown. Remove from muffin cups to cool. Serve warm.

"Christ our Passover lamb was sacrificed for us. Therefore let us keep the feast, not with old leaven, nor with the leaven of malice and wickedness, but with the unleavened bread of sincerity and truth."

1 Corinthians 5:7-8

Soups and Sandwiches

"Trust in the Lord with all your heart and lean not on your own understanding; in all your ways acknowledge Him, and He will make your paths straight."

Proverbs 3:5-6

SOUPS AND SANDWICHES

SOUPS

African Chicken Peanut Soup, 57

Black Bean and Chicken Corn Chowder, 57

Chicken Brunswick Stew, 58

Chicken Tortilla Soup, 58

Cajun Soup, 59

Crab-and-Corn Chowder, 59

Creamy Wild Rice Soup, 60

French Onion Soup, 60

Danish Havarti Cheese Soup
    with Potatoes, 61

New England Clam Chowder, 62

Sausage Jambalaya, 62

Shrimp Bisque, 63

Steak Soup, 63

Spanish Chili, 64

Mushroom Tomato Soup, 64

Taco Soup, 65

Tomato Basil Soup with Feta, 65

Ranch Oyster Crackers, 65

Turnip Green Soup, 66

White Chicken Chili, 66

SANDWICHES

Big Wheel Sandwiches, 67

Mini Fried Tomato Sandwiches, 67

Muffalettas, 68

African Chicken Peanut Soup

1½ cups cubed, peeled sweet potatoes
½ cup chopped onion
½ cup diced red bell pepper
2 cloves garlic
1 jalapeño pepper seeded and minced (optional) or diced chilies, drained
2 cups chopped cooked chicken breast (about 8 ounces)
1 cup bottled salsa
½ teaspoon ground cumin
2 (16 ounce) cans fat free chicken broth
2 cups cooked rice
1 (15 ounce) can black beans drained
⅓ cup creamy peanut butter

Place a large Dutch oven coated with cooking spray over medium-high heat until hot. Add sweet potato, onion, bell pepper, garlic and jalapeño or chilies. Sauté for 5 minutes. Stir in chicken, salsa, cumin, chicken broth, rice and black beans. Bring to a boil. Reduce heat; simmer 10 minutes. Add peanut butter at the end, stir with a whisk. Cook 2 minutes.

Black Bean and Chicken Corn Chowder

2 (14½ ounce) cans low sodium chicken broth
2 (15 ounce) cans black beans
3 cups chopped cooked chicken
1 medium chopped onion
2 (4 ounce) cans chopped green chilies
½ teaspoon ground red (or black) pepper
1 (16 ounce) package frozen white corn
1 teaspoon ground cumin
¾ teaspoon dried oregano
Sour cream, salsa, and cheese for toppings

Mix 1 can of the broth and 1 can of the beans in the blender. Add to bean mixture remaining cans of broth and beans, chicken, onion, chilies, pepper, corn, cumin and oregano. Top with sour cream, salsa and cheese if desired.

"But those who have gathered it shall eat it, and praise the Lord; those who have brought it together shall drink it in my holy courts."

Isaiah 62:9

Chicken Brunswick Stew

1	rotisserie or boiled chicken	1	cup ketchup
1	(28 ounce) can crushed tomatoes	½	cup barbecue sauce
⅓	cup sugar	1	tablespoon liquid smoke
1	onion, chopped	1	tablespoon vinegar
1	tablespoon olive oil	1	tablespoon Worcestershire sauce
1	(14½ ounce) can creamed corn		Salt and pepper, to taste
		¼	teaspoon celery salt

Pick and cut up rotisserie chicken and set aside. To sweeten the tomatoes, combine the crushed tomatoes and the sugar. In a large pot, sauté the onions in olive oil. Add tomatoes, creamed corn, ketchup, barbecue sauce, liquid smoke, vinegar, Worcestershire, salt, pepper and celery salt. Stir well and simmer 20 minutes. Add chicken and simmer for 5 more minutes. Freezes well.

Chicken Tortilla Soup

4	tablespoons butter	½	teaspoon white pepper
1	onion, chopped	½	teaspoon oregano
3	ribs celery, chopped	1	teaspoon salt
2	teaspoons cilantro	1	(4 ounce) can green chilies
3½	cups frozen corn	1	(16 ounce) can diced tomatoes
3	cans chicken broth	1	can tomato soup
1	can creamed corn	2	cups cooked, diced or shredded chicken (rotisserie is fine)
2	cups milk		
1	teaspoon cumin		Toppings: Monterey Jack cheese, sour cream, black olives and tortilla chips
1	clove garlic, minced		
1	teaspoon chili powder		
3	dashes hot sauce		

Sauté butter, onion, celery and cilantro in a large pot. Purée 1 cup of frozen corn with 1 cup of broth. Repeat once. Add purée to the pot with 1 cup frozen corn, 1 can broth, creamed corn, milk, cumin, garlic, chili powder, hot sauce, oregano, salt, chilies, diced tomatoes, tomato soup and cooked chicken. Simmer for 20 minutes. Serve with grated Monterey Jack cheese, sour cream, black olives and tortilla chips.

Freezes well. Seems like a lot of ingredients, but well worth the trouble. Double it and give to a friend.

Crab-and-Corn Chowder

6   bacon slices
2   celery ribs
1   medium green pepper, diced
1   medium onion, diced
1   jalapeño pepper, seeded and diced
1   (32 ounce) container chicken broth
3   tablespoons all-purpose flour
3   cups fresh corn kernels (6 ears)

1   pound fresh jumbo lump crabmeat, drained and picked
1   cup whipping cream
¼   cup chopped fresh cilantro
½   teaspoon salt
¼   teaspoon pepper
    Oyster crackers
    Garnish: chopped fresh cilantro (optional)

Cook bacon in a Dutch oven over medium heat 8 to 10 minutes or until crisp; remove bacon, and drain on paper towels, reserving 2 tablespoons drippings in Dutch oven. Crumble bacon. Sauté celery, peppers, onion and jalapeño pepper in hot drippings for 5 to 6 minutes or until tender. Whisk together broth and flour until smooth. Add to celery mixture. Stir in corn. Bring to a boil; reduce heat, and simmer, stirring occasionally, 30 minutes. Gently stir in crabmeat, whipping cream, cilantro, salt and pepper; cook 4 to 5 minutes or until thoroughly heated. Serve warm with crumbled bacon and oyster crackers. Garnish, if desired.

Cajun Soup

1½   pounds chicken breasts
2   ounces sliced smoked sausage
6   cups water
2   tablespoons salt, divided
1   cup chopped celery
½   teaspoon pepper
½   cup chopped onions
6   scallions, chopped

1   (10 ounce) can tomatoes with chilies
1   (14 ounce) can chopped tomatoes
1   tablespoon chopped fresh parsley
1   cup sliced okra
½   cup rice, uncooked

Simmer chicken, sausage and 1 teaspoon of salt in water for 1 hour; add celery, pepper, onions, scallions, tomatoes, 1 teaspoon salt, parsley and okra. Simmer for 30 minutes. Add ½ cup uncooked rice and cook for 15 minutes. (If this cooks much longer, the rice absorbs all of the moisture.)

Use only ½ can of tomatoes with chilies if you prefer a milder stew.

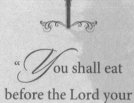

"*You* shall eat before the Lord your God, in the place where he chooses to make his name abide."

Deuteronomy 14:23

Creamy Wild Rice Soup

1 cup butter, divided	½ cup flour
1 large onion, chopped	2 teaspoons salt
3 cups celery, chopped	1½ teaspoons pepper
1 pound fresh mushrooms, sliced	2 quarts whole milk
	3½ cups wild rice, cooked

In a large skillet, sauté onion in ½ cup of butter until tender. Add celery and mushrooms. Sauté until soft. Set aside. Melt remaining ½ cup butter in a large pot or Dutch oven. Mix in flour, salt and pepper. Cook and stir for 1 minute. Stir in milk and cook on low, stirring constantly, until slightly thickened. Add sautéed vegetables and rice. Continue to heat on low for 15 minutes. Do not allow to boil.

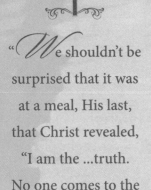

French Onion Soup

¼ cup butter	3 sprigs fresh thyme
5 medium size white onions, thinly sliced	2 sprigs fresh parsley
1 (32 ounce) container chicken broth	Salt and freshly ground pepper to taste
2 (10½ ounce) cans beef consommé, undiluted	6 (¾ inch thick) French baguette slices
¼ cup dry white wine	6 (1 ounce) Swiss cheese slices

Melt butter in a Dutch oven over medium-high heat; add onions, and cook, stirring often, 30 to 40 minutes or until golden brown.

Add chicken broth, beef consommé, white wine, thyme and parsley; bring to a boil. Reduce heat and simmer, stirring occasionally, 20 minutes. Remove and discard herbs. Add salt and pepper to taste.

Ladle into 6 ovenproof bowls; top with bread and cheese slices. Broil 5½ inches from heat, 3 minutes or until cheese is browned and bubbly.

Makes 6 cups

Danish Havarti Cheese Soup with Potatoes

2	medium sized diced potatoes	½	cup very finely chopped onions
1	cup water		
1½	tablespoons dry chicken bouillon	¼	cup finely chopped celery
		3	tablespoons flour
3	cups milk	2	tablespoons fresh minced dill
2	cups heavy cream	½	teaspoon white pepper
3	tablespoons butter	½	pound Havarti cheese
		1	package croutons (optional)

In a small saucepan, cook diced potatoes in water until tender. Drain and set aside. In a 3 quart Dutch oven add 1 cup water, bouillon, milk and heavy cream. Bring to the boiling point but do not let boil. Set aside.

In a small pan, melt butter and sauté onions and celery until very soft and tender, approximately 5 to 7 minutes. Add flour and stir together so that the flour is absorbed. Continue to stir for 1 to 2 minutes, making certain not to let the flour brown. Turn off heat and set aside.

Add dill, white pepper and Havarti cheese cut into small cubes into the Dutch oven (with chicken/milk stock). Stir constantly until the cheese is completely melted and absorbed into the mixture. Add the onion and celery mixture and cook until thickened, stirring fairly constantly, approximately 8 to 10 minutes. Remove soup from heat and purée in blender until smooth. Add cooked potatoes to mixture and serve with croutons.

"Jesus answered, "Are there not twelve hours of daylight? A man who walks by day will not stumble, for he sees by the world's light. It is when he walks by night that he stumbles, for he has no light.

John 15:12-13

New England Clam Chowder

¼ cup butter
¼ cup chopped onion
2 (7 ounce) cans clams
2 cups finely diced potatoes
½ cup water

1 cup heavy cream
1 cup milk
½ teaspoon salt
½ teaspoon pepper

Sauté the butter and onion in a large kettle. Add liquid from the 2 cans of clams, diced potatoes and ½ cup of water. Cook until potatoes are tender. Add clams, heavy cream, milk, salt and pepper. Heat to boiling, but do not boil. Stir occasionally.

"Be devoted to one another in brotherly love. Honor one another above yourselves. Share with God's people who are in need. Practice hospitality."

Romans 12:10,13

Sausage Jambalaya

2 tablespoons minced garlic
1 cup diced onion
1 cup diced celery
2 tablespoons butter
3 fresh tomatoes, diced
3 ears corn, cooked and kernels shaved from ears

2 cups black-eyed peas
  Black pepper to taste
  Creole seasoning to taste
4 cups fresh spinach leaves
14 ounces link smoked jalapeño-cheese sausage
2 cups steamed rice

Sauté the garlic, celery and onions in butter. Add tomatoes and simmer 10 minutes. Add corn and black-eyed peas. Flavor with pepper and Creole seasoning. Add fresh spinach until wilted and blended. Cut sausage links into ½ inch slices. Add sausage to mix. Heat all through and serve over rice.

Shrimp Bisque

3 pounds frozen baby salad shrimp, shelled with tails removed

1 stick butter

1 (26 ounce) can cream of mushroom soup

1 (26 ounce) can cream of chicken soup

1 (26 ounce) can tomato soup

6-8 cups half-and-half

3 heaping tablespoons Cajun seasoning

2 tablespoons chopped parsley

3 tablespoons Worcestershire sauce

3 tablespoons minced garlic

Hot sauce to taste

Place 1 pound of shrimp in food processor or blender and pulse for 1 minute. (Needs to be finely minced, not puréed.) Coarsely chop another pound.

Melt butter in a heavy pot. Add the soups and start with 6 cups of the half-and-half. Whisk until smooth. Add all 3 pounds of shrimp along with the Cajun seasoning, parsley, Worcestershire and garlic. Bring to a boil, stirring often or it will stick. Add additional half-and-half until desired consistency. Reduce heat and simmer, cooking 30 minutes. Add several drops of hot sauce to taste.

Steak Soup

1 pound round steak, finely ground

1 medium onion, finely chopped

1 large carrot, finely chopped

3 stalks celery, finely chopped

2 sticks butter

1 cup flour

3½ cups canned, diced tomatoes

3 quarts beef stock

1 tablespoon Worcestershire sauce

1½ tablespoons seasoned salt flavor enhancer

Salt and pepper to taste

1½ cups half-and-half

Braise meat and onions in a large pot. Add carrot, celery, butter and flour. Mix well and cook 10 minutes. Add tomatoes, beef stock, Worcestershire, seasoned salt, salt and pepper. Simmer for about 1 hour, stirring frequently. Add half-and-half the last 5 minutes before removing from heat. If mixture is too thick, add more beef stock and adjust seasonings.

This soup freezes well.

Makes approximately 4 quarts

"*How lovely is Your tabernacle, O Lord of hosts! My soul longs, yes, even faints for the courts of the Lord; Blessed are those who dwell in Your house; They will be praising You.*"

Psalm 84:1-2,4

"*Be hospitable to one another without grumbling. As each one has received a gift, minister it to one another, as good stewards of the manifold grace of God.*"

1 Peter 4:9-10

Spanish Chili

2	whole chipotle chilies, canned in adobo	2	teaspoons dried oregano
1	cup water	2	teaspoons salt
2	pounds fresh tomatillos	1	green bell pepper, chopped
2	large onions, chopped	2	(4 ounce) cans mild green chilies, chopped and drained well
8	garlic cloves		
3	tablespoons vegetable oil	1	tablespoon cornmeal
2	tablespoons ground cumin	2	(9 ounce) cans white beans, rinsed and drained
2	pounds ground turkey		
2	cups chicken broth		Mozzarella cheese and sour cream as a topping (optional)
1	bay leaf		

Purée the chipotle chilies with water and tomatillos and set aside. In a large Dutch oven, cook the onions and 5 of the garlic cloves in the oil over medium heat until onions are soft. Add the cumin, then the turkey, cooking until no longer pink. Add the chipotle pepper and tomatillo purée, broth, bay leaf, oregano and salt. Simmer uncovered 1 hour. Add more broth as needed to keep the turkey covered.

Stir in the bell pepper, green chilies, and cornmeal. Simmer 30 minutes. Stir in the white beans, the remaining garlic cloves. Simmer 5 minutes or until beans are heated through. Discard the bay leaf.

Serve with tortilla chips and sour cream, mozzarella cheese, or over a baked potato.

Mushroom Tomato Soup

8	ounces sliced mushrooms	1	can beef broth
1	medium onion, finely chopped	1	(28 ounce) can diced tomatoes (plain or Italian)
2	tablespoons butter		Optional: ¾ cup heavy cream
1	can cream of mushroom soup		¼ cup chopped fresh basil
1	cup spicy hot tomato juice		

Sauté onions and mushrooms in butter. Set aside. Mix soup, juice and broth in a large pot and simmer. Whisk to separate. Add tomatoes and mushroom mixture. Simmer 15 minutes.

May add ¾ cup heavy cream and ¼ cup chopped fresh basil, if desired.

Taco Soup

1 pound hamburger meat
1 small onion, chopped
1 can black beans
1 can red beans
1 can kidney beans
2 cans shoepeg corn, drained
1 can tomatoes with chilies

1 can tomato sauce
1 packet taco seasoning mix
1 packet ranch salad dressing seasoning mix
2 cups water
Salt and pepper to taste

Brown meat with the onion. Drain. Add beans, corn, chilies, tomato sauce, taco seasoning mix ranch dressing mix and water. Salt and pepper to taste. Simmer several hours.

Serve with cheese, sour cream and tortilla chips.

Tomato Basil Soup with Feta

6 ripe tomatoes
½ cup olive oil, divided
   Salt and pepper
1 cup chopped onions
1 bay leaf
3 cloves of garlic, minced

½ teaspoon salt
3 cups chicken broth
1 cup crumbled feta cheese
½ cup chopped fresh basil leaves
2 cups tomato sauce

Preheat oven to 400°. Peel, core and remove seeds from tomatoes. Dice tomatoes small. Mix tomatoes with ¼ cup olive oil, salt and pepper. Cover cookie sheet with foil, spray with cooking spray, and roast tomatoes for about 30 minutes, stirring occasionally.

In a deep saucepan, heat remaining oil over medium heat and sauté the onions until transparent, about 3 minutes. Stir in bay leaf, garlic and salt. Continue cooking for another 2 minutes. Add the roasted tomatoes and broth. Bring soup to a boil and simmer for 20 minutes, stirring often.

Remove from stove and remove bay leaf. Slightly purée soup in a blender or food processor, keeping the tomatoes a little chunky. Return the soup to the saucepan and stir in cheese, basil and tomato sauce. Season with black pepper.

Delicious served with Ranch Oyster Crackers

Freezes well.

RANCH OYSTER CRACKERS

¾ cup vegetable oil
1 teaspoon dill seed
½ teaspoon garlic powder
1 teaspoon lemon pepper
1 package ranch dressing mix
1 box or bag oyster crackers

Preheat oven to 275°. Combine all ingredients except oyster crackers and mix well. Line a jellyroll pan with foil. Put oyster crackers in a large bowl. Pour mixture over them and stir to coat. Spread out crackers onto foil and bake 15 minutes.

Turnip Green Soup

1 medium onion, chopped	1 package dried vegetable soup mix
2-3 cloves garlic, minced	1 teaspoon hot sauce
1 tablespoon olive oil	1 tablespoon sugar
2-3 cups water	Salt and pepper, to taste
3-4 cups cooked turnip greens	1 pound hickory smoked sausage, diced
2 cans great Northern beans	

Sauté onions and garlic in oil for 4 to 5 minutes. Add water, turnip greens, beans, soup mix, hot sauce, sugar, salt, pepper and sausage. Cook for 25 to 30 minutes over medium heat.

Top with shredded cheese and enjoy.

Frozen chopped turnips may be used and one packet of ham flavoring while they cook.

"*He* brought me to the banqueting house, and his banner over me was love."

Song of Songs 2:4

White Chicken Chili

1 tablespoon olive oil	¼ teaspoon cayenne pepper
2 medium onions, chopped	4 cups chicken broth
2 large cloves garlic, minced	4 cans great Northern beans
2 (4 ounce) cans chopped green chilies	4 cups diced cooked chicken breasts
2 teaspoons ground cumin	3 cups Monterey Jack cheese, grated
1½ teaspoons dried oregano	

In a large pot over medium heat, sauté onions and garlic in oil until tender. Add chilies and spices, stirring well. Add broth and bring to a boil and simmer for 10 minutes. Add beans and chicken. Simmer 40 minutes, stirring occasionally. Serve with cheese.

May also serve with sour cream, salsa, black olives and tortilla chips. Freezes well.

Big Wheel Sandwiches

1   loaf (round) Hawaiian bread
4   ounces honey baked ham, sliced
4   ounces American cheese, sliced
2   tablespoons Dijon mustard
4   ounces turkey, sliced
2   tablespoons mayonnaise
4   ounces Swiss cheese, sliced
8   ounces bacon, fried crisp and drained
¼   cup margarine, melted
2   teaspoons poppy seeds

Preheat oven to 350°. Slice bread into 3 layers. Place bottom layer on baking sheet. Top with ham, American cheese and 1 tablespoon mustard. Top with middle layer of bread. Layer turkey, mayonnaise, Swiss and bacon. Spread on 1 tablespoon of mustard and put the top layer of bread on. Drizzle with margarine and sprinkle with poppy seeds. Bake 25 minutes. Cut into wedges.

Great for tailgating.

Mini Fried Tomato Sandwiches

¼   cup butter
5-6 ripe Roma tomatoes, sliced (or 3 regular tomatoes)
⅓   cup sugar
    Salt and pepper
1   baguette cut in ¼ inch slices (20 slices)
5   ounces cream cheese, softened

Melt butter in frying pan. Place sliced tomatoes in pan and sprinkle with ½ of the sugar, salt and pepper. Fry for 4 to 5 minutes, flip and sprinkle with remaining sugar, salt and pepper.

Put baguette slices on a cookie sheet and broil until golden. Remove from oven. Spread softened cream cheese and return to oven until cream cheese bubbles. Spread fried tomatoes over open-faced toast.

"You shall eat in plenty and be satisfied, and praise the name of the Lord your God, who has dealt wondrously with you."

Joel 2:26

Muffalettas

2	(12 ounce) jars mixed pickled vegetables	2	tablespoons olive oil	
1	cup pimento stuffed olive slices	¼	pound thinly sliced salami	
3	tablespoons olive oil	¼	pound thinly sliced pastrami	
1	(1 pound) round or long mountain bread	4	ounces thinly sliced mozzarella or provolone cheese	

Preheat oven to 350°. Drain mixed vegetables, reserving 1 tablespoon of liquid. May remove hot peppers. Finely chop vegetables. Combine vegetables, reserved liquid, olives, and 3 tablespoons olive oil; stir well. Slice bread in half horizontally. Drizzle 2 tablespoons olive oil over cut sides of loaf. Layer half of olive mixture, meats and cheese alternately on bottom of loaf. Repeat with remaining ingredients, with olive mixture on top before topping with remaining bread layer. Slice sandwich into wedges or quarters. Wrap sandwich in aluminum foil and place on a baking sheet. Bake 15 to 20 minutes.

Makes 4 sandwiches

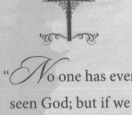

"No one has ever seen God; but if we love one another, God lives in us and his love is made complete in us."

1 John 4:12

Thank you, God, for little things
That often come our way,
The things we take for granted
but don't mention when we pray,
The unexpected courtesy,
the thoughtful, kindly deed.
A hand reached out to help us
in the time of sudden need.
Oh make us more aware, dear God,
of little daily graces
That come to us with "sweet surprise"
from neverdreamed of places.

~Helen Steiner Rice

SALADS

"*But* the fruit of the Spirit is love, joy, peace, patience, kindness, goodness, faithfulness, gentleness and self-control. Against such things there is no law."

Galatians 5:22-23

Asparagus and Artichoke Salad

2 bunches asparagus, bottoms trimmed
1 teaspoon Dijon mustard
½ teaspoon ground black pepper
1 teaspoon lemon zest
2 tablespoons fresh lemon juice
2 tablespoons white balsamic vinegar
2 teaspoons chopped fresh thyme
¼ cup olive oil
2 (14 ounce) cans artichoke hearts, drained
Salt to taste
½ cup crumbled feta cheese

Bring a large pot of water to boil. Set a large bowl of water with ice next to the stove. Place the asparagus in the boiling water and blanch until bright green and just tender, about 4 to 5 minutes. Transfer the asparagus to the ice water to cool and stop the cooking. Drain well.

In a large bowl, whisk together the mustard, pepper, lemon zest, lemon juice, vinegar, thyme and oil. Gently toss the drained asparagus and artichoke hearts in the dressing. Sprinkle with salt and stir again. Top with feta cheese. Chill and serve cold or room temperature.

Shoepeg Salad

¾ cup white vinegar
½ cup vegetable oil
1 cup sugar
1 teaspoon salt
1 teaspoon pepper
2 (11 ounce) cans white shoepeg corn, drained
1 (15 ounce) can Le Sueur English Peas, drained
1 (14½ ounce) can French style green beans, drained
1 cup diced celery
1 cup diced green bell pepper
1 cup chopped onion
1 (2 ounce) jar diced pimento, drained

In a saucepan, combine vinegar, oil, sugar, salt and pepper. Bring to a boil over medium heat. Stir until sugar dissolves. Chill. Combine corn, English peas, green beans, celery, bell pepper, onion and drained pimento. Pour marinade mixture over vegetables; mix well and chill 8 hours. Drain off some of the marinade before serving.

For health and food, For love and friends, For everything Thy goodness sends, We thank thee.

~Ralph Waldo Emerson, 1803-1882

Artichoke and Rice Salad

1	(6 ounce) package chicken-flavored rice	2	(6 ounce) jars marinated artichoke hearts, sliced and drained (reserve liquid)
4	green onions, sliced thinly	¾	teaspoon curry powder
½	bell pepper, chopped	⅓	cup mayonnaise
12	pimento stuffed olives, sliced		

Cook rice according to package directions. Cool and drain in a large bowl. Add green onions, bell pepper and olives. Drain artichokes, reserving marinade; cut into quarters. Combine artichoke marinade, curry powder, and mayonnaise; whisk until smooth. Add artichoke hearts to rice salad. Toss with dressing. Chill.

Makes 8 servings

Asparagus Pasta Salad

1	pound bowtie pasta	¼	teaspoon crushed red pepper flakes
1	pound asparagus, ends trimmed	4	tablespoons olive oil
	Olive oil, for drizzling		Kosher salt and freshly ground black pepper
1	shallot, finely chopped	¼	cup thinly sliced fresh chives
1	clove garlic, finely chopped	1	(4 ounce) container crumbled goat cheese
2	teaspoons Dijon mustard		
	Zest and juice of ½ lemon		

Preheat the oven to 425°. Add pasta to a large pot of boiling, salted water and cook until al dente. Drain in a colander and let cool.

Slice asparagus on the bias into ½ inch pieces. Place the asparagus on a sheet tray. Drizzle with olive oil and season with salt and pepper. Place in oven and roast for 10 minutes until slightly tender. Remove and let cool.

In a small bowl, combine shallot, garlic, mustard, lemon zest, lemon juice and red pepper flakes. Whisk in olive oil and season with salt and pepper. Add chives.

Combine pasta and roasted asparagus in large bowl. Drizzle with dressing and toss. Add the crumbled goat cheese, toss and serve.

Makes 6 to 8 servings

CASHEW CHICKEN SALAD

2 cups cooked, chopped chicken

1 (6.9 ounce) package long grain and wild rice, cooked

¾ cup mayonnaise

2 tablespoons milk

¾ cup chopped celery

2 tablespoons chopped onion

¾ cup cashews

¾ cup red seedless grapes, halved

Combine chicken with remaining 7 ingredients and mix well. Chill and serve cold.

Chicken-Orzo Salad

1¼ cups uncooked orzo
3 cups chopped grilled chicken breast
1½ cups trimmed arugula
1 cup grape tomatoes, halved
½ cup chopped red bell pepper
¼ cup red onion
2 tablespoons chopped fresh basil
1 teaspoon chopped fresh oregano
2 tablespoons red wine vinegar
1 tablespoon extra virgin olive oil
⅛ teaspoon salt
⅛ teaspoon black pepper
6 tablespoons (1½ ounces) crumbled feta cheese

Cook orzo according to package directions, omitting salt and fat. Drain well.

Combine pasta, chicken, arugula, tomatoes, red bell pepper, onion, basil and oregano in a large bowl; toss well. Combine vinegar, oil, salt and pepper in a small bowl, stirring with a whisk. Drizzle vinegar mixture over pasta mixture; toss well to coat. Sprinkle with cheese.

Best with fresh basil. Can substitute dried oregano for fresh.

Makes 6 to 8 servings

Chicken Pasta Salad for a Crowd

8 large chicken breasts
2 bags (or boxes) of bowtie pasta
1½ cups red wine vinegar
1½ cups mayonnaise
1½ cups corn oil
½ jar pesto (3-4 tablespoons)
8 celery stalks, chopped
½ purple onion, chopped
Salt and pepper to taste
½ cup chopped fresh parsley

Cook chicken breasts slowly in crock pot or oven so they will not dry out. Cool and chop chicken. Cook pasta until al dente. Whisk together vinegar, mayonnaise, corn oil and pesto; add celery and onion. Place chopped chicken and pasta in a large bowl, pour ¾ sauce over pasta. Reserve the rest of sauce in refrigerator. Add salt, pepper and parsley. Stir gently to coat well. Cover and refrigerate. Add extra sauce just before serving. Lasts for about a week.

Kind hearts are the gardens,
Kind thoughts are the roots,
Kind words are the flowers, kind deeds are the fruits.
Take care of your gardens and keep out the weeds,
Fill it with sunshine, kind words, and kind deeds.

~Henry Wadsworth Longfellow, 1807-1882

Lulu's Pasta Salad A Greque with Lemon Vinaigrette Dressing

1	pound fettuccini	
1	cup crumbled feta cheese	
1	cup Greek olives	
1	cup pepperoncini	
2	diced tomatoes	
1	cup diced purple onions	

1½ cups walnuts (6 ounce package)
½ cup chopped parsley
1 tablespoon red pepper flakes
Lemon Vinaigrette Dressing
Grilled chicken breast, if desired

Cook pasta according to package directions. For a pretty presentation, place pasta in large individual bowls and layer all ingredients over hot pasta and add dressing to each bowl or combine all ingredients in one large bowl and pour dressing over the entire pasta salad. Add chopped grilled chicken, if desired.

This is a meal all by itself, but also good with a nice green salad and a slice of French bread.

LEMON VINAIGRETTE DRESSING

1 cup olive oil
⅓ cup fresh (not bottled) lemon juice

Salt
Pepper

Mix all ingredients. May be refrigerated for later use.

Noodle Salad

1 box angel hair pasta
1 bunch green onions, diced
4 large carrots, peeled and grated

Salt to taste
1 tablespoon Accent seasoning
¼ cup sugar
¾ cup mayonnaise

Cook angel hair pasta according to directions until al dente. Pour pasta into a strainer and run cold water over until cool, drain well. Add carrots, green onions, salt and Accent seasoning to pasta. Mix mayonnaise and sugar together and then add to pasta mixture. Refrigerate at least 2 hours before serving.

RASPBERRY SALAD DRESSING

1 (10 ounce) jar seedless raspberry preserves
½ cup balsamic vinegar
¼ cup olive oil

Microwave raspberry preserves on low power about 1 minute or until melted. Whisk in vinegar and olive oil until blended well. Let cool. Serve at room temperature over mixed greens.

Black and Bleu Salad

½   cup light olive oil

¼   cup balsamic vinegar

1   teaspoon salt

½   teaspoon freshly ground black pepper

1   (1 pound) flank steak

1   tablespoon plus 1½ teaspoons Creole seasoning, divided

1   pound medium fresh shrimp, peeled and deveined

4   (6 ounce) bags fresh baby spinach, stemmed

1   (5 ounce) package crumbled bleu cheese

In a small bowl, whisk together olive oil, vinegar, salt and pepper. Set aside. Sprinkle flank steak with 1 tablespoon Creole seasoning. Spray grill rack with nonstick nonflammable cooking spray. Preheat grill to medium-high heat (350° to 400°). Grill steak, covered with grill lid, for 4 to 5 minutes per side or until desired degree of doneness. Remove from grill and let stand for 10 minutes. Cut steak across the grain into thin slices.

In a small bowl, combine shrimp and remaining 1½ teaspoons Creole seasoning. Grill shrimp in grill basket, covered with grill lid, for 1 to 2 minutes per side until shrimp are pink and firm.

In a large mixing bowl, combine spinach, sliced steak, shrimp and olive oil mixture, tossing gently to coat. Divide salad mixture among serving plates. Sprinkle each with bleu cheese crumbles. Serve immediately.

Makes 6 to 8 servings

Spinach Pecan Salad

1   large bag mixed lettuce

1   large bag of spinach

6   ounces candied pecans

6   ounces dried cranberries

2   Granny Smith apples, cored and sliced

Poppy seed dressing

Combine lettuce, spinach, candied pecans, cranberries, and apples; add poppy seed dressing and toss to coat. Serve immediately.

See Homemade Poppy Seed Dressing (page 77).

FRITO SALAD

1 pound ground beef, browned and drained

1 package taco seasoning mix

1 cup water

1 head of lettuce

1-2 cups shredded Cheddar cheese

1 onion, sliced

Cherry tomatoes

1 can pinto beans

1 bottle Catalina dressing

1 bag regular Fritos (the small ones)

Mix taco seasoning and water with beef. Simmer until thickened. Shred lettuce and add cheese, onions, beans and tomatoes. Combine with meat and dressing when ready to eat. Add Fritos.

Marinated Flank Steak Salad

JACK'S HOT AND SWEET PECANS

4 tablespoons butter

3 tablespoons sugar

¼ cup Jack Daniels

2 tablespoons hot pepper sauce

1½ teaspoons salt

½ teaspoon garlic powder

4 cups pecan halves

Heat oven to 350°. Combine butter, sugar, Jack Daniels, pepper sauce, salt and garlic powder in a large saucepan. Bring to boil over medium heat, stirring to blend. Boil 3 minutes.

Stir in pecans to coat. Spread nuts in a single layer on baking sheet. Bake 45 minutes.

These are wonderful in a salad!

2	pounds flank steak	1	teaspoon dried oregano
4	tablespoons Dijon mustard	1	sweet red onion, sliced and separated into rings
2	cloves fresh garlic, pressed or minced	1	green bell pepper, sliced and cut into rings
2	tablespoons freshly squeezed lemon juice	1	red and green bell pepper, seeded and cut into strips
1	tablespoon soy sauce	¼	pound fresh bean sprouts
½	cup olive oil		

Lightly score both sides of the steak creating a diamond pattern. This prevents the meat from curling as you cook it. Combine the mustard, garlic, lemon juice and soy sauce in a small bowl. Whisk the oil in gradually until the marinade is creamy. Mix in the oregano. Brush both sides of the steak with marinade and place in the refrigerator several hours or overnight.

Bring to room temperature before cooking. Broil or grill on high, 5 minutes on each side, basting when turning over. Meat will be slightly pink. Let meat sit for a few minutes before slicing. Cut diagonally against the grain into thin slices. Place the onion rings, red and green pepper strips and bean sprouts in a bowl with the steak strips.

DRESSING

¾	cup extra virgin olive oil	1	tablespoon fresh lemon juice
1	large clove garlic, pressed		Salt and pepper to taste
¼	cup rice wine vinegar	2	tablespoons chopped fresh parsley
1	tablespoon soy sauce		Pita pocket bread
2	tablespoons Dijon mustard		

Mix all dressing ingredients, except parsley, in a blender or food processor. Blend for 1 minute. Add parsley. Mix well. Place in pita pockets or serve alone. Keeps for one week in refrigerator.

Chicken may be substituted for the flank steak.

Strawberry Bacon Salad with Homemade Poppy Seed Dressing

3 heads curly red leaf lettuce, cut into pieces	1 cup chopped pecans
2 cups fresh strawberries, sliced	1 pound bacon, cooked and crumbled

Combine all ingredients in a large bowl. Pour desired amount of poppy seed dressing over salad.

HOMEMADE POPPY SEED DRESSING

1½ cups sugar	2 teaspoons dry mustard
⅔ cup white vinegar	2 teaspoons salt
⅔ cup vegetable oil	4 tablespoons poppy seeds
¼ onion, grated or minced	

Combine all ingredients in a jar and shake to combine. Sit in the refrigerator for at least an hour before serving. Shake well. Pour over Strawberry Bacon Salad.

Dressing will keep in the refrigerator for several weeks. Before using, sit dressing out to reach room temperature or put in the microwave for 10 seconds; shake well before serving.

Fruit and Honey Spinach Salad

8 cups loosely packed fresh spinach leaves	2 tablespoons raspberry white wine vinegar
2 cups cantaloupe balls	1 tablespoon honey
1½ cups halved fresh strawberries	2 teaspoons olive oil
2 tablespoons seedless raspberry jam	¼ cup chopped macadamia nuts

Combine spinach, cantaloupe balls and strawberries in a bowl and toss gently. Combine jam, raspberry vinegar, honey and olive oil in a small bowl and whisk until blended. Drizzle over spinach mixture and toss; sprinkle with nuts.

Makes 6 servings

SALAD DRESSING FOR FRUIT AND GREENS

1 cup sugar

2 teaspoons dry mustard

2 teaspoons salt

2 teaspoons grated onion

9 tablespoons cider vinegar, divided

2 cups canola oil

1 tablespoon paprika

Whisk sugar, mustard, salt, onion and 4 tablespoons of cider vinegar in a bowl. Gradually add oil. Beat until thick and light. Continue beating, and slowly add remaining vinegar. Stir in paprika.

Makes 2½ cups

Mandarin Orange and Pear Salad with Toasted Pecan Vinaigrette

10 cups mixed baby lettuce	½ small red onion, thinly sliced
6 fresh Mandarin oranges, peeled, seeded and segmented	Toasted Pecan Vinaigrette (recipe in sidebar)
2 pears, cored and cut into ¼ inch-thick slices	

In a large bowl, combine lettuce, orange sections, pear slices and red onion. Drizzle with Toasted Pecan Vinaigrette Dressing, tossing gently to coat. Serve immediately.

Makes about 6 to 8 servings

TOASTED PECAN VINAIGRETTE DRESSING

2 tablespoons Dijon mustard

1 tablespoon honey

¼ cup extra virgin olive oil

¼ cup balsamic vinegar

1 cup chopped toasted pecans

In a medium bowl, combine Dijon and honey. Slowly add olive oil. Slowly add balsamic vinegar, whisking to combine. Stir in toasted pecans.

Makes about ½ cup

Mandarin Salad

½ cup sliced almonds	1 cup celery
3 tablespoons sugar	2 whole onions, chopped
½ head iceberg lettuce	1 (11 ounce) can Mandarin oranges, drained
½ head romaine lettuce	

Cook almonds and sugar over medium heat, stirring until coated and sugar dissolves. Mix iceberg and romaine lettuce, celery and onions. Just before serving, add almonds and Mandarin oranges. Toss with dressing. Serve.

DRESSING

½ teaspoon salt	2 tablespoons sugar
Dash of pepper	2 tablespoons vinegar
¼ cup vegetable oil	Dash of Tabasco sauce
1 tablespoon chopped parsley	

Mix dressing ingredients and chill.

Greek Salad

SALAD

2	large tomatoes, seeded and cut into chunks	1	cup pitted Kalamata olives
1	English cucumber, cut into chunks	⅓	cup thinly sliced red onion
		5	ounces crumbled feta cheese

In a salad bowl, combine the tomatoes, cucumber, olives, onion and feta cheese. Toss with the dressing and refrigerate. Make ahead several hours for the flavors to blend.

DRESSING

¼	cup red wine vinegar	1	teaspoon sea salt
2	teaspoons lemon juice		Pepper to taste
2	cloves garlic, minced	½	cup extra virgin olive oil
1	heaping teaspoon dried oregano		

For the dressing, combine the vinegar, lemon juice, garlic, oregano, salt, and pepper in a small bowl. Whisk in the oil.

Makes 6 servings

Green Jacket House Salad

4	tablespoons oil		Romaine and iceberg lettuce (enough for four)
2	tablespoons red wine vinegar	2	teaspoons chopped green onion
	Seasoned salt to taste		
1	teaspoon Accent seasoning	2	teaspoons chopped parsley
½	teaspoon oregano	1	piece toasted pita bread (torn in small pieces)
1	tomato, chopped		

In a salad bowl, combine oil, wine vinegar, salt, Accent seasoning and oregano. Add chopped tomato to dressing and refrigerate until ready to serve. When ready to serve, mix lettuce, onion, parsley, and pita bread. Pour dressing over and toss to coat.

It is best to tear up pita bread before toasting so that it will be crunchier.

STRAWBERRY POPPY SEED DRESSING

1¼ cups sugar

⅔ cup vegetable oil

⅔ cup white vinegar

3 tablespoons poppy seeds

½ cup chopped onion

6-8 strawberries

2 teaspoons salt

Combine all ingredients in a blender. Process well.

Will keep in the refrigerator for several weeks.

Makes about 1 quart

Mango Cucumber Slaw

3	cups thinly sliced Napa cabbage
2	cups thinly sliced red cabbage
1	ripe mango, peeled, cut into thin strips
½	cucumber peeled, seeded and cut into thin strips
½	small Vidalia onion, thinly sliced
½	small red bell pepper, thinly sliced
1	carrot, shredded
¼	cup fresh cilantro leaves
3	tablespoons rice vinegar
2	tablespoons fresh lime juice
3	tablespoons vegetable oil
1	tablespoon sweet chili sauce
2	teaspoons sugar
1	teaspoon toasted sesame oil

Combine cabbages, mango, cucumber, onion, bell pepper, carrot and cilantro. Whisk together vinegar, lime juice, vegetable oil, chili sauce, sugar and sesame oil. Pour over slaw mixture and toss well to coat. Cover and chill one hour. Serve immediately.

Makes 7 cups

Asian Slaw

2	packages Ramen beef-flavored noodles (broken up)
¼	cup sugar
½	cup oil
⅓	cup distilled white vinegar
1	(16 ounce) package broccoli slaw
1	cup sunflower seeds
1	cup toasted slivered almonds
4-6	chopped green onions

Mix the flavor packet from the noodles with sugar, oil and vinegar. Set liquid mixture aside. Mix slaw, sunflower seeds, toasted slivered almonds and green onions. Keep chilled. Add the noodles and the dressing immediately before serving. Toss well and serve.

Iceberg Wedge with Creamy Bleu Cheese Dressing

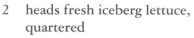

2 heads fresh iceberg lettuce, quartered

1 (4 ounce) container crumbled bleu or Gorgonzola cheese

4 slices bacon, cooked until crisp and chopped coarsely

1 medium tomato, seeded and chopped

Place iceberg wedges on individual salad plates. Drizzle Bleu Cheese Dressing over each wedge and sprinkle each one with crumbled bleu cheese, crumbled bacon and chopped tomato.

CREAMY BLEU CHEESE DRESSING

½ cup mayonnaise

½ cup sour cream

⅓ cup milk

1 (4 ounce) container crumbled bleu or Gorgonzola cheese

½ teaspoon salt

2 teaspoons lemon juice

In a blender process all ingredients until smooth.

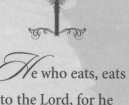

"*He* who eats, eats to the Lord, for he gives God thanks."

Romans 14:6

Crispy Coleslaw

1 small cabbage, shredded (1½ pounds)

1 medium sweet onion, chopped

1 carrot, scraped and shredded

1 small green pepper, chopped

1 small sweet red pepper, chopped

1 small sweet yellow pepper, chopped

1 cup sugar

⅔ cup white vinegar

½ cup vegetable oil

1 teaspoon salt

¼ teaspoon celery seeds

¼ teaspoon mustard seeds

Combine cabbage, onion, carrot, green pepper, red pepper and yellow pepper in a bowl; stir. Combine sugar, vinegar, oil, salt, celery seeds and mustard seeds in saucepan; bring to a boil, stirring until sugar dissolves. Pour vinegar mixture over cabbage mixture, toss gently. Cover and chill at least 2 hours. Serve with slotted spoon.

Makes 8 servings

Viking Ramen Noodle Salad

1	head romaine lettuce, washed and torn into bite-sized pieces	¼	cup slivered almonds, toasted
3	green onions, washed and sliced	3	tablespoons sesame seeds, toasted
1	package chicken-flavor Ramen noodles, crumbled (save seasoning packet for dressing)		

Preheat oven to 300°. Wash lettuce and green onions; toss in salad bowl. Crumble Ramen noodles over salad. Toast almonds and sesame seeds in oven until golden brown. Add to salad; toss with dressing and serve immediately.

DRESSING

¾	cup extra virgin olive oil	½	teaspoon salt
¾	cup white wine vinegar	½	teaspoon pepper
¼	cup sugar		

Whisk together olive oil, vinegar, sugar, salt, pepper and seasoning packet.

Makes 6 servings

Lemon Apple Coleslaw

1	bag coleslaw (cabbage and carrots)	2	tablespoons minced onion
2	apples, chopped	1	teaspoon grated lemon rind
⅓	cup mayonnaise	2	tablespoons fresh lemon juice
1	tablespoon sugar	¼	teaspoon salt
		¼	teaspoon pepper

Combine coleslaw mix and apples in large bowl. Whisk together mayonnaise, sugar, minced onion, lemon rind, lemon juice, salt and pepper, toss with coleslaw. Cover and chill 1 hour.

Napa Coleslaw

2   packages oriental-flavor Ramen noodles and seasoning packet
½   cup butter, melted
1   (2½ ounce) package slivered almonds
6-8 green onions, chopped
1   head cabbage, chopped
1   cup vegetable oil
½   cup sugar
½   cup cider vinegar
2   tablespoons soy sauce
½   teaspoon salt and pepper to taste

Preheat oven to 350°. Reserve seasoning packet from the Ramen noodles. Crush noodles and add almonds. Toss with melted butter. Toast in oven for 20 minutes. Drain and blot.

Combine the cabbage and onions in a large bowl. Mix the oil, seasoning packet, sugar, vinegar, soy sauce, salt and pepper together. Whisk until well blended. Just before serving, mix cabbage with the noodle mixture. Toss with the dressing. Add dried cranberries and chopped Granny Smith apples, if desired.

This is delicious and works very well with barbecue.

Balsamic Apple Salad

DRESSING
1   cup vegetable oil
½   cup sugar
½   cup balsamic vinegar
1   teaspoon paprika
½   teaspoon ground mustard
½   teaspoon salt

Mix all ingredients in a jar and shake well to blend.

APPLE SALAD
2   Granny Smith apples, chopped
1   (10 ounce) bag Italian greens
1   (10 ounce) bag spinach
¼   cup chopped red onion
1   cup crumbled feta cheese
1   cup toasted pecans

Add chopped apples to dressing mixture and marinate for at least 30 minutes in refrigerator. Toss the apples and dressing with Italian greens, spinach, onion, feta cheese and toasted pecans prior to serving.

FROZEN FRUIT SALAD

1 (20 ounce) can crushed pineapple

3 bananas, mashed

¼ cup chopped cherries

1 (16 ounce) container sour cream

2 tablespoons lemon juice

¾ cup sugar

¼ cup finely chopped nuts

⅛ teaspoon salt

Mix all ingredients together. Put cupcake liners in muffin tins. Pour mixture into liners and freeze. After frozen, individual salads may be placed in zip-top plastic freezer bags for storage. Take out of freezer 5 minutes before serving.

ORANGE FLAVORED GELATIN SALAD

1 small can Mandarin oranges

1 (16 ounce) container small curd cottage cheese

1 (20 ounce) can crushed pineapple

1 (3 ounce) box orange flavored gelatin

1 (8 ounce) container nondairy whipped topping

Drain Mandarin oranges and crushed pineapple. Mix the dry flavored gelatin into the cottage cheese. Add oranges and pineapple. Fold in the frozen nondairy whipped topping and fluff up. Ready to serve or you may put in the refrigerator for 5 minutes to stiffen.

Grape Salad

1	(8 ounce) package cream cheese, softened	1-2	pounds seedless grapes (5 cups) halved
1	cup sugar	3	cups toasted pecan pieces
1	cup sour cream		Brown sugar
1	tablespoon vanilla extract		

Rinse grapes and dry on paper towels. Mix cream cheese, sugar, sour cream, and vanilla in large bowl until creamy. Add grapes to mixture and stir well. Put a layer of grape mixture in bottom of serving bowl. Sprinkle brown sugar and pecans over grape mixture. Use as much brown sugar as you like. Alternate layers of grape mixture, brown sugar and pecans until all is used. End with a sprinkle of brown sugar.

Champagne Salad

1	(8 ounce) package cream cheese, softened	1	(10 ounce) package frozen strawberries, partially thawed
¾	cup sugar	2	bananas, sliced
1	(15 ounce) can crushed pineapple, drained	9	ounces whipped topping

Blend the cream cheese and sugar in a large bowl. Add the crushed pineapple and unstrained strawberries and mix well. Fold in the banana slices and whipped topping. Spoon into a 9x13 inch dish, a loaf pan or a ring mold. Cover tightly. Freeze until firm. Cut into squares or unmold the loaf pan or ring mold onto a serving plate and slice into serving portions.

Store any unused salad, tightly wrapped, in the freezer.

Makes 8 servings

Buttermilk Chive Dressing

¾ cup buttermilk
½ cup mayonnaise
2 tablespoons chopped fresh chives
1 tablespoon minced green onion

1 garlic clove, minced
½ teaspoon salt
¼ teaspoon freshly ground pepper

Whisk together all ingredients. Cover, chill until ready to use.

Caesar Salad Dressing

½ cup olive oil
1 small clove garlic
3 tablespoons red wine vinegar
3 tablespoons Parmesan cheese
1 teaspoon salt

Dash pepper
¼ teaspoon dry mustard
1 egg
2 dashes Worcestershire sauce

Combine all ingredients in a blender and process until smooth.

Creamy Basil Vinaigrette

½ cup plain fat free yogurt
2 tablespoons chopped fresh basil
2 tablespoons balsamic vinaigrette

2 tablespoons honey
¼ cup red wine vinegar
½ teaspoon salt
¼ teaspoon pepper

Whisk together all ingredients. Serve immediately or cover and chill up to 8 hours. If chilling, let stand at room temperature 30 minutes before serving.

BLEU CHEESE DRESSING

½ cup mayonnaise

½ cup sour cream

⅓ cup milk

1 (4 ounce) container bleu cheese or Gorgonzola cheese

½ teaspoon salt

2 teaspoons lemon juice

In a blender, process all ingredients until smooth.

Margaret's French Dressing

1 small onion, chopped	2 teaspoons salt
Juice of one lemon	1 teaspoon pepper
½ cup sugar	2 teaspoons paprika
½ cup vinegar	1 cup vegetable oil
½ cup chili sauce	

Place all ingredients except oil in blender. Process on medium speed for 1 minute. With blender on, slowly pour in oil and continue to blend for 20 seconds. Pour dressing into a jar and refrigerate.

Dressing will keep for months in refrigerator. This dressing may be served over avocado and grapefruit salad or any other salad.

Makes 8 to 10 servings

Olive Garden Salad Dressing

½ cup mayonnaise	½ teaspoon Italian seasoning (dry dressing mix)
⅓ cup white distilled vinegar	
1 teaspoon vegetable oil	2 tablespoons fresh parsley, chopped
2 tablespoons white corn syrup	
4 tablespoons Parmesan cheese	1 tablespoon fresh lemon juice
¼ teaspoon garlic salt	

Combine all ingredients in a blender or food processor until well mixed. Chill.

Keeps for 1 to 2 weeks.

Stella's Salad Dressing

½ cup canola oil	5 drops hot sauce
3 tablespoons white vinegar	¼ cup sugar
2 cloves garlic, pressed	Salt and pepper to taste

Mix all ingredients together with a wire whisk or shake in a jar.

HONEY MUSTARD DRESSING

½ cup mayonnaise

2 tablespoons Dijon Mustard

2 tablespoons honey

Stir together all ingredients.

May also be used as a dipping sauce for chicken.

PASTA, RICE AND SAUCES

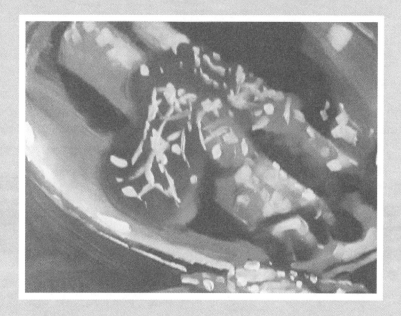

"*L*ove the Lord your God with all your heart and with all your soul
and with all your mind and with all your strength."

Mark 12:30

Baked Penne with Bacon

1 pound package bacon
1 (16 ounce) package mini penne pasta
2 tablespoons olive oil
2 tablespoons all-purpose flour
4 cups chicken broth
1 tablespoon Italian seasoning

Salt and pepper to taste
Garlic powder to taste
1 cup heavy whipping cream
1 cup five blend Italian shredded cheese
1½ cups shredded Parmesan cheese, divided

Preheat oven to 350°. Place bacon on a jellyroll pan and bake for 5 minutes or until crispy. Remove the bacon and place on paper towels to drain. Cook pasta according to package directions.

While pasta is cooking, put olive oil in a frying pan and sprinkle in flour when hot. Whisk for 1 to 2 minutes to get the starchy taste out of the flour. Slowly add in the chicken broth, Italian seasoning, salt, pepper and garlic powder to make white sauce. Cook for 4 to 5 minutes until slightly thickened. Add heavy whipping cream.

Drain pasta and put back in cooking pot. Add crumbled bacon, Italian shredded cheese, 1 cup of shredded Parmesan cheese, and the white sauce. Mix together well. Place into a greased 9x13 inch baking dish. Sprinkle with the rest of the Parmesan cheese. Bake 45 minutes until lightly browned on top.

Linguine with Plum Tomatoes, Steak and Bleu Cheese

8 ounces linguine
6 tablespoons olive oil
2 ounces bleu cheese
2 tablespoons red wine vinegar
1 clove garlic
4 plum tomatoes, cut into ¼ inch slices

1 pound filet, grilled and sliced into thin strips
1 bunch scallions, chopped
½ red bell pepper, cut into ¼ inch slices
½ cup chopped fresh basil

Cook linguine. In a food processor, purée olive oil, bleu cheese, red wine vinegar and garlic. Combine all ingredients and toss.

You only are the maker of all things near and far.

You paint the wayside flower,

You light the evening star.

The winds and waves obey you,

By you the birds are fed.

Much more to us your children,

You give our daily bread.

We thank you then, Creator,

For all things bright and good,

The seed time and the harvest,

Our life, our health, our food. Amen.

~Matthias Claudius, 1740-1815

Baked Spaghetti

1½	pounds ground beef	¼	teaspoon pepper
1	large onion, chopped	1	teaspoon garlic powder
3	tablespoons Worcestershire sauce	½	teaspoon oregano
1	(15 ounce) can crushed tomatoes	½	teaspoon basil
2	(5 ounce) cans tomato sauce	2	teaspoons chili powder
1	can cream of mushroom soup	1	(8 ounce) package thin spaghetti
1	teaspoon salt	½	pound grated cheese

Preheat oven to 350°. Brown ground beef and drain. Add onion, Worcestershire sauce, tomatoes, tomato sauce, soup, salt, pepper, garlic powder, oregano, basil and chili powder. Simmer at least 30 minutes, more if possible. Cook spaghetti for 8 minutes in boiling water. Rinse well and add to beef mixture. Put in 9x13 inch baking dish. Sprinkle with grated cheese and cover with foil. Bake 30 minutes.

Freezes well.

Beef Ravioli in Basil Cream Sauce

4	green onions, sliced	2	roma tomatoes, diced
1	head garlic, crushed	2	cups heavy cream
4	tablespoons butter		Parmesan cheese
1	teaspoon Italian seasoning (or to taste)		Cornstarch to thicken sauce
8	ounces chopped mushrooms	1½	pounds fresh ravioli, any flavor
8	basil leaves, cut up		

In a large skillet, sauté onions and garlic in butter. Add seasonings, mushrooms and basil. Add tomatoes and heavy cream. Simmer about 30 minutes to thicken the sauce. Add some Parmesan cheese. If sauce is too runny, add some cornstarch to a little water and stir into sauce. Boil ravioli according to package directions and add to sauce.

Italian Baked Penne

1 (16 ounce) package penne pasta
1 tablespoon olive oil
1 pound mild ground Italian sausage
1 cup diced onion
1 teaspoon minced garlic
8 ounces fresh mushrooms, sliced
¼ teaspoon ground black pepper
1½ teaspoons Italian seasoning
1 (14½ ounce) can diced tomatoes, Italian style
2 (14½ ounce) cans crushed tomatoes
3 cups chopped fresh spinach
8 ounces mozzarella cheese
½ cup Parmesan cheese

Preheat oven to 425°. Cook pasta. Heat oil and add sausage, onion and garlic; sauté until sausage is cooked. Drain sausage and put back in sauté pan. Add mushrooms and sauté 3 minutes. Add pepper, Italian seasoning and tomatoes. Simmer 8 minutes, stirring occasionally.

Combine sausage mixture with cooked pasta, spinach, mozzarella cheese and ¼ of the Parmesan cheese. Pour into a 9x13 inch baking dish. Sprinkle remaining Parmesan cheese on top. Bake 15 minutes.

"Grace be with you."

Colossians 4:18

Cheesy Italian Tortellini

½ pound ground beef
½ pound Italian sausage
1 (15 ounce) jar marinara sauce
1 cup sliced fresh mushrooms
14 ounces diced tomatoes with Italian seasoning
1 (9 ounce) package refrigerated cheese tortellini
1 cup shredded mozzarella

Cook ground beef and sausage in skillet about 10 minutes or until browned. Spray crock-pot with cooking spray. Mix beef mixture, marinara sauce, mushrooms, and tomatoes in crock-pot. Cover and cook on low heat 7 to 8 hours. Stir in tortellini; sprinkle with cheese. Cover and cook on low heat until tortellini is tender.

Stuffed Manicotti

12 manicotti shells
1 pound ground beef, browned and drained
2 small cans tomato paste
¾ cup chopped onion
⅓ cup parsley
1 tablespoon dried basil

1½ teaspoons salt
½ teaspoon garlic, minced
2 cups water
2 eggs, beaten
3 cups cottage cheese
½ cup grated Parmesan cheese
¼ tablespoon salt

Preheat oven to 350°. Cook manicotti in boiling, salted water until tender, 15 to 20 minutes. Drain. Rinse in cold water and set aside.

Stir tomato paste, onion, parsley, basil, salt and garlic into meat; add water. Simmer for 15 minutes, stirring occasionally. In bowl, combine the eggs, cheeses and salt. Stuff into manicotti shells. Pour half tomato meat sauce into baking dish. Arrange manicotti in dish and top with remaining sauce. Sprinkle with Parmesan cheese. Bake uncovered 40 to 45 minutes.

> "Let your speech always be with grace, seasoned with salt, that you may know how you ought to answer each one."
>
> *Colossians 4:6*

Coconut and Almond Couscous

1½ cups coconut milk
1 cup couscous, uncooked
¼ cup chopped green onions

1 teaspoon salt
½ teaspoon ground red pepper
¼ cup slivered almonds, toasted

Bring coconut milk to a boil in a medium saucepan. Gradually stir in couscous, green onions, salt and red pepper. Remove from heat, cover and let stand 5 minutes. Fluff with a fork. Sprinkle with toasted slivered almonds.

Lasagna Florentine

2	chicken-flavored bouillon cubes	1	cup half-and-half
¼	cup water	¾	cup chopped onions
½	cup butter or margarine	1	tablespoon butter, melted
⅓	cup all-purpose flour	2	(10 ounce) packages frozen chopped spinach, thawed, drained well
⅛	teaspoon salt	1	egg, slightly beaten
⅛	teaspoon Italian seasoning	1½	cups (6 ounces) shredded mozzarella cheese
	Dash garlic powder		
	Dash ground nutmeg	1	(8 ounce) carton sour cream
¼	teaspoon white pepper	9	lasagna noodles
¼	teaspoon lemon pepper	½	cup grated Parmesan cheese
1	cup whipping cream		

Preheat oven to 350°. Dissolve bouillon cubes in ¼ cup water. Set aside.

Melt ½ cup butter in saucepan over low heat. Add flour, salt, Italian seasoning, garlic powder, nutmeg, white pepper and lemon pepper. Stir until smooth. Cook 1 minute, stirring constantly. Gradually add bouillon, cream and half-and-half. Cook over medium heat, stirring until thickened and bubbly. Remove from heat and set aside.

Sauté onion in 1 tablespoon butter until tender. Drain spinach well. Combine spinach, sautéed onion, egg, mozzarella cheese and sour cream. Stir well and set aside.

Cook lasagna noodles as directed on the package. Drain. Layer 3 noodles in lightly greased 12x8 inch dish. Spread with spinach mixture. Repeat 3 noodles. Spread with ½ of the cream sauce. Repeat with remaining noodles. Spread with remaining cream sauce. Sprinkle top with Parmesan cheese. Bake uncovered 30 minutes.

Give us food,
Enough for health
and well-being.
Give us grace
and strength
To forbear and
persevere.
Give us courage
and gaiety
And the quiet mind.
Spare to us our
friends,
Soften to us our
enemies.

*~Robert Louis
Stevenson,
1850-1894*

"*How* precious
is your loving
kindness, Oh God!
Therefore, the
children of men put
their trust under the
shadow of your
wings. They are
abundantly satisfied
with the fullness of
Your house,
And you give them
drink from the river
of your pleasures.
For with you is the
fountain of life;
In Your light we
see light."

Psalm 36:7-9

Orzo with Spinach

2	cloves fresh garlic, minced	½	teaspoon salt
2	tablespoons butter, melted	3	cups tightly packed fresh spinach
1½	cups uncooked orzo		
2½	cups water	½	cup fresh Parmesan cheese (for topping)

In a saucepan, sauté garlic in butter over medium heat about 1 minute. Add orzo and coat with butter and garlic. Stir for a few minutes. Add water and salt and bring to a boil. Reduce heat and cook 12 minutes or until liquid is absorbed. Stir in spinach and most of cheese. May add a little more water to cook spinach down. Serve hot. May add additional cheese on top if desired.

Pasta Shells Florentine

16	jumbo pasta shells	1	cup cottage cheese
10	ounces frozen, chopped spinach (thawed and drained well)	1	egg white
		2	tablespoons Parmesan cheese
		¼	teaspoon nutmeg
4	ounces shredded whole milk mozzarella cheese	1	(24 ounce) jar of spaghetti sauce (your choice)

Preheat oven to 375°. Cook pasta shells according to package directions and set aside.

Mix spinach, mozzarella cheese, cottage cheese, egg white, Parmesan cheese and nutmeg in a medium sized bowl. Fill each shell with spinach mixture and place in a sprayed 9x13 inch dish. Spoon spaghetti sauce over shells. May sprinkle mozzarella and Parmesan cheese over sauce before baking. Cover with foil and cook 30 to 40 minutes.

Makes 4 servings

Penne with Sun-Dried Tomato Pesto

12　ounces penne pasta
1　(8½ ounce) jar sun-dried tomatoes packed in olive oil
2　garlic cloves

Salt and freshly ground black pepper
1　cup (packed) fresh basil leaves
½　cup grated Parmesan cheese

Cook the pasta in a large pot of boiling, salted water until tender but still firm to the bite, stirring occasionally, about 8 minutes. Drain, reserving 1 cup of the cooking liquid.

Blend the sun-dried tomatoes and their oil, garlic, salt and pepper to taste, and basil in a food processor until the tomatoes are finely chopped. Transfer the tomato mixture to a large bowl. Stir in Parmesan cheese. Add the pasta to the pesto and toss to coat, adding enough reserved cooking liquid to moisten. Season the pasta to taste with salt and pepper and serve.

Simple Sesame Noodles

¼　cup soy sauce
2　tablespoons sugar
4　cloves garlic, minced
2　tablespoons rice vinegar
3　tablespoons pure sesame oil
4　tablespoons canola oil

2　tablespoons hot water
½　teaspoon hot chili oil (optional)
12　ounces spaghetti noodles, cooked and drained
4　whole green onions, thinly sliced

Whisk all ingredients (except noodles and green onions) together in a bowl. Taste and adjust ingredients if needed. Pour sauce over warm noodles and toss to coat. Sprinkle with green onions.

Very good with boiled or sautéed shrimp tossed in!

"*Therefore, as God's chosen people, holy and dearly loved, clothe yourselves with compassion, kindness, humility, gentleness and patience.*"

Colossians 3:12

Four Ingredient Tomato Sauce

6   (28 ounce) cans diced or
    whole tomatoes
½   cup extra virgin olive oil

6-10 garlic cloves, finely chopped
2   teaspoons salt

Purée tomatoes in a blender or immersion blender until smooth. Heat olive oil in a large heavy bottomed pot over medium heat. Add finely chopped garlic and stir continuously for one to two minutes, taking care not to let the garlic brown.

Add ½ cup of tomato purée to the pot and stir it into the garlic mixture. Let it cook for a minute and the olive oil will take on a golden color. This will give the sauce a boost of flavor as the tomato sauce caramelizes in the garlic oil.

Add remaining tomato purée and salt. Stir well. Simmer on medium-low heat for at least four hours. Sauce will thicken. Continue cooking if you want a thicker sauce. Freeze in individual batches.

TEN USES FOR BASIC TOMATO SAUCE

PIZZA SAUCE

2   teaspoons sugar
1   can tomato paste
1   teaspoon dried basil

1   teaspoon dried oregano
6   cups tomato sauce

Combine all ingredients and simmer sauce an extra hour until sauce is quite thick.

SHRIMP AND TOMATO CAPELLINI SAUCE

½-1 cup shrimp, peeled
1   garlic clove, minced
2   tablespoons butter
    Tomato sauce

Chopped fresh herbs to taste
½   box Capellini (thinner than
    spaghetti), cooked

Sauté garlic and shrimp in butter until the shrimp are done. Add tomato sauce and fresh herbs. Toss with capellini.

BAKED CAULIFLOWER OR ZUCCHINI

Tomato sauce
Extra virgin olive oil
Parmesan cheese

Spoon sauce over cauliflower florets or chopped zucchini, drizzle with extra virgin olive oil and bake in a casserole dish until vegetables are tender. Sprinkle with Parmesan cheese during the last few minutes of baking (if desired).

This is particularly nice with garlic infused olive oil.

EASY ROSÉ SAUCE

½ cup 35% cooking cream Box of ravioli or manicotti
4 cups tomato sauce

Add cooking cream to tomato sauce and cook an additional 15 minutes over medium-low heat, stirring often. Serve over ravioli or manicotti.

CHICKEN PARMESAN

Tomato sauce Mozzarella cheese, shredded
Breaded chicken cutlets, Spaghetti, cooked
cooked

Spoon tomato sauce generously over cooked breaded chicken cutlets. Top with mozzarella cheese and bake until cheese is melted and sauce is bubbling, about 15 minutes at 350°. Serve with spaghetti.

SAUSAGE RAGOÛT

4 Italian sausages, casings   1 cup button mushrooms,
removed   quartered
1 medium onion, chopped   Green bell peppers, chopped
4-6 cups tomato sauce   (if desired)
Penne pasta

Sauté sausage and onion in a skillet until sausage is done. Add tomato sauce, mushrooms and green peppers (if desired). Cook 15 minutes and serve over penne pasta.

SIMPLE BOLOGNESE

1 pound ground beef, browned Tomato sauce
1 small onion, chopped   Splash red wine
2 stalks celery, chopped   Spaghetti, cooked

Add chopped onion and celery to skillet with ground beef and cook for a few minutes. Add tomato sauce and splash of red wine. Cook over low heat for an hour or so. Serve with spaghetti or as a base for lasagna.

GRILLED VEGETABLE GRATIN

Vegetables such as peppers, Tomato sauce
zucchini, eggplant, or   Freshly grated mozzarella
asparagus, chopped   cheese

Grill vegetables. Place vegetables in a casserole dish, top with tomato sauce and mozzarella. Broil until cheese is melted.

PENNE ARRABBIATA

Chilies to taste, crushed
Tomato sauce
Penne pasta
Romano cheese, grated
Parsley

Add crushed chilies to tomato sauce. Serve over penne pasta. Top with grated cheese and parsley.

MEATBALLS

Favorite meatballs
Tomato Sauce
Spaghetti

Simmer meatballs in tomato sauce and serve with spaghetti.

DIRTY RICE

¾ stick butter,
melted

1 small onion,
chopped

1 cup white rice,
uncooked

1 can beef
consommé soup

1 can French
onion soup

1 small can
mushrooms, sliced
(optional)

Preheat oven to 350°.
Cook butter and onion
in a casserole dish in
the microwave until
the onions are tender
(about 1 minute). Add
rice, beef consommé
soup, French onion soup
and mushrooms to the
casserole dish and bake
45 minutes to 1 hour,
until all liquid is
absorbed.

Tex-Mex Lasagna

¾ cup bottled salsa
1½ teaspoons ground cumin
1 (14½ ounce) can diced tomatoes
1 (8 ounce) can tomato sauce
Cooking spray
6 lasagna noodles, cooked
1 (15 ounce) can whole kernel corn, rinsed and drained
1 (15 ounce) can black beans, rinsed and drained
2 cups shredded four blend Mexican cheese
¼ cup chopped green onions

Preheat oven to 450°. Combine salsa, cumin, diced tomatoes and tomato sauce. Spread ⅔ cup sauce in bottom of an 8 inch square baking dish coated with cooking spray. Arrange 2 noodles over sauce, top with half of corn and half of beans. Sprinkle with ½ cup cheese, top with ⅔ cup sauce. Repeat layers once, top with remaining 2 noodles. Spread remaining sauce over noodles. Sprinkle with remaining 1 cup cheese. Cover and bake 30 minutes or until noodles are tender and sauce is bubbly. Let stand 15 minutes before serving. Sprinkle with onions.

Tomato Gorgonzola Sauce with Pasta Shells

¾ pound medium pasta shells
1 tablespoon olive oil
½ cup finely diced onion
¼ teaspoon ground pepper
¼ teaspoon red pepper flakes
1 teaspoon minced garlic
1 tablespoon tomato paste
2 cans diced tomatoes, undrained
2 tablespoons balsamic vinegar
½ cup heavy cream
½ cup crumbled Gorgonzola cheese
⅓ cup fresh basil

Cook pasta shells. Heat oil; add onion, pepper and pepper flakes. Cook 3 minutes. Add pasta and garlic, sauté 1 minute. Stir in tomato paste, tomatoes and vinegar. Bring to a boil and cook uncovered 5 minutes or until sauce thickens. Add cream, simmer 1 minute. Stir in cheese and basil.

Tomato and Herb Pasta

½ cup rice vinegar

1 tablespoon sugar

½ red onion, thinly sliced

½ (12 ounce) package whole grain spaghetti

2 medium tomatoes, seeded and chopped

1 large cucumber, peeled and thinly sliced into half moons

4 green onions, thinly sliced

⅓ cup firmly packed fresh mint leaves, chopped

⅓ cup firmly packed fresh cilantro leaves, chopped

¼ cup fresh lime juice

2 tablespoons canola oil

1 teaspoon sugar

1 teaspoon salt

½ teaspoon dried crushed red pepper

¼ cup chopped peanuts

Whisk together the vinegar and 1 tablespoon sugar in a bowl. Add onion and let stand 30 minutes; drain, reserving 2 tablespoons vinegar mixture. Prepare pasta according to package directions. Place chopped tomatoes, cucumber, onions, mint, cilantro, lime juice, canola oil, sugar, salt and crushed red pepper in a bowl. Add hot cooked pasta, onion, and reserved vinegar mixture, gently tossing to combine. Sprinkle with peanuts. Serve immediately or cover and chill up to 24 hours.

Makes 6 servings

Macaroni Salad

2 cups elbow macaroni, cooked, rinsed and drained

⅓ cup diced celery

¼ cup minced red onion

1 tablespoon minced flat-leaf parsley

½ cup diced vine-ripened tomato

½ cup mayonnaise

¾ teaspoon dry mustard

1½ teaspoons sugar

1½ teaspoons cider vinegar

3 tablespoons sour cream

½ teaspoon kosher salt, plus more to taste

Freshly ground black pepper to taste

In a large bowl, combine the macaroni, celery, onion, parsley and tomato. Whisk together the mayonnaise, mustard, sugar, vinegar, sour cream and salt. Pour the dressing over the salad and stir to combine. Season with salt and pepper to taste. Serve.

"I know that nothing is better for them than to rejoice, and to do good in their lives, and also that every man should eat and drink and enjoy the good of all his labor–it is the gift of God."

Ecclesiastes 3:12

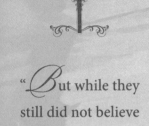

Tomato and Mozzarella Sauce for Pasta

6-8 ripe tomatoes
(seeded and chopped)
½   pound mozzarella cheese,
shredded
¼   cup minced fresh basil leaves
5   tablespoons olive oil

2   cloves fresh garlic, minced
1   tablespoon chopped fresh
parsley
Salt and pepper to taste
½   box spaghetti noodles

Combine tomatoes, cheese, basil, olive oil, garlic, parsley, salt and pepper; let sit at room temperature for about 30 minutes. Cook pasta and drain. Toss with above mixture while pasta is warm so cheese will melt. Serve immediately.

This would also be a great side dish!

Pesto Sauce

3   cups packed fresh basil leaves
½   cup plus 2 tablespoons olive
oil
⅓   cup pine nuts

3   large garlic cloves, chopped
¾   cup Parmesan cheese
Salt and pepper to taste

To make pesto, combine basil, oil, nuts and garlic in a food processor. Process until smooth. Transfer to a small bowl and mix in Parmesan cheese and salt and pepper.

Very good over farfalle pasta with chopped plum tomatoes.

ENTRÉES

BEEF, PORK AND GAME

"In the same way, let your light shine before men, that they may see your good deeds and praise your Father in Heaven."

Matthew 5:16

Beef Bonaparte

1	pound ground chuck	1	bay leaf
1	(14½ ounce) can diced tomatoes	1	(5 ounce) package medium egg noodles
1	(8 ounce) can tomato sauce	1	(8 ounce) carton sour cream
2	teaspoons garlic juice	1	(3 ounce) container cream cheese, softened
2	teaspoons sugar	6	green onions
½	teaspoon salt	1	cup grated Cheddar cheese
¼	teaspoon pepper	1	cup mozzarella cheese
	Dash of hot sauce		

Preheat the oven to 350°. Brown meat and drain grease. Add tomatoes, tomato sauce, garlic juice, sugar, salt, pepper, hot sauce and bay leaf. Stir and simmer 25 minutes. Remove bay leaf.

While meat is simmering, cook noodles according to package instructions. While noodles are cooking, mix cream cheese, sour cream and chopped green onions. Stir cooked noodles into cream cheese mixture. Spray 11x7 inch casserole dish. Layer ½ noodle mixture in bottom of the dish, then layer ½ beef mixture. Sprinkle with ½ cup of each cheese. Repeat layers. Bake 25 minutes.

Perfect Rib Roast

1	(5 pound) standing rib roast	1	teaspoon black pepper
2	teaspoons salt		

Preheat oven to 375°. Allow roast to stand at room temperature for at least an hour. Rub salt and pepper onto roast. Place on a rack in roasting pan fatty side up with ribs on the bottom. Roast 1 hour. Turn oven off and leave roast in the oven. **DO NOT OPEN THE DOOR.** Leave for 3 hours and 30 to 40 minutes. Turn oven back on to 375° until the internal temperature of the meat reaches 145°. Remove from oven and let rest 10 minutes before carving.

GORGONZOLA CREAM SAUCE FOR FILET OF BEEF

1 tablespoon butter

1 shallot, minced

1¼ cups heavy cream

¼ pound Gorgonzola cheese (or bleu cheese)

Salt

Freshly ground black pepper to taste

Heat butter in a medium saucepan over medium heat until melted. Add shallots and sauté until tender. Add the cream and cook until the mixture is reduced by half. Turn down heat to low, add cheese and stir until melted. Season with salt and pepper.

Serve warm over filet or other red meat.

Ground Beef Stroganoff

1	pound ground chuck	1	can sliced water chestnuts
1	small onion, chopped	1	small can sliced mushrooms
¼	teaspoon pepper	1	cup sour cream
¼	teaspoon paprika		Egg noodles, prepared according to package directions
1	teaspoon salt		
2	tablespoons flour		
1	can cream of mushroom soup		

Brown ground chuck and onion, drain. Add pepper, paprika, salt and flour. Cook 5 minutes. Add soup, water chestnuts and sliced mushrooms. Cook 5 minutes on low. Add sour cream and stir in cooked egg noodles.

Makes 6 servings

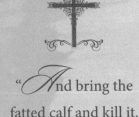

"And bring the fatted calf and kill it. And let us eat, and make merry. For this my son was dead and is alive again; he was lost and is found."

Luke 15:23

Minute Steak with Mushroom Gravy

1	(10¼ ounce) can cream of mushroom soup	1½	pounds cubed steaks
½	cup buttermilk	½	cup all-purpose flour
¼	cup water	2	tablespoons canola oil
¼	teaspoon ground red pepper	1	(8 ounce) package sliced fresh mushrooms
1¼	teaspoons salt	½	teaspoon dried thyme
1½	teaspoons black pepper		

In a bowl, whisk together soup, buttermilk, water and red pepper until smooth; set aside. Salt and pepper steaks. Stir remaining salt, pepper and flour in shallow dish. Dredge steaks in flour mixture. Fry steaks in hot oil in skillet over medium-high heat 2 minutes on each side.

Remove steaks, reserve drippings in skillet. Add mushrooms and thyme, sauté 3 to 4 minutes or until browned. Stir reserved soup mixture into mushroom mixture in skillet; cook 1 minute, stirring to loosen particles from bottom of skillet. Bring to a boil and return steaks to skillet. Cover, reduce heat, and simmer 15 to 20 minutes or until done.

Grilled Beef Fajitas with Fresh Pico de Gallo

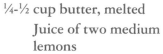

¼-½	cup butter, melted	¼	cup soy sauce
	Juice of two medium lemons	3	pounds flank or round steak
¼	cup Worcestershire sauce	¼	teaspoon pepper
		6	flour tortillas

Combine butter, lemon juice, Worcestershire sauce and soy sauce in a large shallow dish. Sprinkle steak with pepper and add to marinade, turning to coat. Cover and chill 4 to 6 hours.

Remove steak from marinade. Discard marinade. Grill over medium heat (300° to 350°), 5 to 10 minutes on each side. Slice steak on the diagonal into thin strips. Warm tortillas on the grill or in the oven. Divide meat evenly into 6 portions and place on tortillas. Serve with desired toppings and Pico de Gallo.

Toppings: guacamole, diced tomatoes, Pico de Gallo and shredded Cheddar cheese.

Makes 6 servings

PICO DE GALLO

1 medium sweet onion, finely diced

2-3 large tomatoes, finely diced with juice reserved

2-4 jalapeño peppers, seeded, finely diced

⅓ cup finely minced cilantro

Juice of one lime

1 tablespoon sugar

Combine onion, tomatoes, jalapeño peppers, cilantro, lime juice and sugar; mix.

Mock Cabbage Rolls

1½	pounds ground meat	1	bag shredded cabbage
1	onion, chopped	1	(26 ounce) jar pasta sauce
¼	teaspoon pepper	¼	cup brown sugar
3	cups cooked rice	1	cup shredded Cheddar cheese

Preheat oven to 350°. In a skillet, cook meat and onions until done. Drain liquid. Add pepper and cooked rice, mix well.

Spoon the meat mixture into a 4 quart casserole dish coated with nonstick cooking spray. Top with shredded cabbage. Mix pasta sauce and brown sugar. Pour sauce over the cabbage. Bake covered, 1 hour and 15 minutes or until cabbage is tender. Sprinkle with cheese and continue baking 5 minutes.

"So that you may eat and drink at my table in my kingdom."

Luke 22:30

Quesadilla Casserole

1	pound ground beef	2	teaspoons chili powder
½	cup chopped onion	1	teaspoon ground cumin
2	(15 ounce) cans tomato sauce	1	teaspoon minced garlic
1	(15 ounce) can black beans, drained and rinsed (optional)	½	teaspoon oregano leaves
1	(8¾ ounce) can whole kernel corn, drained	½	teaspoon crushed red pepper (optional)
1	(4½ ounce) can chopped green chilies, undrained	6	(8 inch) flour tortillas
		3	cups shredded Cheddar cheese

Preheat oven to 350° and spray a 9x13 inch casserole dish with cooking spray. Brown beef and onion in a large skillet on medium-high heat. Drain. Add tomato sauce, beans, corn and green chilies; mix well. Stir in chili powder, ground cumin, minced garlic and oregano. Bring to a boil. Reduce heat to low, simmer 5 minutes. Add red pepper to taste, if desired.

Spread ⅓ of beef mixture into the bottom of dish. Top with 3 tortillas, overlapping as needed. Spread second ⅓ of the beef mixture over tortillas and half of the cheese over this layer. Repeat with remaining tortillas, beef mixture and cheese. Bake 15 minutes or until heated through. Let stand 5 minutes before serving.

Sloppy Joes

¼	cup chopped green bell pepper	½	teaspoon garlic powder
¼	cup chopped onion	1	teaspoon dry mustard
2	tablespoons butter	¾	cup ketchup
1	pound ground beef	3	teaspoons brown sugar
			Salt and pepper to taste

In a medium skillet over medium heat, sauté the bell peppers and onions in 2 tablespoons butter. Add ground beef and brown, drain liquids. Stir in garlic powder, mustard, ketchup and brown sugar; mix thoroughly. Reduce heat and simmer 30 minutes. Season with salt and pepper.

"As a mother comforts her child, so will I comfort you."

Isaiah 66:13

Meatloaf They Will Eat!

1½ pounds ground chuck
1 egg
1 cup fine bread crumbs
1 onion, finely chopped
1 teaspoon salt
½ teaspoon pepper
½ (8 ounce) can tomato sauce

Preheat oven to 350°. Mix meat, egg, bread crumbs, onion, salt, pepper and tomato sauce together. Form into loaf and place in greased loaf dish.

SAUCE

1½ (8 ounce) cans tomato sauce
½ cup water
3 tablespoons vinegar
3 tablespoons brown sugar .
3 tablespoons prepared yellow mustard
3 teaspoons Worcestershire sauce

Combine tomato sauce, water, vinegar, brown sugar, mustard, Worcestershire sauce in a saucepan. Cook over low heat until sugar melts. Pour ¼ of sauce over meatloaf. Bake 1 hour and 15 minutes. Baste 2 to 3 times with sauce during baking.

Warm remaining sauce and serve with meatloaf.

Winter Meatloaf

1⅓ pounds ground round
⅔ pound ground pork
½ cup panko bread crumbs
1½ tablespoons dried minced onion
2 large eggs, beaten
1 teaspoon garlic salt
1 teaspoon salt
1 teaspoon pepper
1 tablespoon dried Italian seasonings
2-3 slices bacon
⅓ cup molasses
⅓ cup ketchup
¼ cup brown sugar

Preheat oven to 350°. Mix together the meat, bread crumbs, minced onion, eggs, garlic salt, salt, pepper and dried Italian seasonings. Shape into a loaf and place into an 8½x4½ inch loaf pan. Bake 30 minutes. Remove from oven and place bacon slices across the top of meatloaf.

Mix together molasses, ketchup and brown sugar and pour over the bacon. Return to oven and bake 45 minutes more or until no pink is left in the center of the loaf. Let stand for several minutes before slicing.

Makes 6 to 8 servings

"Carry each other's burdens, and in this way you will fulfill the law of Christ."

Galatians 6:2

Mushroom Stuffed Beef Tenderloin

KABOB MARINADE

½ cup olive oil

½ cup red wine vinegar

1 teaspoon salt

1 teaspoon marjoram

1 teaspoon thyme

½ teaspoon pepper

1 clove garlic, minced

½ cup chopped onion

¼ cup fresh parsley, chopped

2 teaspoons Dijon mustard

Juice of ½ lemon

Combine all ingredients. Marinate meat at least 24 hours. After marinated, cut meat into cubes and place on skewers.

Enough for 2 to 3 pounds of meat. Best cooked over charcoal grill. Can be used with chicken, beef, lamb or pork.

STUFFED TENDERLOIN

¼ cup extra virgin olive oil

2 (3.53 ounce) packages prosciutto, finely chopped

3 (8 ounce) packages baby bella mushrooms, finely chopped

1 onion, chopped finely

1 cup Madeira wine

1 tablespoon fresh thyme, minced

1½ teaspoons salt, divided

1 (6 pound) beef tenderloin, trimmed

1 teaspoon ground black pepper

Roasted Garlic Madeira Sauce (recipe follows)

In a large skillet, heat olive oil over medium heat. Add prosciutto and cook 6 to 8 minutes, stirring frequently or until crispy. Using a slotted spoon, remove prosciutto from pan, reserving oil in skillet. Drain prosciutto on paper towels. Add mushrooms and onion to oil in skillet and cook 5 minutes, stirring frequently. Add wine and cook 15 to 20 minutes or until all liquid has evaporated. Remove from heat. Stir in prosciutto, thyme, and ½ teaspoon salt. Set aside to cool slightly.

Butterfly tenderloin by making a lengthwise cut down center of one flat side, cutting to within 1 inch of other side. From bottom of cut, slice tenderloin horizontally to within ½ inch of left side. Repeat procedure on right side.

Open tenderloin and flatten to ½ inch thickness using a meat mallet. Trim edges to make a uniform rectangle. Spread mushroom mixture over tenderloin leaving a ½ inch border at edges. Roll up tenderloin jellyroll style, starting with a long side. Tie tenderloin at 2 inch intervals with kitchen string. Sprinkle remaining 1 teaspoon salt and pepper over tenderloin.

Preheat oven to 375°. Place tenderloin on a lightly greased rack in a shallow roasting pan and bake 35 to 40 minutes or until a meat thermometer inserted in thickest portion registers 145°. Let stand 10 minutes before slicing. Serve with Roasted Garlic Madeira Sauce.

Makes about 12 servings

ROASTED GARLIC MADEIRA SAUCE

Roast garlic bulb while the tenderloin roasts in oven.

1	head garlic	1	cup Madeira wine
2	tablespoons olive oil	1	cup beef broth
2	tablespoons butter	2	teaspoons cornstarch

Preheat oven to 375°. Cut off pointed end of garlic. Place garlic head, cut end up, on a 6-inch square of heavy-duty aluminum foil. Drizzle garlic with oil. Seal garlic in foil and bake 45 minutes or until tender. Set aside and cool.

In a medium skillet, melt butter over medium heat. Squeeze pulp from roasted garlic into skillet. Cook 2 minutes. Add wine. Bring to a simmer and cook 6 to 8 minutes or until wine is reduced by half. Remove mixture from heat. Strain mixture, discarding solids. Return liquid to skillet. In a small bowl, combine beef broth and cornstarch, whisking until smooth. Add to liquid in skillet. Bring to a boil, and boil 1 minute or until thickened.

Makes about ¾ cup

Beef Tenderloin

2	tablespoons seasoned salt	½	tablespoon salt
1	tablespoon cracked black pepper	1	tablespoon soy sauce
1	tablespoon seasoned salt flavored enhancer	1	(7-8 pound) beef tenderloin

Mix seasonings and soy sauce to make a paste. Rub half of the mixture on one side of tenderloin. Place on foil-lined roasting pan. Broil for 7 minutes. Remove from oven and rub paste on the other side of the tenderloin and broil it for 7 minutes. Wrap beef in heavy-duty foil and bake at 350° for 30 minutes. Remove from oven and let stand in foil 1 hour before serving.

The above times will yield medium well meat on both ends and medium rare in the center. For medium in the center, increase bake time to 40 minutes. Keep foil wrapped tightly to continue cooking the meat in the foil during the hour wait time.

Makes 8 to 10 servings

BEEF MARINADE

1 onion, chopped

1 cup vegetable oil

½ cup soy sauce

½ cup lemon juice

2 teaspoons prepared mustard

2 teaspoons Worcestershire sauce

2 teaspoons salt

Combine all ingredients in a zip-top plastic bag. Let meat marinate for several hours.

"From the fullness of his grace we have all received one blessing after another."

John 1:16

Pot Roast

4-5 pound roast (any kind)	1 package dried onion soup mix
Salt and pepper	
1 can cream of mushroom soup	

Preheat oven to 350°. Line a roasting pan with a large piece of aluminum foil. Place ½ of cream of mushroom soup and onion soup mix on foil. Salt and pepper roast. Put roast on top of soup mixture. Cover with remaining soup. Seal foil well and bake 3 hours.

Makes its own gravy.

Standing Rib Roast with Horseradish Cream

1 standing rib roast of beef, approximately 5 to 7 pounds	Salt and pepper

Preheat oven to 350°. Line a roasting pan with aluminum foil. Prepare the roast if it has not already been separated from the bone. (See note.)

Generously salt and pepper the roast and place it in the roasting pan. Bake 20 minutes per pound, plus 20 minutes more for a medium rare roast, or 2 hours and 20 minutes more for a 6 pound roast. Allow the roast to rest for 20 minutes before carving. Serve with horseradish cream.

HORSERADISH CREAM

½ cup sour cream	½ teaspoon salt
3 tablespoons prepared horseradish	Dash of pepper

In a small bowl, mix all ingredients.

With a butcher's knife, slice the bone away from the meat. You may ask the butcher to do this for you. Though separated from the meat, the bone should remain in place during roasting, because the bone contributes to the flavor and tenderness of roast. Use kitchen twine to securely tie the bones and the roast together.

Makes 8 to 10 servings

"Two are better than one, because they have a good return for their work: If one falls down, his friend can help him up. But pity the man who falls and has no one to help him up!"

Ecclesiastes 4:9-10

Holiday Ham

3	teaspoons honey	½	cup brown sugar
3	tablespoons prepared mustard	½	cup granulated sugar
		1	(8 to 10 pound) ham

Preheat oven to 325°. Mix honey and mustard, brush on ham. Mix sugars together, brush on ham and then cover. Bake 18 to 20 minutes per pound.

Garlic Pork Tenderloin with Red Currant Jelly Sauce

½	cup cooking sherry	1	teaspoon ground ginger
½	cup soy sauce	1	teaspoon crushed dried thyme
2	large cloves garlic, minced		
1	tablespoon dry mustard	3	pound boneless pork roast

Preheat oven to 325°. Combine sherry, soy sauce, garlic, dry mustard, ginger and thyme in a large zip-top plastic bag. Shake to mix. Marinate pork tenderloin in marinade at least 2 hours at room temperature. Cook 45 minutes or until meat thermometer reads 160°-165°. Baste occasionally. Let rest 15 minutes.

RED CURRANT JELLY SAUCE

1	(10 ounce) jar red currant jelly	2	tablespoons dry sherry
		1	tablespoon soy sauce

Mix all ingredients and heat in saucepan just until sauce begins to thicken.

"Offer hospitality to one another without grumbling.

Each one should use whatever gift he has received to serve others,

faithfully administering God's grace in its various forms."

1 Peter 4:9-10

ALABAMA WHITE BARBECUE SAUCE

1 cup mayonnaise

1 tablespoon salt

1 tablespoon pepper

3 tablespoons vinegar

4 tablespoons fresh lemon juice

Combine all ingredients in a glass jar with lid. Shake well to mix. Brush half on meat while grilling and save half for dipping

This works well on chicken or pork.

Cherry Almond Glazed Pork

1	(12 ounce) jar cherry preserves	¼	teaspoon nutmeg
¼	cup red wine vinegar	¼	teaspoon cloves
2	tablespoons light corn syrup	¼	teaspoon salt
¼	teaspoon cinnamon	¼	cup slivered almonds, toasted
		3	pound boneless pork roast

Mix preserves, vinegar, corn syrup, cinnamon, nutmeg, cloves and salt. Heat until boiling, add almonds. Baste roast to form a glaze. Bake and serve with remaining sauce.

Sauce is also wonderful with ham.

Pork Tenderloin with Wine Sauce

1	pork tenderloin (about 1 pound)	¼	cup fresh lemon juice
4	cloves garlic, minced		Bacon to wrap tenderloin

Rub meat with minced garlic and drizzle with lemon juice. Wrap tenderloin completely in bacon. Grill (recommended) or broil 6 to 8 inches from heat source about 40 minutes, turning every 10 minutes. Prepare sauce while cooking meat or ahead of time and keep warm.

WINE SAUCE

2	tablespoons butter	1½	cups beef stock or beef bouillon plus 1½ cups water
2	tablespoons olive oil	4	ounces white wine
1	medium onion, chopped		Dash of cayenne pepper
1	tablespoon finely chopped fresh parsley	1	teaspoon fresh lemon juice
2	cups mushrooms, sliced (about ½ pound)	2	teaspoons all-purpose flour

Place butter and oil in a skillet over low heat; add onion, parsley and mushrooms. Sauté over medium heat until tender. Add stock, wine, cayenne and lemon juice. Bring to a boil. Whisk in flour and cook until thickened. Pour sauce over tenderloin and serve.

MIKE'S BARBECUE SAUCE

1 gallon vinegar

1 gallon ketchup

16 ounce bottle steak sauce

16 ounces mustard

16 ounces Worcestershire sauce

4 ounces sugar

4 ounces salt

4 ounces black pepper

Mix all ingredients well. May then put sauce into jars. Shake before using.

Used Heinz Steak Sauce for testing purposes. Makes great Christmas gift.

Pork Tenderloin and Apple Marinade

1	cup apple jelly		Salt to taste
1	cup ketchup		Chili powder to taste
6	tablespoons vinegar	1	pork tenderloin

Mix apple jelly, ketchup, vinegar, salt and chili powder in saucepan and heat thoroughly. Set aside half of marinade to use as a sauce.

Place tenderloin in a shallow, greased baking dish, and baste with heated marinade. Bake uncovered 30 to 60 minutes (according to directions for weight), basting every 10 minutes. Slice thinly and serve with sauce.

Pork Tenderloin with Cherry Glaze

1	teaspoon garlic salt	2	(14½ ounce) cans pitted red tart pie cherries in water, drained
1	teaspoon ground black pepper		
2	(1 pound) pork tenderloins, trimmed	2	tablespoons sugar
		2	tablespoons balsamic vinegar
1	(8 ounce) package cream cheese, softened	¼	cup cherry-flavored brandy
¼	cup mayonnaise	2	tablespoons cornstarch
1	tablespoon green onions, minced	4	dozen toasted French bread rounds
			Garnish with fresh parsley

Preheat oven to 400°. Line broiler pan with heavy-duty aluminum foil. Place rack on top of foil and spray with nonstick cooking spray. Rub garlic salt and pepper over pork. Place pork on prepared pan and bake 40 to 45 minutes or until a meat thermometer inserted in thickest portion reads 155°. Let stand 10 minutes.

Cut pork into ¼ inch-thick slices. In a small bowl, combine cream cheese, mayonnaise and green onions. Cover and chill. In a medium saucepan, combine cherries and sugar. Bring to a simmer over medium-low heat. Simmer 5 minutes. Stir in vinegar.

In a small bowl, combine brandy and cornstarch, stirring to dissolve. Add to cherry mixture. Simmer 1 minute or until thickened. Spread cream cheese mixture over bread rounds. Top each with one slice pork tenderloin. Spoon cherry glaze over pork. Garnish with parsley.

> "Each man should give what he has decided in his heart to give, not reluctantly or under compulsion, for God loves a cheerful giver."
>
> *2 Corinthians 9:7*

Pork Tenderloin with Cream Sauce

Olive oil   Salt and pepper

Rub pork tenderloin with olive oil, salt and pepper. Cook 20 to 30 minutes on the grill.

CREAM SAUCE

1	tablespoon butter	⅛	cup Dijon mustard
½	cup dry white wine	3	green onions, chopped
½	pint heavy cream		

Cook butter and wine on medium heat. Stir until reduced to 2 tablespoons. Add in ½ pint of heavy cream. Cook until thickened. Stir in mustard. Garnish with green onions.

Cannot double.

Pork Tenderloin with Apples and Pears

1	pork tenderloin	1	large pear, sliced thick (or 2 small)
1	bottle teriyaki marinade	½	cup brown sugar
½	cup brown sugar	⅛	teaspoon salt
	Salt and pepper	⅛	teaspoon pepper
1	large apple, sliced thick (or 2 small)	4	tablespoons butter

Preheat oven to 375°. Place tenderloin in a gallon freezer bag and add marinade and brown sugar. Marinate at least 2 hours. Remove tenderloin from bag and place in baking dish sprayed with nonstick cooking spray. Salt and pepper tenderloin. Bake 1 hour.

When tenderloin is half done, place sliced apples and pears in saucepan with butter and brown sugar. Cook on medium-low heat until fruit is softened and butter and sugar are melted. Sprinkle with salt and pepper. Let cooked tenderloin rest 5 minutes. Slice, place on a platter, and serve apples and pears over tenderloin.

Bulgogi for Beef, Venison, Duck or Goose

5	tablespoons sugar	1	small bag shredded carrots
1½	pounds meat, thinly sliced	1	bell pepper, thinly sliced
1	bunch green onions, sliced	5	tablespoons soy sauce
2	cloves garlic, minced	3	teaspoons black pepper
2	tablespoons olive oil	½	teaspoon salt
2	medium onions, thinly sliced		

Place meat and sugar in a gallon size zip-top plastic bag and mix by hand, working sugar into meat. Add green onions, garlic, olive oil, onions, carrots, bell pepper, soy sauce, salt and pepper. Let marinate at least 24 hours. Shake mixture every few hours to mix well. Let mixture reach room temperature before cooking. Stir fry in hot wok, griddle or frying pan until meat and vegetables reach desired degree of doneness.

Serve alone or over steamed rice.

Makes 6 servings

Elk Kabobs

¼	cup cranberry juice	⅛	teaspoon ginger
¼	cup olive oil	1	large container fresh mushrooms, whole
¼	teaspoon fresh garlic		
¼	teaspoon onion salt	2	onions, quartered
¼	teaspoon celery salt	2	(10 ounce) packages cherry tomatoes
¼	teaspoon black pepper		
¼	teaspoon sweet basil	2	green peppers, cut in large pieces

Mix cranberry juice, oil, garlic, onion salt, celery salt, pepper, basil and ginger. Slice the elk into chunks that will fit securely onto skewers. Marinate elk overnight.

Alternate skewered meat with mushrooms, onions, green peppers and cherry tomatoes. Place on hot grill 8 to 10 minutes or until done. Do not overcook. Baste meat and vegetables several times with remaining marinade.

Works nicely with venison kabobs.

"I know that there is nothing better for men than to be happy and do good while they live. That everyone may eat and drink and find satisfaction in all his toil-this is the gift of God."

Ecclesiastes 3:12-13

Boots' Dove

12-18	dove breasts	2	teaspoons dried parsley
2-3	chicken bouillon cubes		Salt and pepper to taste
2	onions, quartered		Cornstarch
2	stalks celery, diced		Cooking sherry to taste

Place dove breasts in pot and cover with water. Add bouillon cubes, onion, celery, parsley, salt and pepper. Cook until tender with fork. Not too done. Remove birds and keep warm.

Add cornstarch to 1 cup of the bouillon mixture and stir to thicken. Slowly add thickened mixture until the gravy is a nice consistency. Use a whisk to prevent lumps.

Return birds to the thickened gravy and heat approximately 20 minutes. Add sherry to taste.

May transfer to chafing dish to serve warm.

"A man can do nothing better than to eat and drink and find satisfaction in his work. This too, I see, is from the hand of God."

Ecclesiastes 2:24

Quail in Cream

8	quail	4	cups fine bread crumbs, warmed and buttered
3	sticks of butter		Red currant jelly
	Salt and pepper to taste		
1	cup heavy cream		

Melt the butter in a fry pan and over a medium flame, sauté and baste the quail 30 minutes, spooning the butter over and into the cavity of the birds. Sprinkle with salt and black pepper, reserve on a warm platter.

Pour the heavy cream into the same fry pan that the quail were cooked in. Stir up the browned particles and butter. Stir well and bring to a simmer for just less than 5 minutes. Place two quail on a bed of warm, buttered bread crumbs with a dollop of currant jelly on the side. Serve the hot cream separately.

Makes 4 servings

Duck Breasts in Wine Sauce

WINE SAUCE

½	cup butter	3	tablespoons flour
1	cup mushrooms	½	teaspoon salt
1	cup chopped ham	½	teaspoon pepper
1	cup finely chopped green onions	¾	cup canned beef bouillon
		¾	cup Burgundy wine

1-2 garlic cloves, minced

Make the sauce by lightly sautéing the mushrooms, ham, onions and garlic in the butter. When the onion is tender, add the flour, salt and pepper. Stir, then add the bouillon and wine; cover and simmer for 45 minutes. While the sauce is simmering, prepare the breasts.

DUCK BREASTS

6	duck breasts	2	teaspoons paprika
½	cup flour	½	cup butter
2	teaspoons salt		

Preheat oven to 450°. Combine the flour, salt and paprika in a bowl. Coat the ducks in the flour mixture. Melt the butter in a shallow baking pan in the oven. Remove the baking pan and coat the floured duck pieces in the melted butter. Arrange them in a single layer in the pan and bake 30 minutes. Turn. Pour the wine sauce over the breasts. Cover the pan with foil and cook the breasts until they are tender (another 45 minutes).

Venison Sloppy Joes

1	pound ground venison	2	tablespoons yellow mustard
½	cup diced onion	¾	cup ketchup
¼	cup chopped red pepper	3	teaspoons brown sugar
½	teaspoon garlic powder		Black pepper to taste

Brown venison, onion and red pepper. Add garlic powder, mustard, ketchup, brown sugar and pepper; simmer 30 minutes.

"Only be careful, and watch yourselves closely so that you do not forget the things your eyes have seen or let them slip from your heart as long as you live. Teach them to your children and to their children after them."

Deuteronomy 4:9

Stuffed Venison

1-2 pounds venison tenderloin or backstrap pounded to ¼ inch thickness or thinly sliced
Dash of salt
½ cup finely chopped fresh basil or 1 tablespoon dried basil
1 head garlic, roasted, casings removed and smashed

½ cup thinly sliced smoked Gouda or goat cheese (optional)
2 tablespoons olive oil
¼ cup shallots (may use yellow onion)
¼ cup white wine
¼ cup chicken stock
1 tablespoon honey mustard or Dijon mustard
1 tablespoon butter

Preheat oven to 350°. Sprinkle venison with salt and basil. Spread garlic in center of tenderloin, add cheese, then roll up and secure with kitchen twine or toothpicks.

Sear tenderloins on all sides in a large ovenproof skillet with the olive oil over high heat. Place the pan in the oven and roast for 20 minutes or until desired degree of doneness, being careful not to overcook.

Remove meat from pan, cover with foil and set aside. Place the pan with meat drippings back on stove over medium heat. Add the shallots and sauté until translucent. Add the wine and deglaze the pan. Add the chicken stock and bring to a boil. Reduce heat and stir in the mustard and butter. Pour sauce over venison and serve.

To roast 1 head of garlic, pour 2 tablespoons of olive oil over the garlic and wrap in foil. Place in oven and bake at 400° for 20 to 30 minutes or until soft. (Can be done ahead of time.)

ENTRÉES

POULTRY

"*Delight yourself in the Lord and He will give you the desires of your heart.*"

Psalm 37:4

Apricot-Dijon Glazed Chicken

8	chicken thighs	1	(12 ounce) jar apricot jam
	Coarse salt and freshly	2	tablespoons honey
	ground pepper	2	tablespoons Dijon mustard

Preheat oven to 425°. Rinse chicken. Pat dry and transfer to a baking dish. Season well with salt and pepper, set aside. Bring jam, honey and mustard to a boil in a small saucepan over medium heat. Reduce heat to medium-low, simmer until thickened and reduced by half, about 15 minutes. Spoon apricot mixture evenly over the chicken. Bake chicken, basting with sauce from bottom of dish every 10 minutes, until juices run clear when chicken is pricked with a fork, about 30 minutes.

Cheesy Chicken Enchiladas

4	chicken breasts	1	(8 ounce) package sharp Cheddar cheese, shredded
2	cans cream of chicken soup		
1	(8 ounce) container sour cream	1	(8 ounce) can chicken broth
2	(8 ounce) packages Pepper Jack cheese, shredded	1	package flour tortillas

Preheat oven to 350°. Boil chicken until cooked thoroughly. Shred chicken into small pieces. Put aside.

In a large bowl, mix cream of chicken soup, sour cream and 1½ packages of Pepper Jack cheese and ½ package of Cheddar cheese. Add shredded chicken and chicken broth to mixture and stir. Fill tortillas with chicken mixture, roll and place in a greased 13x9 inch baking dish. Pour remaining chicken mixture over enchiladas and sprinkle with remaining Cheddar and Pepper Jack cheese. Bake 30 minutes.

Makes about 8 to 10 enchiladas

Oh Lord, that lends me life, Lend me a heart replete with thankfulness.

~William Shakespeare, 1564-1616

Cheesy Chicken Gnocchi

4	baking potatoes	1	tablespoon extra virgin olive oil
1	tablespoon salt		Salt and pepper to taste
½	tablespoon baking powder	1	teaspoon thyme
1	egg white	2	tablespoons unsalted butter
1½	cups all-purpose flour	1	cup grated Gruyère cheese
1	package chicken tenders, chopped into pieces		

Preheat oven to 400°. Bake the potatoes 1 hour or until fork tender. Peel the potatoes while they are still hot and mash. Place the potatoes in a large bowl; add the salt, baking powder, and egg white. Add the flour a little at a time and mix with hands until the mixture forms dough. Transfer the dough to a lightly floured surface. Gently knead the dough until smooth, adding a little more flour if necessary, to keep it from sticking. Break off a piece of the dough and roll it back and forth into a rope, about the thickness of one's index finger. Cut the rope into 1 inch pieces. Gently roll each piece over the end of a fork to create the signature gnocchi ridges. This will allow the gnocchi to hold the buttery cheese sauce when served. Boil the gnocchi in batches of salted water. The gnocchi are done about 2 minutes after floating to the surface.

While the gnocchi are cooking, sauté the chopped chicken in olive oil over medium-high heat. Add salt, pepper, thyme, butter and cooked gnocchi. Toss to coat in butter and stir in the Gruyère cheese until melted.

Serve hot with some crispy Parmesan cheese bread.

"And God is able to make all grace abound to you, so that in all things at all times, having all that you need, you will abound in every good work."

2 Corinthians 9:8

Chicken with Artichokes and Pasta Salad

2	chicken bouillon cubes	1	box vermicelli
2	cups boiling water	1	(14 ounce) can artichoke hearts, quartered
4-6	boneless chicken breast halves	1	pint cherry tomatoes, halved
¼	cup chopped onions		Herbed Dressing
1	cup water		

Dissolve bouillon cubes in 2 cups boiling water. Add chicken and onions. Cover chicken with additional water. Simmer chicken and onions until done. Remove chicken, reserving broth. Set aside and allow to cool. When chicken has cooled, chop coarsely. Strain and set aside.

Break vermicelli into 2 inch pieces. Pour reserved broth into pot. Add enough water to cook the vermicelli according to package directions. Drain vermicelli thoroughly. Combine vermicelli, chicken and Herbed Dressing. Add artichoke hearts and toss. Refrigerate for at least 2 hours. Add tomatoes and serve.

Chicken Divan

3	(10 ounce) packages frozen, chopped broccoli	1	tablespoon lemon juice
2	(10 ounce) cans cream of chicken soup		Parmesan cheese
			Salt and pepper to taste
1	cup mayonnaise	3	whole chicken breasts, boiled and chopped
1	(8 ounce) carton sour cream		Paprika
1	cup grated sharp cheese		Butter

Preheat oven to 350°. Cook and drain broccoli. Mix soup, mayonnaise, sour cream, grated cheese, lemon juice, salt and pepper. In a 9x13 inch casserole dish, layer broccoli first and top with chicken. Sprinkle with Parmesan cheese. Pour soup mixture over all. Sprinkle more Parmesan cheese and paprika on top. Put several pats of butter on top. Bake uncovered 35 to 40 minutes.

Freezes well.

HERBED DRESSING

1½ tablespoons grated onion

⅓ cup oil

3 tablespoons red wine vinegar

3 tablespoons fresh lemon juice

1½ teaspoons seasoned salt

1½ teaspoons dried crushed basil

1½ tablespoons whole basil

Combine all ingredients and mix well.

Chicken and Asparagus Crêpes

CRÊPES

¾	cup all-purpose flour	1	tablespoon butter, melted
½	teaspoon salt	1	large egg
1¼	cups milk	1	egg yolk

In a medium bowl, combine flour and salt. In another medium bowl, whisk together milk, butter, egg and egg yolk. Gradually add flour mixture to milk mixture, whisking until smooth. Heat an 8 inch nonstick skillet over medium-high heat. Spoon 2½ tablespoons of batter into skillet. Cook 30 to 45 seconds. Loosen crêpe with a spatula and carefully turn over. Cook 30 to 45 seconds. Transfer to plate. Repeat procedure with remaining batter, stacking crêpes on a plate.

CHICKEN AND ASPARAGUS FILLING

½	cup butter	¼	cup dry sherry
1	(8 ounce) package sliced fresh mushrooms	1	(3 ounce) package cream cheese
1	small onion, chopped	¾	cup shredded fontina cheese
2	cloves garlic, minced	2	cups cooked chicken, chopped
¼	cup all-purpose flour	12	asparagus spears, steamed until crisp tender
1½	cups chicken broth	½	cup shredded Swiss cheese
1	cup milk		

In a large skillet, melt butter over medium heat. Add mushrooms, onion and garlic. Cook 6 to 8 minutes or until mushrooms are tender. Stir in flour, and cook 2 minutes, stirring frequently. Stir in broth, milk and sherry. Bring to a simmer, and cook 10 minutes. Add cream cheese and fontina cheese, stirring until cheeses melt. Stir in chicken.

Preheat oven to 400°. Lightly grease two 13x9 inch baking dishes. Spoon ¼ cup chicken mixture down center of each crêpe, top each with one asparagus spear. Fold edges of crêpes over filling. Place seam up in prepared baking dishes. Sprinkle Swiss cheese over crêpes. Bake 10 minutes or until cheese melts and crêpes are hot. Serve immediately.

"*Yet the inward man is being renewed day by day.*"

2 Corinthians 4:16

Chicken Cambridge

½	teaspoon flour	¼	cup finely chopped celery
½	teaspoon salt	¼	cup finely chopped onions
½	teaspoon freshly ground black pepper	2	tablespoons chopped fresh parsley
6	(6 ounce) boneless, skinless chicken breast halves	¼	cup chicken stock
		1	(10 ounce) jar red pepper jelly
3	tablespoons butter	1	cup crumbled goat cheese
3	tablespoons olive oil		

In a large bowl, combine flour, salt and pepper. Roll chicken in flour mixture and shake off excess. In a heavy 12 inch skillet, heat butter and oil. Lightly sauté celery, onions and parsley. Remove from pan with a slotted spoon and reserve.

In the same butter and oil, sauté chicken breasts until lightly browned, about 3 to 4 minutes per side. Sprinkle reserved sautéed vegetables on top of each chicken breast. Add chicken stock. Cover skillet and simmer 5 minutes. Remove from heat and spread each chicken breast with red pepper jelly. Place under broiler until jelly melts, basting often with melting jelly. Place chicken breasts on a large platter and sprinkle with goat cheese.

"Let your conversation be always full of grace, seasoned with salt, so that you may know how to answer everyone."

Deuteronomy 4:6

Chicken Fajita Pizza

1	tablespoon olive oil	1	green pepper, chopped
1	pound skinless, boneless chicken, chopped	1	(10 ounce) can pizza crust
		¾	cup picante sauce
1	teaspoon chili powder	1	cup shredded cheese
	Salt and pepper to taste	½	cup black beans, drained
1	small onion, chopped		

Preheat oven 425°. In large skillet, sauté chicken in olive oil over medium heat until done. Stir in chili powder, salt and pepper. Add onion and green pepper until tender, about 3 minutes.

On a nonstick pizza pan coated with nonstick cooking spray, unroll dough. Press out to the edges. Bake 6 to 8 minutes until lightly brown. Remove from oven and spoon picante sauce over the crust. Top with chicken mixture, black beans and cheese. Bake 10 to 12 minutes.

Chicken Cakes

4   tablespoons butter, divided
⅓   cup minced red bell pepper
⅓   cup minced celery
⅓   cup minced onion
3   cups chopped cooked chicken
1¾   cups Japanese panko
     (bread crumbs)

½   cup mayonnaise
2   large eggs, lightly beaten
2   tablespoons Dijon mustard
1   tablespoon Worcestershire
     sauce
1½   teaspoons seasoned salt

In a small skillet, melt 2 tablespoons butter over medium heat. Add red bell pepper, celery and onion. Cook 5 minutes until tender. In a large bowl, combine chicken, panko and red bell pepper mixture. Set aside.

In a small bowl, combine mayonnaise, eggs, mustard, Worcestershire sauce and seasoned salt. Add to chicken mixture, tossing gently to combine. Form mixture into 10 patties.

In a large skillet, melt remaining 2 tablespoons butter over medium heat. Cook chicken cakes 3 to 5 minutes per side or until browned. Serve with Tzatziki Sauce or Creole Sauce.

Makes 4 to 6 servings

CREOLE SAUCE

½ cup mayonnaise

½ cup sour cream

1 clove garlic, minced

1 tablespoon prepared
mustard

1 tablespoon fresh
lemon juice

½ teaspoon Creole
seasoning

In a small bowl,
combine all ingredients.
Cover and chill up to
3 days.

Tzatziki Sauce

1   English cucumber, finely
     grated
     Dash of salt
1   cup Greek yogurt
1   teaspoon lemon juice

1   teaspoon lemon zest
1   clove garlic, minced
½   teaspoon salt
1   teaspoon chopped fresh dill

Finely grate English cucumber on small side of grater. Place in a sieve and sprinkle with a dash of salt. Combine yogurt, lemon juice, lemon zest, garlic, salt and dill; mix well. Press cucumber with a spoon to remove as much liquid as possible. Add to yogurt mixture and stir well. Cover and place in refrigerator until ready to serve.

Chicken Kabobs

MARINADE

1 cup plain yogurt	1 teaspoon salt
⅓ cup extra virgin olive oil	1 teaspoon pepper
4 teaspoons fresh garlic, minced	¼ teaspoon cayenne pepper
1 tablespoon dried thyme	2 pounds boneless chicken breasts, cut into 1 inch cubes
1 tablespoon dried oregano	

LEMON DRESSING

6 tablespoons fresh lemon juice (about 3 lemons)	2 fresh garlic cloves, minced
½ cup extra virgin olive oil	3 tablespoons chopped fresh basil

SKEWERS

2 red onions	1 yellow pepper
2 red peppers	1 green pepper

YOGURT-HERB DIPPING SAUCE

1 cup plain yogurt	1 tablespoon fresh mint, finely chopped
3 tablespoons extra virgin olive oil	1 garlic clove, minced
2 tablespoons fresh lemon juice (about 1 lemon)	½ teaspoon salt
1 tablespoon fresh basil, finely chopped	½ teaspoon pepper
	1 large cucumber, peeled, halved, seeded and chopped finely

Whisk together marinade ingredients, add chicken and refrigerate 4 to 6 hours.

Whisk together lemon dressing ingredients, cover and refrigerate while chicken marinates.

Whisk together all dipping sauce ingredients except cucumber. Stir in cucumber after all whisked together. Cover and refrigerate at least 30 minutes.

Chop onion and peppers into chunks. Alternate on skewers peppers, onion and chicken. Grill over medium hot coals, uncovered, turning ¼ turn every 2 minutes. Remove and brush with lemon dressing and serve with dipping sauce.

May God be praised that all things be so good.

~John Donne, 1572-1631

Chicken Lettuce Wraps

1 tablespoon olive oil	3 green onions
3 boneless, skinless chicken breasts, chopped	2 tablespoons brown sugar
1 cup mushrooms	3 tablespoons soy sauce
1 small can sliced water chestnuts	Rice noodles for garnish
	Lettuce for serving

In a large skillet, heat one tablespoon of oil over medium heat. Add chicken and stir while cooking until cooked thoroughly. While chicken is cooking, finely dice mushrooms, water chestnuts, and green onions. Add to skillet. Stir in brown sugar and soy sauce. Cook and stir over medium heat until heated thoroughly.

If garnishing with rice noodles, place 1 to 2 inches of oil in a small saucepan. Heat over medium heat for several minutes. Break a handful of rice noodles and drop into pot, immediately removing to a paper towel lined plate when noodles puff up. Serve chicken mixture in lettuce leaves topped with crunchy rice noodles.

Eat like a taco.

Chicken Pockets

1 (3 ounce) package cream cheese, softened	⅛ teaspoon pepper
3 tablespoons butter, softened	2 tablespoons milk
2 cups diced cooked chicken	1 (8 ounce) can refrigerated crescent rolls
1 tablespoon chopped onion	¾ cup crushed seasoned croutons
1 tablespoon chopped chives	
¼ teaspoon salt	

Preheat oven to 350°. In a mixing bowl, combine cream cheese and 2 tablespoons of butter. Add chicken, onion, chives, salt, pepper and milk. Blend well. Fill each rectangle of crescent rolls with ¼ of the chicken mixture. Pull up corners and twist dough tightly. Pinch all seams closed. Melt remaining butter and brush on dough. Dip lightly in crushed croutons. Place on an ungreased baking sheet and bake 25 minutes or until golden brown.

Makes 4 servings

CHICKEN MARINADE

1 cup vinegar

1 stick butter, melted

1 cup water

¼ cup soy sauce

2 teaspoons liquid smoke

2 teaspoons fresh lemon juice

½ teaspoon garlic powder

1 tablespoon lemon pepper

1 teaspoon salt

½ teaspoon poultry seasoning

Mix all ingredients in a boiler and cook on medium-high heat until boiling. Let marinade cool. Put marinade and chicken into a zip-top plastic bag and let marinate at least 8 hours. Baste chicken with marinade while cooking.

This marinade works well on chicken cooked in the oven or on the grill.

Chicken Picatta

4	thin boneless, skinless chicken breasts or pound thin Kosher salt and fresh ground pepper	3	tablespoons butter, divided
¾	cup all-purpose flour	2	fresh garlic cloves, pressed or minced well
1	teaspoon salt and ½ teaspoon pepper divided	½	cup freshly squeezed lemon juice (3 lemons), reserve the lemon halves
1	large egg	¾	cup dry white wine
½	tablespoon water	3	tablespoons chopped fresh parsley
¾	cup Italian seasoned dry bread crumbs		Fettuccini noodles, cooked according to package directions
2	tablespoons olive oil		

Preheat oven to 300°. Pound chicken breast halves until thin, about ¼ inch thick. Sprinkle both sides of chicken pieces with salt and pepper. Set up three plates. Mix the flour, ½ teaspoon salt and ¼ teaspoon of pepper on the first plate. Beat the egg and water together and put on the second plate. Place the bread crumbs on the third plate.

Dip chicken breasts in the flour mixture, making sure to cover both sides. Shake off excess. Next, dip each chicken breast in the egg and then the bread crumb mixture. Heat olive oil in a large sauté pan over medium to medium-low heat. Add chicken breasts and brown on each side for about 2 to 3 minutes. Place chicken on sheet pan and bake for about 10 minutes in the oven while making the sauce. Wipe the saucepan out with a dry paper towel.

Over medium heat, melt 1 tablespoon of butter. Add garlic and stir. Add lemon juice, wine, reserved lemon halves, ½ teaspoon salt and ¼ teaspoon pepper. Boil over medium-high heat until reduced by half, about 2 to 3 minutes. Take off heat and add remaining butter and stir. Remove lemon halves. Serve chicken on top of noodles and spoon sauce over chicken. Sprinkle with parsley.

Serve with a salad and garlic bread.

> "For we walk by faith, not by sight."
>
> *2 Corinthians 5:7 (KJV)*

Chicken Scaloppine with Spinach and Linguine

1 pound fresh asparagus	2 tablespoons all-purpose flour
1 (16 ounce) package linguine	2½ cups chicken broth
1 (9 ounce) package clean, fresh spinach	1 tablespoon lemon zest
¾ cup all-purpose flour	3 tablespoons fresh lemon juice
2½ teaspoons salt, divided	¼ cup capers, rinsed and drained
2½ teaspoons pepper, divided	2 roma tomatoes, seeded and chopped
6 chicken cutlets	Freshly grated Parmigiano Reggiano cheese, or Parmesan cheese
3 tablespoons butter	
3 tablespoons olive oil	

Snap off and discard tough ends of asparagus. Cut asparagus in half crosswise. Prepare linguine according to package directions, adding asparagus during the last 2 minutes of cooking. Drain and return to pan. Stir in spinach. Cover and keep warm over low heat.

Combine flour, 2 teaspoons salt and 2 teaspoons pepper in a large zip-top plastic bag. Add chicken cutlets; seal bag, and shake to lightly coat. Melt 1½ tablespoons butter and 1½ tablespoons olive oil in a large nonstick skillet over medium-high heat. Cook 3 cutlets in skillet 2 to 3 minutes on each side or until lightly browned and done. Remove from skillet and repeat procedure with remaining 1½ tablespoons butter, 1½ tablespoons oil and 3 cutlets. (Chicken may be kept warm in a 250° oven on a wire rack.)

Whisk 2 tablespoons flour into skillet and cook 30 seconds. Whisk in chicken broth, lemon zest, lemon juice, capers and remaining ½ teaspoon salt and pepper. Cook over medium-high heat 6 to 8 minutes or until slightly thickened, whisking to loosen particles from bottom of skillet. Pour over warm pasta mixture, toss to combine. Transfer to serving plates. Sprinkle with tomatoes, chicken and freshly grated cheese. Serve immediately.

Makes 6 servings

Chicken Spectacular

3   cups cooked diced chicken
1   box Original Uncle Ben's Long Grain and Wild Rice, cooked
1   can cream of celery soup, undiluted
1   (4 ounce) jar chopped pimentos
1   medium onion, chopped
1   (14½ ounce) can French style green beans, drained
1   cup mayonnaise
1   (8 ounce) can sliced water chestnuts
    Salt and pepper to taste
1   can French onions

Preheat oven to 350°. Combine chicken, rice, soup, pimentos, onion, green beans, mayonnaise, sliced water chestnuts, salt and pepper. Pour into a 9x13 inch casserole dish. Bake 30 minutes. After 30 minutes, turn the oven off and sprinkle can of French onions on top and leave in the oven for about 4 minutes or until onions are browned.

"*Not that we are sufficient of ourselves.*"

2 Corinthians 3:5

Chicken with Olives

4   bone-in chicken breasts with skin
4   ounces soft cream cheese with herbs
2   tablespoons capers
½   cup pimento stuffed green olives
½   cup pitted Kalamata black olives
½   cup Italian salad dressing
    Salt and pepper to taste

Preheat oven to 400°. Rinse and pat dry chicken breasts. Loosely separate skin from breast to form a pocket and stuff each with 1 ounce of cheese, spreading under skin and over meat. Place in 9x12 inch baking dish and sprinkle capers and olives over chicken.

Pour dressing over all and season with salt and pepper. Bake 1 hour and 15 minutes.

Serve with yellow rice.

Makes 4 servings

Chicken with Herbed Goat Cheese

3 whole (6 split) chicken breasts, bone-in, skin on	Fresh basil leaves
12 ounces Montrachet goat cheese, with garlic and herbs	Olive oil
	Kosher salt
	Freshly ground black pepper

Preheat oven to 375°. Place the chicken breasts on a baking sheet. Loosen the skin from the meat using fingers, leaving one side attached. Cut 12 thick slices of the Montrachet and place 2 slices plus a large basil leaf under the skin of each chicken breast. Rub each piece with olive oil and sprinkle generously with salt and pepper. Bake the breasts 35 to 40 minutes, until just cooked through.

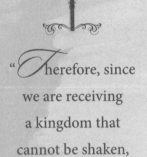

"Therefore, since we are receiving a kingdom that cannot be shaken, let us be thankful, and so worship God acceptably with reverence and awe."

Hebrews 12:28

Chinese Chicken Casserole

2 cups cooked chicken, diced	1 teaspoon salt
1 cup chopped celery	1 (10 ounce) can cream of chicken soup
1 cup cooked rice	
¾ cup mayonnaise	4 ounces water chestnuts, sliced and drained
1 cup sliced fresh mushrooms	
1 teaspoon lemon juice	

Preheat oven to 350°. Mix all ingredients and pour mixture into lightly greased 2 quart casserole dish.

TOPPING

½ cup softened butter	1 cup crushed round buttery crackers
½ cup slivered almonds	

Mix butter, almonds and crackers. Spread mixture on top of casserole. Bake approximately 40 minutes.

Cilantro Grilled Chicken

1	cup finely chopped fresh cilantro	2	teaspoons ground cumin	
1	cup mayonnaise	1	teaspoon salt	
½	cup extra virgin olive oil	6	boneless, skinless chicken breasts	
¼	cup fresh lime juice			

In a large resealable plastic bag, combine cilantro, mayonnaise, oil, lime juice, cumin and salt. Add chicken. Seal bag, and refrigerate at least 4 hours.

Spray grill rack with nonstick nonflammable cooking spray. Preheat grill to medium heat (300° to 350°). Remove chicken from marinade, discarding marinade. Grill chicken, covered with grill lid, 4 to 5 minutes per side or until chicken is done. Let stand 5 minutes before slicing.

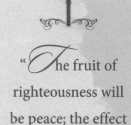

Citrus Marinated Chicken

1	cup soy sauce		Salt and pepper
1	cup orange marmalade	12-14	boneless chicken thighs, skin on
1	cup lemon juice		

Combine soy sauce, orange marmalade, lemon juice, salt and pepper. Place the chicken in a zip-top bag or container with a lid. Seal the container and refrigerate for 2 hours or longer.

May substitute lime juice for lemon juice in the marinade for a more intense citrus flavor The longer the chicken marinates, the stronger the flavor will be.

FOR GRILLING
Rub the grill with oil to avoid sticking. Preheat the grill to medium-high heat. Remove the chicken from the marinade. Sprinkle with salt and pepper. Grill, skin side down, 6 to 8 minutes. Flip the chicken and cook an additional 4 to 6 minutes or until the juices run clear.

FOR ROASTING
Preheat oven to 400°. Remove the chicken from the marinade. Sprinkle with salt and pepper and place in a shallow baking pan, skin side up. Roast 25 to 30 minutes or until the juices run clear. Discard any unused marinade.

"The fruit of righteousness will be peace; the effect of righteousness will be quietness and confidence forever."

Isaiah 32:17

Creamy Chicken and Cheese Enchiladas

4 boneless, skinless chicken breast halves	¼ cup butter or margarine
3 tablespoons olive oil	¼ cup flour
3 cups shredded Monterey Jack cheese	1 cup sour cream
½ cup chopped onion	2 cups chicken broth
10 flour tortillas	1 (4 ounce) can chopped green chilies, drained

Preheat the oven to 350°. Rinse chicken and pat dry. Cut into thin slices. Sauté the chicken in olive oil in a skillet until browned, drain. Combine the chicken, cheese and onion in a bowl. Mix well. Spoon the chicken mixture onto the center of each tortilla. Roll the tortilla to enclose the filling. Place the enchiladas seam side down in a greased 9x13 inch baking dish.

Heat the butter in a saucepan until melted. Stir in the flour until blended. Add the chicken broth. Mix well. Cook until thickened, stirring constantly. Stir in the sour cream and green chilies. Spoon the sauce over the enchiladas. Bake 20 minutes or until bubbly.

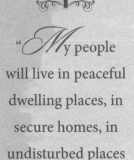

"*My* people will live in peaceful dwelling places, in secure homes, in undisturbed places of rest."

Isaiah 32:18

Poppy Seed Chicken

4 chicken breasts, cooked and chopped	1 can cream of chicken soup
½ cup chopped onion	½ cup sour cream
1 teaspoon minced garlic	¼ cup butter, melted
1 tablespoon butter or olive oil	1 pack buttery round crackers
Salt and pepper, to taste	2 tablespoons poppy seeds

Preheat oven to 350°. Sauté onions and garlic in butter. In a large bowl, mix chicken, sautéed onions, salt, pepper, soup, sour cream and butter. Place in a greased 9x9 inch glass dish. Crumble buttery round crackers on top and sprinkle with poppy seeds. Bake 30 minutes.

Curry Chicken Salad

1 large roasted chicken cut into 1 inch cubes

¾ cup chopped celery

1 (8 ounce) can sliced chopped water chestnuts, drained

2 cups seedless red grapes, halved

1 (2 ounce) package slivered almonds

Gently combine the chicken, celery, water chestnuts, grapes and almonds in a large bowl.

DRESSING

1 cup mayonnaise

1 tablespoon soy sauce

1 tablespoon fresh lemon juice

1½ teaspoons curry powder

1 tablespoon prepared mango chutney

Salt

Combine all ingredients and mix well. Add to the chicken mixture and stir gently to combine. Season with salt and pepper to taste.

Rosemary Grilled Chicken

1 garlic clove, pressed

1 tablespoon olive oil

2 tablespoons Dijon mustard

2 tablespoons honey

1 teaspoon salt

1 teaspoon chopped fresh rosemary

1 teaspoon pepper

1½ pounds skinned and boned chicken thighs or breasts

½ lemon

Combine garlic, olive oil, mustard, honey, salt, rosemary and pepper in a large zip-top plastic freezer bag, squeezing bag to combine ingredients. Add chicken, turning to coat, and seal bag. Chill 1 to 24 hours.

Preheat grill to 350° to 400° (medium-high) heat. Remove chicken from marinade, discarding marinade. Grill chicken, covered with grill lid, 5 to 7 minutes on each side. Transfer chicken to a large piece of aluminum foil. Squeeze juice from lemon over chicken. Fold foil around chicken, covering chicken completely. Lct stand 10 minutes.

Great with honey mustard sauce.

"Is any among you suffering? Let him pray. Is any cheerful? Let him sing praise."

James 5:13

Fancy Chicken Phyllo Breasts

1½ cups mayonnaise

1 cup green onions, chopped, using green part also

⅓ cup freshly squeezed lemon juice

2 cloves fresh garlic, minced

2 teaspoons dried tarragon

12 skinless, boneless chicken breasts
Salt and pepper to taste

24 sheets phyllo dough (about 2 packages)

1⅓ cups butter, melted

⅓ cup freshly grated Parmesan cheese

Preheat oven to 375°. Mix mayonnaise, onions, lemon juice, garlic and tarragon in a bowl and set aside. Sprinkle chicken with salt and pepper on both sides.

Place sheet of phyllo dough on work surface and quickly brush with melted butter. Keep remaining dough covered with a damp cloth while working. Place a second sheet on top of the first and brush with melted butter. Place a breast in one corner, spread 1½ tablespoons of sauce mixture on each side of breast (3 tablespoons per breast). Fold corner over breast, then fold sides over and roll breast up in the sheets to form a package. Place on lightly sprayed baking sheet or dish. Repeat for each breast. Brush packets with rest of butter and sprinkle with Parmesan cheese. Bake 20 to 25 minutes or until golden brown.

Can dress these up by cutting strips of phyllo, brush with melted butter and pleat like a fan into a bow. Bake the bows at 375° about 5 minutes or until browned. Place them on top of "chicken breast package."

"*And* whatever you do, do it heartily."

Colossians 3:23

French Vinegar Chicken

½	cup all-purpose flour	1	(8 ounce) package fresh mushrooms
¼	teaspoon salt	2	medium tomatoes, chopped
¼	teaspoon pepper	1	cup cream
½	teaspoon garlic powder	¼	cup white wine vinegar or champagne vinegar
4	thin boneless, skinless chicken breasts or pounded thin	1-2	cans quartered artichokes (not marinated), cut in half
3	tablespoons olive oil, divided	1	(16 ounce) box fettuccini, cooked
3	tablespoons butter		

Preheat oven to 300°. Mix flour, salt, pepper and garlic powder on a plate. Dip chicken in mixture, coating well. Sauté about 2 to 3 minutes on each side in 1½ tablespoons olive oil.

Place chicken in oven about 40 minutes while making the sauce. Put butter and other 1½ tablespoons of olive oil in skillet and sauté mushrooms. Cut stem end off tomatoes and squeeze to release the seeds, then chop. Add cream, white vinegar, chopped artichokes. Stir well. Place the chicken in the sauce and cook about 5 minutes on medium-low. Serve over fettuccini.

Skillet Chicken Cordon Bleu

½	cup Italian seasoned bread crumbs	1	tablespoon butter
1	teaspoon pepper	1	tablespoon olive oil
½	teaspoon salt	8	Canadian bacon slices, cut into thin strips
8	chicken tenders	4	Swiss cheese slices, halved

Combine bread crumbs, pepper and salt in a large zip-top plastic freezer bag. Rinse chicken tenders and add to freezer bag. Seal bag and shake to coat.

Melt butter with oil in an ovenproof skillet over medium heat. Cook chicken 3 to 4 minutes on each side or until done. Arrange Canadian bacon strips over chicken in skillet and top each with one cheese slice. Broil 5½ inches from heat for 2 minutes or until cheese is melted.

"Choose for yourselves today the one you will worship... As for my family, and me we will worship the Lord."

Joshua 24:15

Herb-Roasted Chickens with Mushroom-Parsley Noodles

6	tablespoons olive oil	4	teaspoons fresh minced garlic
½	cup poultry seasoning	2	teaspoons salt
¼	cup finely chopped fresh rosemary	1	teaspoon freshly ground black pepper
¼	cup finely chopped fresh thyme	2	(3 pound) whole chickens

Preheat oven to 425°. Mix together olive oil, poultry seasoning, rosemary, thyme, garlic, salt and pepper. Remove giblets from chickens, then rinse and dry the chickens. Loosen and lift the skin from the chickens and rub oil and herb mixture evenly under the skin of each chicken. Replace skin and rub remaining oil mixture over both chickens.

Place the chickens on a greased rack in a pan. Bake 30 minutes. Cover loosely with aluminum foil and bake 45 to 50 minutes or until a meat thermometer registers 165°. Let chicken stand for 15 minutes before slicing. Serve with Mushroom-Parsley Noodles.

MUSHROOM-PARSLEY NOODLES

1 (8 ounce) package medium egg noodles

3 chicken bouillon cubes

5 tablespoons butter

1 (8 ounce) package sliced fresh mushrooms

¼ cup finely chopped parsley

Salt to taste

¼ teaspoon freshly ground black pepper

Prepare pasta according to package directions, adding chicken bouillon cubes to pasta water. Melt 4 tablespoons of butter in pan. Add sliced mushrooms, sauté 5 minutes until golden. Remove from heat and stir in chopped parsley, noodles, 1 tablespoon butter, salt and pepper.

Rosemary Roasted Chicken with Potatoes

2	tablespoons olive oil	½	teaspoon black pepper
1	teaspoon salt	6	bone-in chicken thighs or breasts (skin removed)
2	teaspoons paprika	1½	pounds small red potatoes cut into 1 inch cubes
1½	teaspoons crushed rosemary leaves		
1	teaspoon minced garlic		

Preheat oven to 425°. Mix oil, salt, paprika, rosemary, garlic and pepper. Add chicken and potatoes, toss to coat well. Arrange chicken and potatoes in a single layer on foil-lined 15x10 inch baking dish sprayed with nonstick cooking spray. Roast in oven 45 minutes or until chicken is cooked through and potatoes are tender, turning potatoes occasionally.

Lattice Topped Chicken Pot Pie

3 chicken breasts, cooked and chopped	1 can cream of chicken soup
1 stalk celery, coarsely chopped	1 stick butter, melted
½ cup coarsely chopped onion	3 tablespoons flour
Salt and pepper	2½ cups chicken broth
2 large carrots, peeled and chopped	Salt and pepper to taste
1 large potato, peeled and chopped into cubes	1 can of cut green beans, drained
1 egg	½ teaspoon dried thyme, optional
	2 ready pie crusts

Preheat oven to 350°. Cook chicken breasts in water with celery, onion, salt and pepper over low heat. Boil carrots and potato together until just tender when pricked with a fork. Hard-boil the egg and chop. Combine soup, butter, flour and broth. Add chicken, carrots, potatoes, eggs and beans; mix well. The mixture will be "soupy".

Place in a greased 9x13 inch glass dish. Cut pie crusts into strips and lattice them on top of pie. Bake 30 to 40 minutes or until bubbling and slightly brown.

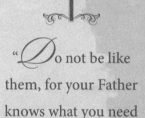

"*Do not be like them, for your Father knows what you need before you ask him.*"

Matthew 6:8

Sweet Chili Chicken

½ cup sweet chili sauce	1½ teaspoons minced fresh ginger
3 tablespoons orange juice	Vegetable cooking spray
2 tablespoons honey	4 boneless, skinless chicken breasts
1 tablespoon lite soy sauce	
1½ teaspoons minced jalapeño pepper	

Whisk together chili sauce, orange juice, honey, soy sauce, jalapeño pepper and ginger in a small bowl until blended. Reserve half of the sweet chili sauce mixture for dipping.

Coat cold cooking grate with cooking spray and place on grill. Preheat grill to 350° to 400° (medium-high) heat. Lightly spray chicken with cooking spray and place on cooking grate. Grill chicken 6 minutes on each side or until done, basting with sweet chili sauce mixture during last few minutes on each side.

Nana's Smothered Chicken and Rice with Rich Vinegar Gravy

4-5 chicken breasts (skin and bone-in)	1¼ tablespoons distilled white vinegar
Water to boil chicken	Salt and pepper to taste
1 stick butter	Browning Sauce (optional)
3-4 tablespoons all-purpose flour	Rice

In a large double boiler, cover the chicken with water and boil about 45 minutes until tender. Turn the stove off and allow the chicken to sit in broth until cool. This makes a rich broth and moist chicken. Remove the chicken. Reserve the broth for the gravy.

Melt butter in a large saucepan over medium-high heat and whisk in flour. Whisk constantly until flour mixture turns light brown. Be careful not to let mixture burn. When it turns light brown, add about 4 cups of reserved broth. Whisk constantly until the gravy thickens. Add vinegar, salt and pepper to taste.

To make the sauce a richer color, a dash of browning sauce may be used. Remove the skin and bone from the chicken and place chicken in gravy. Simmer for about 20 to 25 minutes. If gravy gets too thick, more broth may be needed.

Serve the vinegar gravy over chicken and prepared white rice.

For a lower calorie dish, make the following substitutions: Skinned chicken breasts, light margarine, 98% fat free cream of chicken soup.

"In the same way, let your light shine before men, that they may see your good deeds and praise your Father in heaven."

Matthew 5:16

ENTRÉES

SEAFOOD

"If I take the wings of morning, and dwell in the uttermost parts of the sea, even there your hand shall lead me, your right hand shall hold me."

Psalm 139:9-10

Apricot and Mustard Glazed Grilled Salmon

SALMON

4	(6 ounce) salmon filets	¼	teaspoon freshly ground black pepper
1½	teaspoons bottled minced garlic		Cooking spray
½	teaspoon kosher salt		

Prepare grill. Sprinkle filets evenly with garlic, salt and pepper. Cover and refrigerate 15 minutes.

GLAZE

¼	cup apricot nectar	1½	teaspoons honey
¼	cup apricot preserves	¼	teaspoon kosher salt
1	tablespoon Dijon mustard	¼	teaspoon freshly ground black pepper
1½	teaspoons white wine vinegar		

To prepare glaze, combine apricot nectar, apricot preserves, Dijon mustard, vinegar, honey, salt and pepper in a small saucepan. Bring to a boil. Reduce heat and simmer until reduced to ¼ cup (about 10 minutes). Remove from heat, set aside.

Place filets, skin side up, on a grill rack coated with cooking spray. Grill 2 minutes. Carefully turn over and grill 4 minutes or until fish flakes easily when tested with a fork or until desired degree of doneness. Brush each filet with 1 tablespoon glaze, grill 30 seconds.

4 servings

"*Do not store up for yourselves treasures on earth, where moth and rust destroy, and where thieves break in and steal.*"

Matthew 6:19

Asian Marinated Salmon

1	clove garlic	6	tablespoons olive oil
2	tablespoons Dijon mustard	2-3	cuts of salmon
3	tablespoons soy sauce		

Mix together garlic, mustard, soy sauce, and olive oil in a bowl. Pour ½ of mixture over salmon pieces and marinate for several hours in a gallon size zip-top plastic bag in the refrigerator. Grill salmon pieces on medium heat for 5 minutes on each side. Pour remaining mixture on cooked fish.

If more salmon is used, double the marinade.

Tilapia with Vegetables and Basil Cream Sauce

3	tablespoons butter, divided	½	cup all-purpose flour
1	(16 ounce) package frozen whole kernel shoepeg corn, thawed	¼	cup yellow cornmeal
		1	tablespoon Creole seasoning
1	medium onion, chopped	4	(6 to 8 ounce) tilapia filets
1	medium green bell pepper, chopped	⅓	cup buttermilk
		1	tablespoon vegetable oil
¾	teaspoon salt	½	cup whipping cream
¾	teaspoon pepper	2	tablespoons chopped fresh basil

Melt 2 tablespoons butter in large skillet over medium-high heat. Add corn, onion and peppers and sauté 6 to 8 minutes, until tender. Stir in salt and pepper. Spoon onto serving dish and keep warm. Combine flour, cornmeal and Creole seasoning in a large shallow dish. Dip filets in buttermilk, dredge in flour mixture. Melt remaining 1 tablespoon butter with oil in skillet over medium-high heat. Cook filets 2 to 3 minutes on each side until golden brown. Remove. Arrange with vegetables. Add cream to skillet, stirring to loosen particles from the bottom of the skillet. Add chopped basil and cook stirring often, until thickened. Serve sauce with filets and vegetables.

Any white fish may be used for this dish. It is also very good using catfish.

Grilled Glazed Salmon with Orange Salsa

MARINADE

1	(15 ounce) can Mandarin oranges	1	clove garlic, minced
2	tablespoons brown sugar	2	teaspoons fresh ginger, minced
2	tablespoons soy sauce	4	(6 ounce) salmon filets

For the marinade, drain the Mandarin oranges, reserving the juice. Set the Mandarin oranges aside to use in the Orange Salsa.

In a small bowl, combine the reserved orange juice, brown sugar, soy sauce, garlic and ginger. Place the salmon in a shallow dish. Pour the marinade over the salmon and refrigerate for several hours.

ORANGE SALSA

1	medium ripe tomato, seeded and chopped	1	tablespoon chopped jalapeño chile
	Reserved Mandarin oranges, chopped	¼	cup chopped red bell pepper
		1	teaspoon sugar
			Salt to taste

For the salsa, in a bowl combine the tomato, Mandarin oranges, jalapeño, bell pepper, sugar and salt. Refrigerate the salsa until ready to serve.

Preheat the grill to medium. Remove the salmon from the marinade, reserving the marinade. Place skin side down in a grill basket on the grill. Turn the fish after a couple of minutes and baste with the marinade. Continue grilling until the desired degree of doneness. Serve topped with the orange salsa.

Makes 4 servings

"Again the kingdom of heaven is like a dragnet that was cast into the sea and gathered some of every kind, which when it was full, they drew to shore; and they sat down and gathered the good into vessels..."

Matthew 13:47-48

"*I* will refresh the weary and satisfy the faint."

Jeremiah 31:25

Sesame-Crusted Tuna Steaks with Ginger-Soy Sauce

¾	cup sesame seeds	3	tablespoons vegetable oil
4	tuna steaks (yellow fin, Ahi or black fin) about 1 inch thick		Salt and ground black pepper

Spread the sesame seeds in a shallow baking dish or pie plate. Pat the tuna steaks dry with a paper towel. Use 1 tablespoon of the oil to rub both sides of the steaks, sprinkle with salt and pepper. Press both sides of each steak in the sesame seeds to coat. Heat the remaining 2 tablespoons oil in a 12 inch nonstick skillet over high heat until just beginning to smoke and swirl to coat the pan. Add tuna steaks and cook 30 seconds without moving the steaks. Reduce the heat to medium-high and continue to cook until the seeds are golden brown, about 1½ minutes.

Using tongs, flip the tuna steaks carefully and cook, without moving them, until golden brown on the second side, about 1½ minutes for rare or 3 minutes for medium rare. To serve, cut into ¼-inch-thick slices. Serve with Ginger-Soy Sauce or Avocado-Orange Salsa, if desired.

Cooking times are estimates. Check for desired degree of doneness by nicking with a paring knife. Remember to cut right away if desired degree of doneness has been obtained. If steaks are almost ready, do not cut immediately, and let the residual heat finish the cooking.

Avocado-Orange Salsa

1	large orange, cut into segments	1	small jalapeño chile, stemmed, seeded and minced
1	ripe avocado, diced medium	2	tablespoons minced fresh cilantro leaves
2	tablespoons minced red onion		Salt
4	teaspoons fresh lime juice		

Combine all ingredients a small bowl.

To keep the avocado from discoloring, prepare this salsa just before cooking tuna steaks.

Makes about 1 cup

Tilapia with Citrus Vinaigrette

4	(6 ounce) tilapia filets	2	tablespoons fresh lemon juice
2	teaspoons salt, divided	2	tablespoons fresh orange juice
2	teaspoons freshly ground black pepper, divided	4	teaspoons extra virgin olive oil
½	cup dry white wine	2	teaspoons sherry vinegar
2	tablespoons finely chopped shallots		

Heat a large nonstick skillet over medium-high heat. Coat pan with cooking spray. Sprinkle fish evenly with 1 teaspoon salt and 1 teaspoon pepper. Add filets to pan. Cook 4 minutes on each side or until fish flakes easily when tested with a fork or until desired degree of doneness.

Remove from pan, keep warm. Add white wine to pan and cook 30 seconds or until liquid almost evaporates. Combine shallots and the remaining ingredients, stirring well. Stir in remaining 1 teaspoon salt and 1 teaspoon pepper. Add shallot mixture to pan. Sauté 1 minute or until thoroughly heated, stirring frequently. Top each serving with about 3 tablespoons of sauce.

Makes 4 servings

Skillet Filets with Cilantro Butter

¼	teaspoon salt	2	tablespoons butter, softened
¼	teaspoon ground cumin	2	tablespoons finely chopped fresh cilantro
⅛	teaspoon ground red pepper		
4	(6 ounce) tilapia filets	½	teaspoon grated lemon zest
	Cooking spray	¼	teaspoon paprika
1	lemon, quartered	⅛	teaspoon salt

Combine salt, cumin and pepper. Sprinkle over both sides of fish. Heat a large nonstick skillet over medium-high heat. Coat pan with cooking spray. Coat both sides of fish with cooking spray, place in pan. Cook 3 minutes on each side or until fish flakes easily when tested with a fork or until desired degree of doneness. Place fish on a serving platter. Squeeze lemon juice quarters over fish. Place butter, cilantro, lemon zest, paprika and salt in a small bowl. Stir until well blended. Serve with fish.

SALMON STEAKS WITH TARRAGON BUTTER

¼ cup butter, softened

1 shallot, minced

1 tablespoon chopped fresh tarragon

1 tablespoon chopped fresh chives

1½ tablespoons chopped fresh parsley

⅛ teaspoon ground pepper

1 tablespoon Dijon mustard

4 (1½ inch thick) salmon steaks

Combine butter, shallot, tarragon, chives, parsley, pepper and Dijon mustard. Mix well. Brush salmon steaks with butter mixture, saving a little to baste with. Prepare grill and place salmon in a wire fish basket. Grill 8 minutes on each side or until salmon flakes easily with a fork. Brush frequently with remaining butter mixture while grilling.

Broiled Tilapia with Thai Coconut-Curry Sauce

1	teaspoon dark sesame oil, divided	4	teaspoons low sodium soy sauce
2	teaspoons fresh ginger, peeled and minced	1	tablespoon brown sugar
2	garlic cloves, minced	½	teaspoon salt, divided
1	cup finely chopped red bell pepper	1	(14 ounce) can light coconut milk
1	cup chopped green onions	2	tablespoons chopped fresh cilantro
1	teaspoon curry powder	4	(6 ounce) tilapia filets
2	teaspoons red curry paste		Cooking spray
½	teaspoon ground cumin	3	cups cooked basmati rice
		4	lime wedges

Heat ½ teaspoon oil in a large nonstick skillet over medium heat. Add ginger and garlic. Cook 1 minute. Add pepper and onions, cook 1 minute. Stir in curry powder, curry paste, and cumin. Cook 1 minute. Add soy sauce, sugar, ¼ teaspoon salt and coconut milk; bring to a simmer (do not boil).

Remove from heat, stir in cilantro. Brush fish with ½ teaspoon oil, sprinkle with ¼ teaspoon salt. Place fish on a baking sheet coated with cooking spray. Broil 7 minutes or until fish flakes easily when tested with a fork. Serve fish with sauce, rice and lime wedges.

Crispy Flounder Filets with Apricot Sauce

6	(6 ounce) flounder filets	⅓	cup water or milk
	Salt and pepper	3	cups panko breadcrumbs
2	cups flour		Vegetable oil for frying
3	eggs		

Generously sprinkle flounder filets with salt and pepper. Place the following into three shallow pans. 2 cups flour in pan 1. Whisk together 3 eggs and milk or water in pan 2. 3 cups panko breadcrumbs in pan 3.

Fill a 10 to 12 inch skillet with oil to a depth of ½ inch. Heat the oil until hot, but not smoking. Prepare the flounder by dipping each filet into the flour first, followed by the egg wash and then the breadcrumbs. Press the filets firmly into the breadcrumbs to ensure a thick coating.

Place the filets 2 or 3 at a time into the hot oil and cook for 3 minutes on each side until golden brown. Using a pair of tongs, gently remove the filets onto a platter and place in a warm oven. Repeat this process with the remaining filets.

Delicious with Apricot Sauce (recipe below), Creamy Caper Dill Sauce (page 151) or Lemon Rémoulade (sidebar).

Any mild tasting fish, such as halibut, cod or tilapia will work well using this method.

APRICOT SAUCE

2	(10 ounce) jars apricot jam	1	tablespoon fresh ginger, minced (fresh preferred, but may substitute 1 teaspoon ground ginger)
1	cup rice vinegar		
¼	cup mustard seed		

Combine all ingredients in a medium skillet and bring to a boil over medium-high heat. Reduce heat slightly and continue simmering, stirring frequently, until the mixture is thickened and reduced to 2 cups, about 8 to 10 minutes. Allow to cool before serving.

Store in airtight container in the refrigerator.

Great on toasted French baguette slices with cream cheese and a spoonful of sauce. Also pairs nicely with grilled chicken, fish or pork tenderloin.

LEMON RÉMOULADE

2 cups mayonnaise

¼ cup Creole mustard

2 garlic cloves, pressed

2 tablespoons chopped fresh parsley

1 tablespoon fresh lemon juice

2 teaspoons paprika

¾ teaspoon ground red pepper

Whisk together all ingredients until blended. Cover and chill 30 minutes or up to 3 days.

This sauce may also be used as a dip for boiled shrimp or steamed asparagus. Add a small amount of milk to make a delicious salad dressing.

Heavenly Fish

1½ pounds white fish	2 tablespoons chopped green onions
1 tablespoon lemon juice	¼ teaspoon salt
⅓ cup Parmesan cheese	⅛ teaspoon hot sauce
3 tablespoons softened butter	Paprika
2 tablespoons mayonnaise	

In a 13x9 inch casserole dish, arrange fish with thick meaty areas to the outside. Brush fish with the lemon juice and let stand 10 minutes. Cover fish with plastic wrap and cook in microwave oven 4 minutes. Combine Parmesan cheese, butter, mayonnaise, green onions, salt and hot sauce. Spread cheese mixture over fish and cook 3 to 4 more minutes. Sprinkle with paprika.

For testing purposes, tilapia was used. Best to double the sauce recipe because it is so yummy, this will probably not be enough.

Barbecue Shrimp

8 pounds unpeeled shrimp	1½ teaspoons Tabasco sauce
1 pound butter	1 tablespoon Italian seasoning
2 cups olive oil	3 cloves garlic, minced
¾ cup Worcestershire sauce	1 teaspoon paprika
6 tablespoons black pepper	4 teaspoons salt
4 lemons (sliced)	

Preheat oven to 450°. In saucepan, heat butter and olive oil. Add Worcestershire sauce, pepper, lemon, Tabasco, Italian seasoning, garlic, paprika and salt. Simmer in saucepan 5 to 7 minutes. Place shrimp in a large pot and pour butter mixture over shrimp. Cook shrimp just until pink, about 6 minutes. Pour shrimp into a large aluminum pan or large casserole dish and cover with foil. Bake in oven 10 minutes and turn once.

These barbecue shrimp are very good peeled and deveined and poured over cooked white rice with some of the shrimp pan sauce and chopped tomatoes on top. Very similar to Bubba Gump's Accidental Tourist dish.

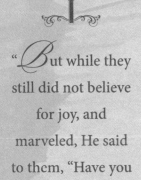

"But while they still did not believe for joy, and marveled, He said to them, "Have you any food here?" So they gave Him a piece of broiled fish and some honeycomb. And He took it and ate in their presence."

Luke 24:41-43

Maryland Crab Cakes

2	pounds fresh lump crabmeat	1	tablespoon fresh lemon juice
½	cup minced green onion	1½	teaspoons Old Bay seasoning
½	cup minced red bell pepper	½	teaspoon pepper
1	tablespoon olive oil		Dash of Worcestershire sauce
½	cup Italian seasoned breadcrumbs	4	tablespoons butter
1	large egg, lightly beaten		Lemon wedges
½	cup mayonnaise		Garnish with dill sprigs (optional)

Rinse, drain and flake crabmeat, being careful not to break up lumps, and remove any bits of shell. Set crabmeat aside.

Sauté green onion and bell pepper in hot olive oil in a large nonstick skillet eight minutes or until tender. Stir together green onion mixture, breadcrumbs, egg, mayonnaise, lemon juice, Old Bay seasoning, pepper and Worcestershire sauce. Gently fold in crabmeat.

Shape mixture into 14 (2½ inch) cakes (about ⅓ cup for each cake). Place on an aluminum foil-lined baking sheet. Cover and chill at least 1 hour or up to 8 hours. Melt butter in a large nonstick skillet over medium heat. Add crab cakes and cook in two batches 4 to 5 minutes on each side or until golden. Drain on paper towels. Serve with a squeeze of lemon and Sweet White Corn and Tomato Relish (below), Creamy Caper Dill Sauce (sidebar) or Lemon Rémoulade (page 149).

This is wonderful with either sauce.

Sweet White Corn and Tomato Relish

4	ears fresh sweet white corn	1	tablespoon olive oil
2	large tomatoes, peeled and chopped	½	teaspoon salt
3	green onions, sliced	½	teaspoon pepper
2	tablespoons lemon juice	¼	teaspoon garlic salt
		¼	teaspoon hot sauce

Cook corn in boiling water for 1 minute, drain and cool. Cut kernels from cobs. Stir together corn, tomato, onion, lemon, olive oil, salt, pepper, garlic salt and hot sauce. Cover and chill 3 hours.

Excellent served over Maryland Crab Cakes.

CREAMY CAPER DILL SAUCE

¼ cup mayonnaise

½ cup sour cream

¼ teaspoon lemon zest

2 tablespoons fresh lemon juice

1 tablespoon drained capers

2 teaspoons chopped fresh dill

1 teaspoon Dijon mustard

½ teaspoon salt

½ teaspoon pepper

Stir together all ingredients. Cover and chill up to three days.

Boiled Shrimp

2½ pounds shrimp	2 teaspoons celery seed
Old Bay seasoning pouch	2½ teaspoons capers and juice
1 beer	Dash Tabasco sauce
1¼ cups salad oil (vegetable)	1 large onion, sliced
¾ cup white vinegar	Bay leaves
1½ teaspoons salt	

Boil deveined shrimp in Old Bay seasoning pouch and beer until the shrimp begin to float and turn pink. Drain. Layer cleaned, boiled shrimp, sliced onion and bay leaves in covered container. Mix salad oil, vinegar, salt, celery seed, capers with juice and Tabasco sauce. Pour mixture over shrimp. Cover and refrigerate for at least 24 hours for best flavor.

Will keep one week in refrigerator.

Louie Sauce for Boiled Shrimp

1 (12 ounce) jar chili sauce	1½ teaspoons Greek seasoning
2 cups mayonnaise	1½ teaspoons Worcestershire sauce
2 tablespoons grated onion	¼ teaspoon ground red pepper
2 tablespoons lemon zest	½ teaspoon hot sauce
3 tablespoons lemon juice	Garnish with lemon zest
1 tablespoon prepared horseradish	

Stir together all ingredients. Cover and chill until ready to serve. Garnish if desired.

Cocktail Sauce

2 cups chili sauce	3 tablespoons freshly grated horseradish
2 cups ketchup	
3 tablespoons fresh lemon juice	

Whisk together all ingredients; chill, if desired.

3 tablespoons prepared horseradish may be substituted.

TARTAR SAUCE

4 cups mayonnaise

1½ cups finely chopped onion

¾ cup sweet pickle relish

⅓ cup plus 1 tablespoon fresh lemon juice

2 tablespoons dried parsley flakes

¾ teaspoon hot sauce

1 teaspoon Worcestershire sauce

Whisk together all ingredients. Chill until ready to serve.

Crab and Shrimp Casserole

1 (6 ounce) package wild and white rice mix
1 pound sliced fresh mushrooms
1 stick butter, divided
6 tablespoons flour
3½ cups half-and-half
1 tablespoon Worcestershire sauce
Juice of one lemon
Salt and pepper to taste
1 (14 ounce) can artichoke hearts, drained and quartered
2 pounds medium shrimp, peeled and partially cooked
1 pound cooked lump crabmeat
½ cup shredded Parmesan cheese
Paprika for color

Preheat oven to 375°. Cook the rice mix according to the directions for firmer rice. Set aside.

In a small saucepan, sauté the mushrooms in 2 tablespoons of butter until tender. Set aside. In a medium saucepan, heat the remaining 6 tablespoons butter. Add the flour and cook, stirring for about 1 minute. Remove the pan from the heat and stir in the half-and-half until smooth. Return to heat and cook, stirring constantly, until slightly thickened.

Season with the Worcestershire sauce, lemon juice, salt and pepper. Adjust seasonings to taste.

In a 3 quart casserole dish, layer the cooked rice, artichokes, mushrooms, shrimp and crabmeat. Pour the sauce over the mixture, making sure all of the ingredients are covered. Sprinkle with the Parmesan cheese and paprika. Bake uncovered for about 40 minutes or until bubbly and hot in the center.

Makes 10 to 12 servings

"Those who go down to the sea in ships,
Who do business on great waters,
They see the works of the Lord,
And His wonders in the deep."

Psalm 107:23-24

Old Athens Pickled Shrimp

3 pounds fresh large Georgia shrimp, boiled, peeled and deveined

1 Vidalia onion, sliced thinly into rings

1 lemon, sliced

7-8 bay leaves

1 tablespoon capers

2 tablespoons Worcestershire sauce

⅓ cup ketchup

⅓ cup cider vinegar

1 cup salad oil

Hot sauce to taste

2 tablespoons sugar

1 tablespoon salt

½ tablespoon dry mustard

Prepared horseradish and lemon juice to taste

Place shrimp, onion slices, lemon slices, bay leaves and capers into a 2 gallon zip-top bag. Combine Worcestershire sauce, ketchup, vinegar, salad oil, hot sauce, sugar, salt, mustard, horseradish and lemon juice in a jar and replace lid. Shake until well blended. Pour over shrimp mixture in bag and seal. Marinate in refrigerator for up to two weeks.

Serve with toothpicks in a glass bowl as a delicious cold hors d'oeuvre.

Caution: Never put them all out at once, they disappear in a hurry!

"*Jesus then came and took the bread and gave it to them, and likewise the fish.*"

John 21:13

Shrimp and Green Noodles

4 ounces spinach fettuccini, cooked and drained

2 pounds shrimp, peeled and deveined

½ cup butter

1 (10¾ ounce) can cream of mushroom soup

½ cup sour cream

½ cup mayonnaise

1½ teaspoons Dijon mustard

1 tablespoon chopped chives

4 tablespoons dry sherry or white wine

½ cup shredded sharp Cheddar cheese

Preheat oven to 350°. Place cooked and drained noodles in a 9x13 inch casserole dish. Sauté shrimp in butter until done, about 5 minutes. Place over noodles. Combine mushroom soup, sour cream, mayonnaise, mustard, chives and sherry. Pour over shrimp. Top with cheese. Bake for 30 minutes or until cheese is bubbly.

Roasted Shrimp with Orzo

1	pound unpeeled, jumbo raw shrimp	2	garlic cloves, minced
2	teaspoons hot chili sesame oil	1	teaspoon canola oil
6	tablespoons fresh cilantro, divided	2	cups water
1	teaspoon salt	½	stalk lemongrass, diced
1½	cups uncooked orzo	¼	teaspoon curry powder
1	small carrot, chopped	2	tablespoons coconut milk
1	celery rib, chopped	1	tablespoon lite soy sauce
1	large shallot, chopped	1	teaspoon grated fresh ginger

Peel shrimp, leaving tails on. Devein, if desired. Toss together shrimp, chili sesame oil, 2 tablespoons cilantro and salt in a large bowl. Cover and chill 1 hour.

Cook orzo according to package directions, drain. Spoon hot orzo into 4 lightly greased custard cups, pressing slightly with the back of a spoon. Set aside.

Sauté carrot, celery, shallot and garlic in hot canola oil over medium-high heat in a large nonstick skillet 3 minutes. Add 2 cups water and bring to a boil. Add lemongrass, and curry powder. Reduce heat and simmer 20 minutes. Remove from heat and cool slightly.

Process mixture in a food processor. Pour through a fine wire mesh strainer in a saucepan, pressing with the back of a spoon. Discard solids. Stir in coconut milk, soy sauce, ginger and remaining cilantro. Bring to a boil. Remove from heat. Heat a nonstick skillet over high heat. Add shrimp, and cook 3 minutes or just until shrimp turn pink. Unmold orzo. Spoon coconut milk mixture around orzo. Arrange shrimp around orzo.

Lemongrass is used often in Asian cooking. Can be found in large supermarkets and Asian markets.

"*Nevertheless He did not leave Himself without witness, in that He did good, gave us rain from heaven and fruitful seasons, filling our hearts with food and gladness.*"

Acts 14:17

Shrimp and Artichoke Casserole

2½ tablespoons butter	¾ cup whipping cream
½ pound fresh mushrooms	½ cup dry sherry
¾ pound frozen shrimp, cooked	1 tablespoon Worcestershire sauce
1 can artichoke hearts	Salt and pepper to taste
4½ tablespoons butter	½ cup Parmesan cheese
4½ tablespoons flour	Paprika
¾ cup milk	

Preheat oven to 350°. Melt butter and sauté mushrooms. Place in 2 quart casserole, 1 layer each of artichoke, shrimp and mushrooms. Melt 4½ tablespoons butter and flour and stir with wire whisk. Stir in milk and cream. Stir and cook until thickened. Add sherry, Worcestershire sauce, salt and pepper. Pour sauce over layered ingredients. Sprinkle with grated Parmesan and paprika. Bake 30 minutes.

Serve over rice. ¼ pound crab can be added for a heartier dish.

Makes 6 servings

Shrimp Creole

½ cup chopped onion	1½ teaspoons salt
½ cup chopped celery	1 teaspoon sugar
½ cup chopped green pepper	1 teaspoon chili powder
1 clove garlic, minced	1 tablespoon Worcestershire sauce
3 tablespoons oil	Dash of hot sauce
1 (15 ounce) can tomatoes, diced	2 cups shrimp
1 (15 ounce) can tomato sauce	

Sauté onion, celery, green pepper and garlic in oil until tender. Add tomatoes, tomato sauce, salt, sugar, chili powder, Worcestershire sauce and hot sauce. Simmer on low about 10 minutes. Add shrimp and cook for about 3 more minutes, until shrimp are pink.

Serve over rice.

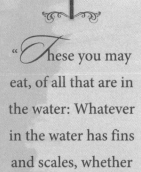

"*These you may eat, of all that are in the water: Whatever in the water has fins and scales, whether in the seas or in the rivers, that you may eat.*"

Leviticus 11:9

Shrimp and Creamy Cheddar Grits

SHRIMP

6	slices applewood-smoked bacon	1	pound large fresh shrimp, peeled and deveined
½	cup diced red bell pepper	2	tablespoons fresh chives, minced
½	cup diced yellow bell pepper		
2	cloves garlic, minced	1	tablespoon fresh lemon juice
1	tablespoon Creole seasoning		Creamy Cheddar Grits
½	cup dry white wine		Garnish with thinly sliced chives

In a large skillet, cook bacon over medium heat until crisp. Using a slotted spoon, remove bacon. Drain on paper towels. Reserve 2 tablespoons drippings in skillet. Add bell peppers, garlic and Creole seasoning to hot drippings in skillet. Cook 2 minutes, stirring frequently. Add wine and cook 2 minutes.

Increase heat to medium-high. Add shrimp and cook, stirring occasionally, 1 to 2 minutes or until shrimp are pink and firm. Remove from heat. Stir in minced chives and lemon juice. Serve shrimp mixture over Creamy Cheddar Grits. Crumble bacon and sprinkle over shrimp. Garnish with thinly sliced fresh chives, if desired. Serve immediately.

CREAMY CHEDDAR GRITS

1	(32 ounce) carton reduced sodium chicken broth	1½	cups shredded extra-sharp white Cheddar cheese
1	cup water	3	tablespoons butter
1	cup stone-ground white grits	¼	teaspoon ground white pepper
1	cup half-and-half		

In a medium saucepan, combine chicken broth and 1 cup water. Bring to a boil over medium-high heat. Stir in grits. Return to a boil. Reduce heat and simmer, stirring frequently, for 1 hour. Stir in half-and-half. Cook for 45 minutes, stirring frequently or until thickened. Remove from heat. Stir in cheese, butter and white pepper, stirring until cheese melts.

Makes 4 servings

"*Teach me your way, O Lord; lead me in a straight path.*"

Psalm 27:11

Shrimp and Pasta with Creole Cream Sauce

1½ pounds unpeeled, medium-size raw shrimp	2 garlic cloves, minced
2 teaspoons Creole seasoning	1½ cups whipping cream
12 ounces uncooked penne pasta	1 teaspoon hot sauce
2 tablespoons butter	¼ cup chopped fresh parsley
4 green onions, sliced	½ cup freshly grated Parmesan cheese

Peel shrimp and devein, if desired. Toss shrimp with Creole seasoning, set aside. Prepare pasta according to package directions, drain. Keep warm. Melt butter in a large skillet over medium-high heat. Add shrimp and cook, stirring constantly, 5 minutes or just until shrimp turn pink. Remove shrimp from skillet. Add green onions and garlic to skillet. Sauté 2 to 3 minutes or until tender. Reduce heat to medium. Stir in cream and hot sauce. Bring to a boil. Reduce heat and simmer, stirring constantly, 8 to 10 minutes or until sauce is slightly thickened. Stir in shrimp and parsley. Toss with pasta. Sprinkle with cheese.

1½ pounds of thawed frozen shrimp may be substituted.

Shrimp Tortellini

1 pound medium-sized fresh shrimp	1 shallot, minced
1 (9 ounce) package fresh tortellini with cheese filling	2 tablespoons chopped fresh basil or 2 teaspoons dried basil
⅓ cup butter	½ cup Parmesan cheese

Peel and devein shrimp. Cook pasta as directed. Drain and set aside. Melt butter in a large skillet over medium-high heat. Add shrimp, minced shallot and basil. Cook about 5 minutes, stirring constantly. Add pasta and Parmesan cheese. Toss gently.

Makes 4 servings

Sun-Dried Tomato Spiced Shrimp

1   (8 ounce) jar oil-packed
    sun-dried tomato halves
1   cup chopped fresh cilantro
½   teaspoon grated lemon zest
2   tablespoons fresh lemon juice

1¼ teaspoons curry paste
1½ pounds large shrimp, peeled
    and deveined
    Cooking spray

Drain sun-dried tomatoes in a sieve over a bowl, reserving oil. Place 1 tablespoon reserved oil in a food processor. Coarsely chop 1 cup tomatoes, add to food processor. Place remaining oil and sun-dried tomatoes in sun-dried tomato jar. Reserve for another use.

Add cilantro, zest, juice and curry to food processor. Process until smooth. Combine tomato mixture and shrimp in a large zip-top plastic bag. Seal and marinate in refrigerator 30 minutes, turning bag occasionally. Remove shrimp from bag, discard marinade. Prepare grill. Place shrimp on grill rack coated with cooking spray. Grill 3 minutes on each side or until done.

Makes 4 servings

In him, he will bear much fruit; apart from me you can do nothing.

John 15:5

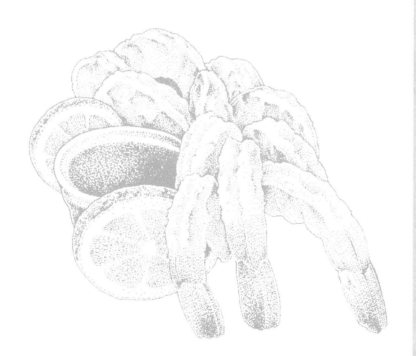

Oyster Casserole

1 stick butter
4 green onions, chopped
4 ribs celery, chopped
2 pints raw oysters, drained and rinsed
 Salt

Dash of cayenne pepper to taste
1 sleeve saltine crackers, crushed
1 cup half-and-half cream
1 cup grated Monterey Jack cheese

Preheat oven to 400°. Melt butter in an 8 to 10 inch sauté pan. Add onions and celery and cook over medium heat 5 to 8 minutes until softened but not brown. Place a layer of oysters on the bottom of a 2 quart ovenproof dish. Using ⅓ of onion-celery mixture, top each oyster. Sprinkle lightly with salt and cayenne pepper. Top with a thick layer of cracker crumbs. Repeat layers ending with the cracker crumbs on top.

Insert a knife blade around the edge of the dish and in the center in several places, pour cream around the blade until all the cream is used. Bake 30 minutes. Remove from oven and carefully drain any excess liquid. Top with cheese and bake uncovered 10 minutes or until cheese is bubbly.

Oysters are best from the Gulf or Georgia Coast.

Makes 6 to 8 servings

"You did not choose me, but I chose you and appointed you to go and bear fruit-fruit that will last."

John 15:16

VEGETABLES AND SIDE DISHES

"Be joyful always; pray continually; give thanks in
all circumstances, for this is God's will for you in Christ Jesus."
1 Thessalonians 5:16-18

Almond Peas

1   (10 ounce) package frozen peas
1   cup sour cream
1   (2½ ounce) can sliced mushrooms, drained
1   (2½ ounce) package slivered almonds
2   tablespoons butter
1   teaspoon sugar
½   teaspoon salt

Cook peas according to package directions and drain. Combine peas, sour cream, mushrooms, slivered almonds, butter, sugar and salt in a medium-sized saucepan. Heat but do not allow to boil. Serve immediately.

Makes 4 to 6 servings

Asparagus with Tarragon and Lemon Sauce

3-4 cups water
1   teaspoon salt
2   pounds asparagus, ends trimmed

Pour 3 to 4 cups of water into a 12 inch saucepan (covering asparagus). Add salt and bring to a boil. Add asparagus and return to a boil. Lower temperature to simmer and cook until crisp but tender, about 3 to 5 minutes. Drain. Place in a bowl of ice water to cool and retain color. Drain again and remove asparagus from ice. Place on a platter and serve at room temperature with Tarragon and Lemon Sauce.

Makes 1¼ cups

TARRAGON AND LEMON SAUCE

½   cup mayonnaise
½   cup sour cream
1   tablespoon fresh tarragon, minced or ½ teaspoon dry tarragon
2   teaspoons fresh lemon juice
1   teaspoon grated lemon zest
1   teaspoon Dijon mustard
    Salt and freshly ground pepper to taste

Whisk together mayonnaise, sour cream, tarragon, lemon juice, lemon zest and mustard. Season with salt and pepper to taste and transfer to a small serving bowl.

The sauce may be made ahead and will keep in the refrigerator for two weeks.

Makes 6 to 8 servings

"He makes grass grow for the cattle, and plants for man to cultivate-bringing forth food from the earth... and bread which strengthens man's heart."

Psalms 104: 14-15

Lemon Roasted Asparagus

2	pounds fresh asparagus	¼	cup olive oil
3	garlic cloves, minced	¾	teaspoon salt
¼	cup lemon juice	¼	teaspoon pepper

Preheat oven to 400°. Trim asparagus ends. Place asparagus on a lightly greased baking sheet. Whisk together garlic, lemon juice, olive oil, salt and pepper. Drizzle mixture over asparagus, tossing to coat. Bake 15 minutes until tender, turning halfway through baking time.

Makes 8 servings

Fluffy Broccoli Casserole

2	(10 ounce) boxes frozen, chopped broccoli	1	(10 ounce) block Velveeta cheese, grated
2	stalks celery, diced	1	(10 ounce) can cream of celery soup
1	medium onion, diced		
3	garlic cloves, minced	1	cup mayonnaise
½	stick butter	1	tablespoon parsley flakes
		3	egg whites

Preheat oven to 350°. Cook broccoli in salted water until very tender. Sauté celery and onion in butter until tender. Do not brown. Add garlic and cook another 3 minutes, stirring so it does not brown. Mix in the broccoli and cheese. Stir in the soup, mayonnaise and parsley. Blend well. Pour into a 9x13x2 inch greased baking dish. Allow to cool for an hour.

Whip egg whites until stiff peaks form and fold into the casserole. The egg whites should be incorporated throughout the casserole without overmixing. Bake 30 to 40 minutes. The top of the casserole should be fluffy and light brown.

Makes 8 to 10 servings

This can be made a day ahead and the egg whites added just before cooking.

HOLLANDAISE SAUCE

3 egg yolks
1 tablespoon fresh lemon juice
2 sticks butter, cut into tablespoons
Salt to taste

In a large, heavy saucepan, beat the egg yolks and lemon juice with a whisk over low heat until very light and creamy. Whisk in the butter 1 tablespoon at a time, making sure the pan never gets hot enough to melt the butter. (You are creaming the butter into the eggs.) Take off of heat from time to time if needed, to prevent the pan from getting too hot. Continue whisking until all the butter has been added. The sauce should be thick and creamy, and the butter not melted. Season with salt and serve warm, not hot.

Great on eggs, vegetables and fish.

Classic Green Bean Casserole

4	cans French style green beans	¾	pound sharp Cheddar cheese, shredded
½	pound mushrooms, sliced or finely chopped	1	teaspoon Tabasco sauce
1	onion, chopped	2	teaspoons soy sauce
1	stick butter	1	can water chestnuts, sliced
¼	cup flour		French fried onions
1	pint half-and-half		

Preheat oven to 350°. Sauté onions and mushrooms in butter. Add flour and half-and-half until thickened. Add cheese, Tabasco and soy sauce. Stir until cheese melts. Add beans and water chestnuts. Pour into greased 9x13x2 inch baking dish. Bake 20 minutes. Top with French fried onions and bake another 10 minutes.

Makes 8 servings

Cabbage Casserole

1	small cabbage	¼	cup mayonnaise
1	medium Vidalia onion	1	cup grated sharp Cheddar cheese
1½	sticks butter, divided		
	Salt and pepper to taste	1	stack round buttery crackers, crushed
1	(10¾ ounce) can mushroom soup or chicken soup		

Preheat oven to 350°. Coarsely chop cabbage and place in a lightly greased 2 to 3 quart casserole dish. Chop onion and place on top of cabbage. Melt ½ stick of butter and pour over cabbage. Sprinkle with salt and pepper. Mix soup and mayonnaise together. Spread over cabbage mixture.

To make topping, melt the remaining stick of butter. Mix in grated cheese and crushed crackers. Sprinkle mixture on top of casserole. Bake 45 minutes or until top is browned and inside is bubbly.

Makes 6 servings

"He will make her wilderness like Eden, and her desert like the garden of the Lord. Joy and gladness will be found in it, thanksgiving and the voice of melody."

Isaiah 51:3

Irish Carrots

1	(5 pound) bag carrots	2	bunches scallions, chopped
3	tablespoons butter	3	tablespoons sour cream

Peel and cut carrots into ½ inch pieces. Melt butter in sauté pan. Add carrots. Cover and cook on low heat until tender. Add scallions and stir on low heat 2 minutes. Add sour cream and stir until coated.

Be careful to not overcook carrots.

May add additional sour cream to taste.

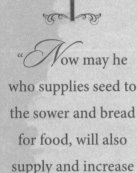

Red Pepper Jelly-Glazed Carrots

1	(2 pound) package baby carrots	2	tablespoons butter
1	(10½ ounce) can condensed chicken broth	1	(10½ ounce) jar red pepper jelly

Combine carrots and chicken broth in a skillet over medium high heat. Bring to a boil and cook, stirring often, 6 to 8 minutes or until carrots are crisp-tender and broth is reduced to ¼ cup. Stir in butter and red pepper jelly. Cook, stirring constantly, 5 minutes or until mixture is thickened and glazes carrots.

Makes 8 servings

Jalapeño Corn Casserole

4	(11 ounce) cans white shoepeg corn	4	ounces cream cheese, softened
1	stick butter, melted	2	tablespoons chopped pickled jalapeño peppers

Preheat oven to 350°. In a large bowl, combine corn, melted butter, cream cheese, jalapeños and jalapeño juice to taste. Bake 30 minutes. Stir, then serve.

VEGETABLES AND SIDE DISHES

Creamy Corn Pudding

2 rolls frozen white creamed corn, thawed	1 cup grated Cheddar cheese
3 tablespoons sugar	2 tablespoons flour
½ cup milk	3 eggs, beaten

Preheat oven to 350°. In a medium bowl, combine all ingredients. Pour into a greased 2 quart baking dish. Bake 45 minutes or until set in the middle and golden.

Rolls of frozen white creamed corn can be found in the freezer section of the grocery store.

For Mexican Corn Pudding, add 1 small can chopped green chilies and substitute Mexican blend cheese for the Cheddar cheese.

Essie's Onion Pie

1 ready-made pie crust	2 tablespoons plain flour
4 sweet onions, thinly sliced	1 teaspoon salt
1 tablespoon olive oil	⅛ teaspoon pepper
3 tablespoons butter	Pinch of nutmeg
2 eggs	2 ounces Swiss cheese, grated
1 cup half-and-half	Chopped parsley

Preheat oven to 350°. Spray 9 inch pie pan with nonstick spray and partially bake.

Sauté onions in oil and butter over low heat until golden yellow. Beat together eggs, half-and-half, flour, salt, pepper and nutmeg. Add onions and half of the grated cheese. Pour into crust. Sprinkle remaining cheese on top and bake for 25 to 30 minutes or until golden brown.

Garnish with parsley, if desired.

"...Thou shalt eat the herbs of the field."

Genesis 3:18

Grilled Okra

Fresh okra pods, 3 to 4 inches long

1-2 tablespoons olive oil

1 garlic clove, minced

Salt and pepper to taste

Preheat grill to high. Toss okra, olive oil, garlic, salt and pepper in a bowl, coating each pod. Spread pods in a single layer on the hot grill. Close the lid and cook 3 to 4 minutes per side, turning when grill marks are visible and okra is soft.

If cooking in oven, preheat to 400°. Place the okra on a cookie sheet and roast 15 minutes, turning halfway through the cooking time to brown evenly.

"As long as the earth endures, seedtime and harvest, cold and heat, summer and winter, day and night will never cease."

Genesis 8:22

Spinach Parmigiana

1 tablespoon butter

¾ cup chopped sweet onion

10 ounces baby spinach, coarsely chopped

1 tablespoon water

2 large eggs, slightly beaten

1 cup milk

1 cup grated Parmigiano Reggiano cheese, divided

½ teaspoon salt

¼ teaspoon pepper

⅛ teaspoon ground nutmeg

Preheat oven to 350°. Melt butter in a large skillet over medium-high heat and sauté the onion until tender. Add the spinach and water and cook until just wilted. Drain in a large sieve, pressing with a wooden spoon until all the liquid is drained.

In a bowl, whisk together the eggs, milk, ¾ cup cheese, salt, pepper and nutmeg. Stir into the spinach mixture. Pour into a lightly greased 1½ quart baking dish. Sprinkle with the remaining ¼ cup cheese and bake uncovered about 30 minutes or until set in the center.

Serve warm or at room temperature.

Makes 4 to 6 servings

Spinach and Artichoke Casserole

2   (10 ounce) packages frozen
    spinach, chopped
1   stick butter, melted
1   (8 ounce) package cream
    cheese

1   teaspoon lemon juice
2   (14 ounce) cans artichokes,
    drained
    Ritz cracker crumbs
    Parmesan cheese, grated

Preheat oven to 350°. Cook spinach according to package directions. Drain well. Combine cooked spinach, butter, cream cheese and lemon juice. Place artichokes in the bottom of a greased 9x13x2 inch pan. Add spinach mixture and spread evenly. Top with cracker crumbs and Parmesan cheese. Dot with butter and bake 25 minutes.

Spinach Soufflé

1   (10 ounce) package frozen
    chopped spinach, thawed
2   tablespoons butter
1   medium onion, chopped
2   garlic cloves, minced
3   eggs
2   tablespoons all-purpose flour

½   teaspoon salt
    Dash of nutmeg
¼   teaspoon pepper
1   cup milk
1   cup freshly grated Parmesan
    cheese

Preheat oven to 350°. Drain spinach well, pressing between paper towels to remove all excess liquid. Melt butter in a large skillet over medium heat. Add onion and garlic. Sauté 5 minutes or until garlic is lightly browned and onions are tender. Remove from heat and stir in spinach. Cool. Whisk together eggs, flour, salt, nutmeg and pepper in a large bowl. Stir in milk, Parmesan cheese and spinach mixture.

Pour into a lightly greased 8 inch square baking dish. Bake 30 to 35 minutes or until set. Let stand 5 minutes before serving.

Makes 6 servings

"I will bless them and the places surrounding my hill. I will send down showers in season, there will be showers of blessing. The trees of the field will yield their fruit and the ground will yield its crops; the people will be secure in their land. They will know that I am the Lord when I break the bars of their yoke and rescue them from the hands of those who enslaved them."

Ezekiel 34:26-27

Squash Casserole

1	pound squash, sliced	¼	cup milk
1½	cups grated sharp Cheddar cheese, divided	1	egg
¼	stick butter, melted	2	onions, chopped finely
8-10 Ritz crackers, crushed			Salt and pepper to taste

Preheat oven to 350°. Boil squash and onion in salted water until tender. Drain water and mash. Add ½ cup of grated cheese, butter, egg, milk, crushed crackers, salt and pepper. Pour mixture into a lightly greased 8x8 inch baking pan. Top with remaining cheese. Bake 30 minutes or until casserole is set and lightly browned on top.

Makes 6 servings

"Now faith is being sure of what we hope for and certain of what we do not see."

Hebrews 11:1

Balsamic Tomatoes with Basil

1	small onion, thinly sliced	½	teaspoon pepper
4	cups ice water	2	garlic cloves, minced
¾	cup balsamic vinegar	½	cup chopped fresh basil
¾	cup olive oil	6	tomatoes, thinly sliced
2	tablespoons water		Parmesan cheese curls
2	teaspoons sugar		French bread (optional)
½	teaspoon salt		

Combine onion slices and 4 cups ice water in a large bowl. Soak onions 30 minutes. Drain and pat dry with paper towels.

Whisk together vinegar, olive oil, 2 tablespoons water, sugar, salt, pepper and garlic. Stir in basil. Layer a shallow dish with half of the tomato slices then half of onion slices. Drizzle with half of the dressing. Repeat with remaining tomato, onions and dressing. Cover and chill 30 minutes.

Sprinkle with Parmesan cheese curls, and serve with bread, if desired. Serve at room temperature. Recipe may be prepared up to three hours ahead.

Makes 12 servings

VEGETABLES AND SIDE DISHES

Tomato Pie

4-5 tomatoes, peeled and sliced

10 fresh basil leaves, rolled and chopped

½ cup chopped green onion

1 (9 inch) prebaked deep-dish pie shell

2 cups grated cheese, mozzarella and Cheddar

1 cup mayonnaise

Salt and pepper

Preheat oven to 350°. Place the sliced tomatoes in a colander. Sprinkle with salt and allow to drain 10 minutes. Pour out onto several layers of paper towels and pat lightly to remove as much liquid as possible. Layer the tomato slices, basil and onion in pie shell. Season with salt and pepper.

Combine the grated cheeses and mayonnaise and spread mixture on top of the tomatoes. Bake 30 minutes or until lightly browned. To serve, cut into slices and serve warm or at room temperature.

This can also be baked in individual tart shells.

This can be a side dish for any meal, bringing the flavors of a tomato sandwich to the dinner plate. It can also be served as a lunch dish, along with a fresh salad or Grilled Okra (page 168).

Tomato Aspic

24 ounces tomato juice

1 bay leaf

½ teaspoon salt

¼ teaspoon pepper

1 teaspoon Worcestershire sauce

1 teaspoon grated onion

1 stalk celery

2 tablespoons (2 envelopes) unflavored gelatin, dissolved in 3 tablespoons cool water

1 tablespoon vinegar

Juice of one lemon

½ cup sliced green olives

½ cup diced celery

Bring tomato juice, bay leaf, salt, pepper, Worcestershire sauce, onion, and celery to a boil. Remove from heat and discard stalk of celery and bay leaf. Immediately add both envelopes of gelatin (which have been dissolved in 3 tablespoons cool water), vinegar and lemon juice. Cool. Add olives and celery. Pour into mold and chill until set. Serve with a dollop of mayonnaise.

White pepper can be substituted for better appearance.

"*L*and that drinks in the rain often falling on it and that produces a crop useful to those for whom it is farmed receives the blessing of God."

Hebrews 6:7

Broiled Tomatoes

Tomatoes	Garlic, minced
Salt	Oregano
Chili powder	Butter
Parmesan cheese	Ritz or saltine crackers

Preheat oven to 350°. Slice desired amount of tomatoes in half. Sprinkle tomatoes with salt, chili powder, Parmesan cheese, garlic and oregano to taste. Crush crackers and sprinkle on top. Place a pat of butter on each tomato half. Bake 10 minutes.

Tomato and Onion Strata

8	plum tomatoes, quartered lengthwise	2	cups shredded sharp Cheddar cheese, divided
2	tablespoons olive oil	2	cups shredded Colby Jack cheese
1½	teaspoons salt		
1	teaspoon pepper	⅓	cup chopped onion
⅓	tablespoon dried thyme		Sourdough bread, cut in 1 inch cubes (about 8 cups)
8	eggs		
3	cups whole milk		

Preheat oven to 350°. In a bowl, toss tomatoes with thyme, olive oil, ½ teaspoon each of salt and ½ teaspoon pepper. Spread on baking sheet and bake 1 to 1¼ hours, stirring twice during baking. Tomatoes will be dry and lightly browned. Cool completely.

Mix together milk, eggs, 1 teaspoon salt, ½ teaspoon pepper, 1¾ cups Cheddar cheese and 2 cups Colby Jack cheese. Set aside. Layer bread cubes in baking dish. Top with tomatoes and onions. Pour egg and cheese mixture over bread. Cover and refrigerate overnight.

Take out of the refrigerator and preheat oven to 350°. Sprinkle the rest of the cheese on top. Bake uncovered 45 minutes or until golden brown and almost set. Turn off oven for an additional 10 minutes.

Makes 16 servings

Red Peppers Stuffed with Grits

4	red bell peppers, tops cut out and seeds removed
2	cups milk
2	cups water
1	teaspoon salt
1	cup quick grits
2	eggs, slightly beaten
⅛	teaspoon pepper

1½ cups Cheddar cheese, shredded
1 large garlic clove, pressed
1 teaspoon Worcestershire sauce
1 tablespoon chopped green chilies (in can)
Tabasco sauce, to taste
1 stick butter

Preheat oven to 350°. Place peppers in a lightly greased 9x13x2 inch baking dish. Boil milk, water and salt in a deep pot. Slowly add grits while stirring until mixture is as thick as mashed potatoes. Remove from heat and add eggs, pepper, cheese, garlic, Worcestershire sauce, chilies and Tabasco. Stuff peppers with the grits mixture; place a pat of butter on top of each pepper. Bake 1 hour. This may be made a day ahead and kept in the refrigerator until ready for cooking.

Hash Brown Casserole

1 (2 pound) package frozen country hash browns, thawed
1 stick butter, melted
1 cup onion, chopped
1 (10 ounce) can cream of chicken soup
1 (8 ounce) container of sour cream

½ teaspoon pepper
1 teaspoon salt
2 cups shredded sharp Cheddar cheese, divided
2 cups crushed cornflakes
2 tablespoons melted butter

Preheat oven to 350°. Sauté onions in melted butter. Mix butter, onions, hash browns, soup, sour cream, salt and pepper in a large mixing bowl. Fold in 1¼ cups of the shredded cheese. Put in a greased 9x13x2 inch pan. Top with remaining Cheddar cheese. Place cornflakes and melted butter in a zip-top plastic bag and crush cornflakes with hands. During the last 20 minutes of baking, spread the cornflakes on top of the casserole. Bake 1 hour.

"Then I realized that it is good and proper for a man to eat and drink, and to find satisfaction in his toilsome labor under the sun during the few days of life God has given him—for this is his lot."

Ecclesiastes 5:18

Bleu Cheese Zucchini Boat

4	small zucchini	¼	teaspoon garlic salt
	Salt to taste	¼	cup Parmesan cheese
⅔	cup mayonnaise		Dash of cayenne pepper
2	tablespoons crumbled bleu cheese		Oregano to taste

Preheat oven to 350°. Parboil whole zucchini in salted water just until tender and drain. Cut zucchini in half lengthwise and sprinkle with salt. Cool slightly. Combine mayonnaise with bleu cheese, garlic salt, Parmesan cheese and cayenne pepper. Spread mayonnaise mixture on zucchini halves. Sprinkle with oregano. Bake 20 minutes.

Makes 8 servings

"But the one who received the seed that fell on good soil is the man who hears the word and understands it. He produces a crop, yielding a hundred, sixty or thirty times what was sown."

Matthew 13:23

Pepper Jack Potato Casserole

1	(30 ounce) package frozen shredded hash browns, thawed	1½	cups milk
		1	(10¾ ounce) can cream of chicken soup
1	(8 ounce) package shredded Monterey Jack cheese with peppers	2	tablespoons butter, melted
		1½	teaspoons salt
1	teaspoon garlic, minced	½	teaspoon pepper

Preheat oven to 350°. Combine hash browns, cheese and garlic in a bowl. Stir together milk, soup, butter, salt and pepper. Pour over hash brown mixture and stir. Pour into a lightly greased 9x13x2 inch baking dish. Bake 45 to 50 minutes until bubbly.

Makes 8 servings

New Potato Salad in Bacon and Bleu Cheese

2	pounds red-skinned new potatoes
	Kosher salt
¼	pound thick cut bacon (6 strips)
¾	cup mayonnaise
¾	cup sour cream
½	cup chopped onion
¼	pound bleu cheese
	Salt and freshly ground black pepper to taste
	Garnish with tomatoes and parsley, optional

Scrub potatoes and place them in a pot filled with water to cover. Salt water with approximately 1 tablespoon of salt per gallon. Bring to a boil. Simmer for 20 minutes. Check for tenderness at 5-minute intervals until ready. Should be tender but not mushy.

Drain, and run cold water over potatoes, but do not soak in cold water. Set aside. Cook bacon in skillet. Drain thoroughly on paper towels. Chop in ¼ inch pieces.

Mix mayonnaise, sour cream, onion and bleu cheese in a bowl large enough to hold the whole recipe. Mix the dressing together, adding pepper. Wait to add salt until the final stir. When the potatoes are cool, cut potatoes into quarters and place into the dressing bowl. Stir gently. Add salt and stir.

Makes 8 servings

Parmesan Cheese Potatoes

6-8 small red potatoes

3-4 tablespoons butter

2-3 teaspoons dried parsley

3-4 tablespoons freshly grated Parmesan cheese

Salt and pepper to taste

Wash and quarter potatoes, leaving peel on. Boil until tender. Drain and mix with butter, parsley, Parmesan cheese, salt and pepper.

Makes 4 servings

"For Jehovah thy God bringeth thee into a good land, a land of brooks of water, of fountains and springs, flowing forth in valleys and hills; a land of wheat and barley, and vines and fig trees and pomegranates; a land of olive trees and honey; a land wherein thou shalt eat bread without scarceness, thou shalt not lack anything in it. And thou shalt eat and be full, and thou shalt bless Jehovah thy God for the good land which he hath given thee."

Deuteronomy 8:7-10

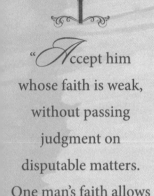

Sweet Potato Casserole

4-5	large sweet potatoes	⅓	cup milk
½	cup butter, softened	1	teaspoon vanilla extract
1	cup sugar		Pinch of cinnamon
2	eggs		

Preheat oven to 350°. Peel and boil potatoes until soft. Place warm potatoes and butter in a large mixing bowl and beat with an electric mixer at low speed. Slowly add sugar, eggs, milk, vanilla and cinnamon. Mix well until smooth. Pour into greased 9x13x2 inch baking dish.

TOPPING

1	cup light brown sugar	5	tablespoons butter, cold
½	cup self-rising flour	½	cup chopped nuts

Make topping by stirring together brown sugar and flour. Cut 5 tablespoons of cold butter in, using a fork, until crumbly. Add chopped nuts and sprinkle topping over sweet potato mixture. Bake 45 minutes.

Makes 12 servings

Sweet Potato Delight

3	cups cooked sweet potatoes	½	cup dark brown sugar
½	cup sugar	¼	cup flour
½	teaspoon salt	⅓	stick butter
2	eggs, beaten	½	cup pecans, chopped
½	stick butter, softened	1	teaspoon cinnamon
½	cup milk	10	large marshmallows
½	teaspoon vanilla		

Preheat oven to 350°. Using a 4 quart mixing bowl, mix together potatoes, sugar, salt, eggs, butter, milk and vanilla. Pour into a greased 2 quart ovenproof casserole dish. Combine the brown sugar and flour. Add butter and mix together with fingers or a fork. Add nuts and cinnamon. Place topping on sweet potatoes. Bake for 35 minutes. Remove from oven. Top with marshmallows and cook an additional 8 to 10 minutes until marshmallows brown.

Makes 8 to 10 servings

Twice Baked Potato Casserole

2 cups potatoes, peeled and cut	1 cup shredded Cheddar cheese, divided
½ stick butter, melted	½ cup milk
1 package Ranch Buttermilk Dressing mix	Salt and pepper to taste
8 strips of fried bacon, crumbled	

Preheat oven to 350°. Boil potatoes until tender. Drain potatoes and place in large bowl with butter, dressing mix, crumbled bacon, ½ cup shredded cheese, milk, salt and pepper. Mix well with electric mixer. Place in a greased 9x13x2 inch pan and sprinkle with remaining ½ cup of cheese. Bake 30 minutes.

Makes 4 servings

Loaded Baked Potato Pizza

1 (12 inch) pizza crust	2 medium red skin potatoes, thinly sliced and cooked
1 tablespoon butter	6 slices lean bacon, cooked and crumbled
1 (10 ounce) package frozen chopped spinach, thawed, rinsed and well drained	1¼ cups grated sharp Cheddar cheese
½ cup crumbled Gorgonzola cheese	1 tablespoon chopped fresh chives
¼ cup sour cream	

Melt butter in nonstick skillet. Add spinach and Gorgonzola. Stir until melted. Remove from heat and blend in sour cream. May add salt and pepper to taste. Spread mixture evenly over crust. Top with sliced potatoes and sprinkle with Cheddar cheese, chives and bacon. Bake at 425° for 12 to 15 minutes or until cheese is melted.

"Do not forget to entertain strangers, for by doing, some people have entertained angels unaware."

Hebrews 13:2

Crockpot Macaroni and Cheese

8	ounces elbow macaroni	1	cup shredded medium cheese
1	regular can evaporated milk	¼	cup melted margarine
1½	cups plain sweet milk	2	eggs
1	teaspoon salt		Black pepper to taste
2	cups shredded sharp cheese		

Cook and drain macaroni. Mix all ingredients together and put in greased crockpot. Cut several thin slices of cheese and put on top. Sprinkle with paprika. Cook 3 to 4 hours on low.

Perfect Macaroni and Cheese

1	pound dry penne pasta	12	ounces Gruyère cheese, grated
4	cups milk		
1	stick butter	1	medium onion, finely chopped
1	tablespoon dry mustard		
½	cup all-purpose flour		

Preheat oven to 375°. In a pot of boiling, salted water, cook the penne pasta according to directions. In a large pot, melt the butter. Add the flour and cook, stirring with a whisk for 2 minutes. Whisk in the milk, onion, dry mustard and continue cooking over medium-high heat until the mixture is thick and smooth.

Remove from heat and add cheese, stirring with a spoon until the cheese melts. Add the drained pasta to the cheese mixture and toss gently. Pour into a greased 3 to 4 quart baking dish. Add topping.

TOPPING

1½	cups panko bread crumbs	4	tablespoons butter, melted

Combine the bread crumbs and melted butter and sprinkle on top. Bake 30 minutes.

Makes 12 servings

Cranberry Chutney

2	oranges	¼	teaspoon ground cloves
2	cups fresh cranberries	2	teaspoons ginger
1	large apple	1	tablespoon curry powder
½	cup orange marmalade	½	cup white raisins
½	cup cider vinegar		Dash of allspice
1½	cups sugar		Dash of salt
¾	teaspoon cinnamon	1	cup water

Peel oranges, removing membrane and seeds. Section oranges, and cut sections in half. Wash cranberries and drain well. Peel, core, and dice apple. Combine all ingredients in saucepan. Bring to a boil over medium heat. Reduce heat to low, cover pan, and simmer for 30 minutes, stirring occasionally. Seal in sterilized jars.

Makes 6 to 8 cups

Bread and Butter Pickles

4	quarts sliced cucumbers	3	cups cider vinegar
8	medium white onions, sliced	2	tablespoons mustard seed
3	cloves garlic	1½	teaspoons turmeric
⅓	cup pickling salt	1½	teaspoons celery seed
5	cups sugar		

In a large bowl, combine first 4 ingredients. Stir in a large amount of cracked ice. Let stand 3 hours; drain well. Remove garlic. In a large kettle, combine remaining ingredients; add drained mixture. Bring to a 5-minute boil. Pack pickles and liquid into hot, clean jars, leaving ½ inch space at the top of the jar. Wipe rims; adjust lids. Process 5 minutes for pints or half-pints. (Start timing when water boils.)

Makes 6 pints.

"But you are a forgiving God, gracious and compassionate, slow to anger and abounding in love."

Nehemiah 9:17

BLUEBERRY JAM

1½ quarts stemmed blueberries

¼ cup lemon juice

1 cinnamon stick

7 cups sugar

1 (6 ounce) liquid pectin

Combine blueberries, lemon juice, cinnamon stick and sugar. Bring to a boil stirring often until sugar dissolves. Boil 5 minutes longer. Remove from heat. Discard cinnamon stick. Add pectin. Pour jam into sterilized hot jars being sure to wipe the lids clean before you lightly screw on the tops. Let sit for 24 hours. Check to make sure the lids sealed by listening for the "pop."

Cranberry Relish

1	(12 ounce) bag fresh cranberries	1	(15 ounce) can crushed pineapple
	Rind of one grated orange	½	cup sugar
1	navel orange		

Grate the orange rind, then peel the orange and section it. Place the cranberries, orange rind, orange, crushed pineapple and sugar in a food processor and pulse until minced. If not sweet enough for your taste, add ¼ cup more sugar. Chill at least 2 hours.

This is wonderful by itself as a side dish, added as a topping to ice cream, with turkey or chicken.

Chow Chow

5	green bell peppers	2	cups white vinegar (5% acidity)
5	red bell peppers	1	cup water
2	large green tomatoes	1	tablespoon mustard seeds
2	large onions	1½	teaspoons celery seeds
½	small cabbage	¾	teaspoon turmeric
¼	cup pickling salt		
3	cups sugar		

Chop red and green bell peppers, green tomatoes, onions and cabbage. Stir together chopped vegetables and salt in a large Dutch oven. Cover and chill 8 hours. Rinse and drain; return mixture to Dutch oven. Stir in sugar and remaining ingredients. Bring to a boil; reduce heat, and simmer 3 minutes. Pack hot mixture into hot jars, filling to ½ inch from top. Remove air bubbles; wipe jar rims and cover at once with metal lids. Process in boiling water bath 15 minutes.

For more heat, add chopped jalapeño to the vegetables.

Makes 5½ pints

DESSERTS

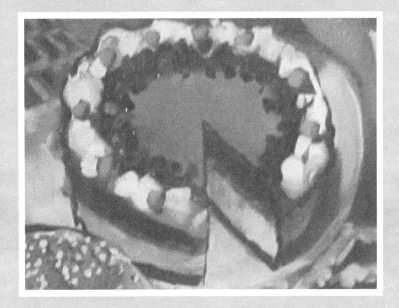

"My son, eat honey because it is good, and the honeycomb which is sweet
to your taste; so shall the knowledge of wisdom be to your soul."

Proverbs 24:13-14

Apple Cake with Hot Buttered Rum Sauce

1	stick butter, softened	½	teaspoon salt
2	cups sugar	½	teaspoon nutmeg
2	eggs	½	teaspoon cinnamon
2	cups all-purpose flour	½	cup chopped walnuts
1	teaspoon baking powder	4	medium to large apples, peeled, cored and chopped
1	teaspoon baking soda		

Preheat oven to 350°. Generously grease a tube pan. In a large bowl, combine butter and sugar until light and fluffy. Add eggs and combine.

In another bowl, whisk together flour, baking powder, baking soda, salt, nutmeg and cinnamon. Gradually add to egg mixture, combining thoroughly. Stir in apples and nuts. Mixture will be very thick. Scrape batter into the tube pan and bake 45 to 50 minutes, or until toothpick inserted in the center comes out clean.

Cool 15 minutes and invert cake onto a serving plate. Serve warm or room temperature. Spoon Hot Buttered Rum Sauce over individual slices when serving.

HOT BUTTERED RUM SAUCE

1	cup sugar	½	cup light cream or half-and-half
1	stick butter	1	teaspoon rum extract

Combine sugar, butter, cream and extract in small saucepan over medium heat until smooth and hot.

The Hot Buttered Rum Sauce is also delicious served over vanilla ice cream.

"*Strengthen me with raisins, refresh me with apples, for I am faint with love.*"

Song of Songs 2:5

Banana Torte

FIRST LAYER

| 1 | cup flour | 1 | cup finely chopped pecans |
| 1 | stick butter, melted | | |

SECOND LAYER

| 1 | (8 ounce) package cream cheese, softened | ½ | large (13 ounce) container nondairy whipped topping |
| 1 | cup powdered sugar | | |

THIRD LAYER

3-4 sliced bananas

FOURTH LAYER

| | Large box instant vanilla pudding | 2½ cups milk |

FIFTH LAYER

Remaining ½ container nondairy whipped topping

For first layer, mix flour, butter and pecans and press into a greased 9x13 inch ovenproof glass baking dish. Cool before adding next layer.

For second layer, cream together cream cheese and powdered sugar and add ½ container nondairy whipped topping. Mix well; spread over crust.

For third layer, layer sliced bananas.

For fourth layer, mix instant vanilla pudding with milk until thick. Spread evenly over bananas.

For fifth layer, cover with remaining nondairy whipped topping.

"Those who possess the spirit of God through faith are granted "spiritual fruit," the first being love, the second joy."

Galatians 5:22

Key Lime Cake

1	box lemon cake mix	¾	cup orange juice
1	(6 ounce) lime flavored gelatin	5	eggs
		1¾	cups oil

Preheat oven to 350°. Combine cake mix and gelatin; add orange juice. Add eggs one at a time. Add oil, and mix thoroughly. Bake in three prepared 9 inch cake pans 20 to 30 minutes or until toothpick inserted in middle comes out clean. Ice cake when cooled.

ICING

1	stick butter, softened	1	(1 pound) box powered sugar
1	(8 ounce) package cream cheese, softened		

Prepare icing by mixing butter, cream cheese and powered sugar until smooth.

Chocolate Ice Cream Cake

1	cup butter	6	(2.07 ounce) chocolate-coated caramel-peanut-nougat candy bars, chopped and divided
8	(1 ounce) squares semisweet chocolate		
1	cup sugar	¾	cup chocolate sauce
5	large eggs		Garnish with chocolate sauce or caramel sauce
½	cup all-purpose flour		
½	gallon vanilla ice cream, softened		

Preheat oven to 350°. In a large microwave-safe bowl, combine butter and chocolate. Microwave on high in 30-second intervals, stirring between each until melted and smooth. Whisk in sugar. Add eggs, one at a time, whisking well after each addition. Whisk in flour until smooth.

Pour batter into an ungreased 10 inch springform pan. Place pan on a rimmed baking sheet. Bake 25 minutes. Let cool completely. In a large bowl, combine ice cream and ½ of chopped candy bars. Spread ¾ cup chocolate sauce over cake layer. Spread ice cream mixture over chocolate sauce. Cover and freeze 4 hours or until firm. Drizzle cake with chocolate sauce and caramel sauce, if desired. Sprinkle with remaining chopped candy bars.

EARTHQUAKE CAKE

1 box German chocolate cake mix

1½ cups chopped pecans

1½ cups shredded coconut

½ cup margarine

1 (8 ounce) package cream cheese

4 cups powdered sugar

Preheat oven to 325°. Grease and flour 9x13 inch pan. Prepare cake according to directions. Combine pecans and coconut, sprinkle in bottom of pan. Pour prepared cake mixture over pecan/coconut mixture. Melt margarine and cream cheese in saucepan. Add powdered sugar. Mix well; pour mixture over cake batter. Bake 45 minutes or until a toothpick inserted in the center comes out clean. Remove cake from pan, cool and serve.

Shortcut Carrot Cake

1 (26½ ounce) package cinnamon streusel coffee cake mix
3 large eggs
1¼ cups water
⅓ cup vegetable oil

3 large carrots, finely grated
½ cup chopped pecans, toasted
1 cup sweetened flaked coconut
2 tablespoons orange juice

Preheat oven to 350°. Grease 3 (8 inch) round cake pans. Line with wax paper; grease and flour pans. Combine cake mix and streusel packet in mixing bowl, reserving glaze packet, if there is one. (If no glaze packet is included with mix, just omit this step.) Cake is also very good without it.

Add eggs, water and oil; beat at medium speed with electric mixer for 2 minutes. Stir in carrots, pecans and coconut. Pour batter evenly into prepared pans. Bake 18 to 20 minutes. Cool in pans on wire racks 10 minutes. Remove from pans; place on racks. Stir together reserved glaze and juice; brush evenly over warm cake layers. Cool completely on wire racks.

CREAM CHEESE FROSTING

1 (8 ounce) package cream cheese, softened
1 (3 ounce) package cream cheese, softened

¾ cup butter, softened
7 cups powdered sugar
1 tablespoon vanilla extract
3-4 tablespoons milk

Beat cream cheese and butter at medium speed with an electric mixer until fluffy; gradually add powdered sugar, beating well. Stir in vanilla. Add milk, 1 tablespoon at the time, until frosting reaches desired consistency.

Spread cream cheese frosting between layers and on top and sides of cake. Chill frosted cake at least 2 hours.

If you have a sweet tooth, but are short on time, this cake only takes about 45 minutes to prepare.

"So I have come down to deliver them out of the hand of the Egyptians,

and to bring them up out of that land into a good and spacious land,

a land flowing with milk and honey..."

Exodus 3:8

"Pretty in Pink" Strawberry Cake

1   (18¼ ounce) box white cake mix
1   (3 ounce) box strawberry-flavored gelatin
1   (10 ounce) package frozen strawberries in syrup, thawed and puréed
4   large eggs
½   cup vegetable oil
¼   cup water
    Strawberry Cream Cheese Frosting
    Garnish with sliced fresh strawberries

Preheat oven to 350°. Lightly grease 2 (9 inch) round cake pans. In a large bowl, combine cake mix and gelatin. Add puréed strawberries, eggs, oil and ¼ cup water. Beat at medium speed with a mixer until smooth. Pour into prepared pans.

Bake for 20 minutes or until a wooden toothpick inserted in center comes out clean. Let cool in pans for 10 minutes. Remove from pans and cool completely on wire racks. Spread Strawberry Cream Cheese Frosting between layers and on top and sides of cake. Garnish with sliced fresh strawberries, if desired. Store cake covered in the refrigerator up to three days.

STRAWBERRY CREAM CHEESE FROSTING

1   (8 ounce) package cream cheese, softened
¼   cup butter, softened
1   (10 ounce) package frozen strawberries in syrup, thawed, puréed and divided
½   teaspoon strawberry extract
7   cups powdered sugar

In a large bowl, beat cream cheese and butter at medium speed with a mixer until creamy. Beat in ¼ cup strawberry purée. Reserve remaining purée for another use. Beat in extract. Gradually add powdered sugar, beating until smooth.

For pinker frosting, add 2 to 3 drops of red food coloring to frosting.

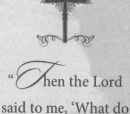

"Then the Lord said to me, 'What do you see Jeremiah?' And I said, 'Figs, the good figs, very good.'"

Jeremiah 24:3

 Red Velvet Cake

2	cups sugar	2	tablespoons cocoa
1½	cups oil	1	teaspoon vinegar
2	eggs	1	(1 ounce) bottle red food coloring
2½	cups cake flour	1	cup buttermilk
1	teaspoon baking soda	1	teaspoon vanilla extract
¼	teaspoon salt		

Preheat oven to 350°. Cream sugar and oil with electric mixer. Add eggs one at a time; beat well after each.

Sift flour, baking soda, and salt together and set aside. Add cocoa to sugar mixture. Mix well, add vinegar. Slowly add food coloring; beat well. Add flour mixture and buttermilk alternately, beating well after each addition. Add vanilla extract and mix well.

Pour into 3 greased and floured (9 inch) pans. Bake 20 to 25 minutes or until cake begins to pull away from the sides of the pan. Do not overcook or the edges will be crusty. Cool completely and frost layers.

CREAM CHEESE FROSTING

½	cup butter or margarine, softened	1	(16 ounce) box powdered sugar
1	(8 ounce) package cream cheese, softened	1	teaspoon vanilla extract
		1	cup chopped pecans

Cream butter and cream cheese. Slowly add sugar. When creamy, add vanilla extract. Sprinkle pecans on top and sides.

"A friend loves at all times."

Proverbs 17:17

Hummingbird Cake

3 cups all-purpose flour
2 cups sugar
1 teaspoon baking soda
1 teaspoon salt
1½ cups canola oil

3 eggs
1 (8 ounce) can crushed pineapple, drained
2 cups bananas, mashed
1 cup chopped nuts, pecans or black walnuts

Preheat oven to 350°. Grease and flour 2 (9 inch) cake pans. Sift together the flour, sugar, baking soda and salt. Set aside.

In a large bowl, combine oil, eggs, pineapple, bananas and nuts. Add flour mixture and mix by hand. Pour batter into prepared pans and bake 1 hour until a toothpick inserted in the center comes out clean. Remove from oven and cool on racks.

FROSTING

1 (8 ounce) package cream cheese, softened
½ cup butter, softened

1 pound box powdered sugar, sifted
1 teaspoon vanilla extract
1 teaspoon orange extract

Prepare the frosting by mixing cream cheese, butter, sugar and extracts until smooth.

This recipe also makes beautiful cupcakes. One recipe makes 24 cupcakes. Double the frosting to cover all of the cupcakes.

"*Let love and faithfulness never leave you; bind them around your neck, write them on the tablet of your heart. Then you will win favor and a good name in the sight of God and man.*"

Proverbs 3:3-4

Chocolate Roulade

1½ cups semisweet chocolate morsels
9   eggs, separated
1¾ cups sugar, divided
1   teaspoon vanilla
2   teaspoons cocoa
1½ cups whipping cream
2   tablespoons powdered sugar
    Strawberries for garnish

Preheat oven to 350°. Grease bottom and sides of 15x10x1 inch jellyroll pan with vegetable oil; line with wax paper; grease wax paper with oil. Set aside.

Melt chocolate morsels in top of double boiler. Cool. Beat egg whites until foamy. Gradually add 1 cup sugar and beat until stiff peaks form. Set aside.

Beat egg yolks until foamy. Gradually add remaining sugar, beating until thick and lemon colored. Add vanilla and gradually beat in cooled chocolate. Fold chocolate mixture and egg white mixture together until no streaks remain.

Pour chocolate into prepared pan and spread evenly. Bake 20 to 22 minutes. Do not over bake. Let cool 20 minutes. Sift cocoa over top.

Place 2 lengths of wax paper (longer than jellyroll pan) on counter. Overlap edge of paper nearest you over second sheet. Loosen sides and invert roulade onto wax paper, long side nearest you. Peel off wax paper.

Beat cream until soft peaks form. Add powdered sugar, and spoon onto chocolate, spreading evenly. Roll beginning on long side, using wax paper to support roulade. Secure roulade with wax paper and cool in refrigerator until serving time.

This dessert should be completed and refrigerated at least 3 hours prior to serving. Garnish with strawberries. Sift powdered sugar over roulade, if desired.

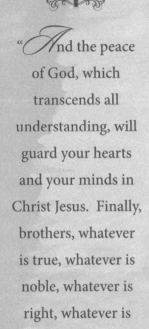

"*And the peace of God, which transcends all understanding, will guard your hearts and your minds in Christ Jesus. Finally, brothers, whatever is true, whatever is noble, whatever is right, whatever is pure, whatever is lovely, whatever is admirable- if anything is excellent or praiseworthy-think about such things.*"

Philippians 4:7-8

Chocolate Sheet Cake

2 cups all-purpose flour
2 cups sugar
½ teaspoon salt
1 cup water
3 tablespoons cocoa
2 sticks butter

½ cup vegetable oil
½ cup buttermilk
2 eggs
1 teaspoon baking soda
1 teaspoon vanilla extract

Preheat oven to 350°. Mix flour, sugar and salt in large bowl; set aside. Bring water, cocoa, butter and oil to a boil. Pour hot mixture over flour mixture. Add buttermilk, eggs, baking soda and vanilla. Bake in greased and floured 11x16 inch jellyroll pan 30 minutes.

GLAZE

1 stick butter
3 tablespoons cocoa
6 tablespoons buttermilk
½ cup chopped nuts (optional)

1 tablespoon vanilla extract
1 (1 pound) box powdered sugar

Bring butter, cocoa and buttermilk to boil over low heat. Add powdered sugar, nuts and vanilla. Remove from heat and mix very well until lumps are removed and glaze is smooth. Pour over hot cake.

> "In his heart a man plans his course, but the Lord determines his steps."
>
> *Proverbs 16:9*

Death by Chocolate

1 package brownie mix
1 package chocolate-covered toffee candy bar bits
1 (6 ounce) box instant pudding (chocolate or vanilla)

1 (12 ounce) container frozen nondairy whipped topping
½ cup coffee-flavored liqueur or substitute (see below)

Mix and bake brownies according to box directions. Punch holes in warm brownies with a fork and pour coffee-flavored liqueur over brownies; set aside.

Mix pudding according to directions on box. Break up half of the brownies and place at the bottom of a glass trifle dish. Cover with half of the pudding, half of the toffee bits and then half of the whipped topping. Repeat layers with the remaining ingredients. Save some of the toffee bits to sprinkle on top.

Liqueur substitute: mix 1 tablespoon sugar with 4 tablespoons coffee.

Frosted Chocolate Sour Cream Pound Cake

3	sticks butter, softened	1	teaspoon baking soda
3	cups sugar	¼	teaspoon salt
5	eggs (room temperature)	1	(8 ounce) carton sour cream
3	cups all-purpose flour	1	cup boiling water
½	cup cocoa	2	teaspoons vanilla

Preheat oven to 325°. Cream together softened butter and sugar. Mix in eggs one at a time. Set aside. Mix flour, cocoa, baking soda, and salt together. Add creamed mixture alternately with sour cream, beginning and ending with flour mixture. Carefully stir in boiling water, a little at a time. Stir in vanilla and mix well.

Pour into buttered and floured 10 inch tube pan or 2 prepared 8 inch pound cake pans. Bake large pan for 1 hour and 20 minutes or 2 small pound cake pans (in same oven on same rack) for 50 minutes, until toothpick inserted in center comes out clean.

Cool in pan for 15 minutes before removing to cooling rack. Cool completely before frosting.

CHOCOLATE FUDGE FROSTING

1 stick butter, softened

4 tablespoons cocoa

6 tablespoons milk

3¾ cups powdered sugar or 1 box

1 teaspoon vanilla

1 cup chopped nuts (optional)

Prepare frosting by melting butter in double boiler; stir in cocoa. Remove from heat and quickly mix in milk. Beat in powdered sugar and vanilla for 1 to 2 minutes.

Frost cooled cake(s) and sprinkle with nuts if desired. Let frosting set before serving.

This is a chocolate lovers dream come true!

Kahlúa Pound Cake

1	box butter cake mix	1	cup oil
1	small box instant chocolate pudding	½	cup sugar
		½	cup Kahlúa
4	eggs	¾	cup water

Preheat oven to 350°. Mix all ingredients together in large bowl; beat for 2 minutes. (Batter will be thin.) Bake 50 minutes. Let cool and then turn out of pan.

GLAZE

¼	cup Kahlúa	½	cup powered sugar

Prepare glaze by mixing liqueur and powered sugar in a small saucepan over low heat. Poke holes in cake and pour glaze over cake.

Coca Cola Cake

1   cup cola-flavored drink
½   cup buttermilk
1   cup butter or margarine,
    softened
1¾ cups sugar
2   large eggs, lightly beaten
2   teaspoons vanilla extract
2   cups all-purpose flour

¼   cup unsweetened cocoa
1   teaspoon baking soda
1½ cups miniature
    marshmallows
    Cola Frosting
    Garnish with ¾ cup chopped
    pecans, toasted

Preheat oven to 350°. Combine cola and buttermilk; set aside.

Beat butter at low speed with an electric mixer until creamy. Gradually add sugar, beat until blended.

Add eggs and vanilla; beat at low speed until blended.

Combine flour, cocoa, and baking soda. Add to butter mixture alternately with cola mixture, beginning and ending with flour mixture. Beat at low speed just until blended.

Stir in marshmallows. Pour batter into a greased and floured 13x9 inch pan. Bake 30 to 35 minutes. Remove from oven; cool 10 minutes. Spread Cola Frosting over warm cake.

Makes 12 servings

COLA FROSTING

½ cup butter or
margarine

⅓ cup cola-flavored
drink

3 tablespoons
unsweetened cocoa

1 (16 ounce) package
powdered sugar

1 tablespoon vanilla
extract

Bring butter, cola
flavored drink and
unsweetened cocoa to a
boil in a large saucepan
over medium heat,
stirring until butter
melts. Remove from
heat; whisk in sugar
and vanilla.

Makes 2¼ cups

Virginia Clark's Pound Cake

3   cups sugar
2   sticks butter (do not soften)
½   cup solid vegetable
    shortening
3   cups flour, sifted (soft as silk)
1   level teaspoon baking powder

¼   teaspoon salt
1   cup milk
6   eggs
1   teaspoon vanilla flavoring
1   teaspoon almond flavoring

Cream sugar, butter and shortening. In a separate bowl, mix flour, baking powder and salt. Alternately add milk, eggs, flour and then add flavoring. Pour into greased and floured Bundt pan. Place in cold oven and bake at 325° for 1 hour.

Chess Cake

| 1 | box yellow cake mix | 1 | egg |
| 1 | stick butter, softened | | |

Preheat oven to 350°. Lightly grease 9x13 inch baking pan. Add butter to cake mix. Add egg and mix well. Press into greased pan.

TOPPING
| 1 | (8 ounce) package cream cheese, softened | 3¾ | cups powdered sugar |
| 3 | eggs | ½ | cup chopped pecans (optional) |

Prepare topping by beating cream cheese until smooth. Add the eggs, one at a time, beating well after each addition. Add powdered sugar, mix. Add pecans, mix. Pour over cake mixture. Bake 40 to 50 minutes.

Cream Cheese Pound Cake

3	sticks salted butter, softened	6	large eggs
1	(8 ounce) package cream cheese, softened	3	cups all-purpose or cake flour
3	cups sugar	⅛	teaspoon salt
		1	tablespoon vanilla extract

For best results. All ingredients need to be at room temperature.

Preheat oven to 300°. In a large mixing bowl, cream butter and cream cheese until fluffy. Slowly add sugar, beating well. Mixture should still be fluffy. Beat in one egg at a time, beating just until yellow disappears.

Combine flour and salt. Gradually add to butter mixture, beating at low speed just until blended after each addition. Stir in vanilla. Pour into a well-greased and floured 10 inch Bundt pan or tube pan. Bake 1 hour and 35 minutes or until toothpick inserted near center comes out clean. Cool in pan on wire rack 15 minutes. Remove from pan and cool completely on wire rack.

For a Chocolate Cream Cheese Pound Cake, use 2½ cups flour and ½ cup cocoa in place of 3 cups flour.

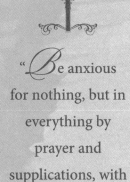

"*Be* anxious for nothing, but in everything by prayer and supplications, with thanksgiving, let your requests be made known to God. And the peace of God, which surpasses all understanding, will guard your hearts and minds through Jesus Christ."

Philippians 4:6-7

Simply Delicious Birthday Cake with Buttery Icing

1 cup butter, softened	½ teaspoon baking powder
½ cup solid vegetable shortening	¼ teaspoon salt
	1 cup whole milk
3 cups sugar	1 teaspoon vanilla
5 eggs	1 teaspoon almond extract
3 cups flour, unsifted	

Beat butter, shortening, and sugar until fluffy. Add eggs one at a time. Set aside.

Sift together dry ingredients; add to batter alternating with milk. Begin and end with flour. Blend in vanilla and almond extract on low speed. Pour in greased and floured cake pans. May use 3 (8 inch) rounds, 2 (9 inch) rounds or 9x13 inch pan. Bake 1 hour at 325°.

BUTTERY ICING

½ cup butter, at room temperature	4 cups powdered sugar, sifted
	1 teaspoon vanilla
½ cup solid vegetable shortening	2 teaspoons whole milk

Beat butter and shortening. Slowly add powdered sugar. Add vanilla and milk. If icing is too thick to spread, add another teaspoon of milk. If icing is too thin, add more sugar.

"Here I am! I stand at the door and knock.

If anyone hears my voice and opens the door,

I will come in and eat with him, and he with me."

Revelation 3:20

A birthday is an occasion for prayer, a holy time. A journey began. God blessed someone with life. Remember the gift of life, we thank God and celebrate.

Rave Reviews Coconut Cake

1	package yellow cake mix	1⅓	cups water
1	(6 ounce) box vanilla pudding	¼	cup vegetable oil
		2	cups sweetened coconut
4	eggs	1	cup chopped pecans

Preheat oven to 350°. Blend cake mix, pudding mix, eggs, water and oil in large mixing bowl. Beat at medium speed with mixer for 4 minutes. Stir in coconut and pecans. Pour into three greased and floured (9 inch) layer pans. Bake 35 minutes. Cool in pans 15 minutes. Remove from pans and cool.

Wu Wu's Tiramisu Cake

1	box white (Moist Deluxe) cake mix	4	egg whites
3	cups brewed coffee (with coffee-flavored liqueur) at room temperature	1	(8 ounce) package toffee bits

Preheat oven to 350°. Grease and flour 2 (8 inch) cake pans. Beat cake mix with coffee and 4 egg whites. Fold in ¾ package of toffee bits. Bake 20 to 25 minutes. Let cake cool 15 minutes. Take out of pans and cool completely. Slice layers horizontally making 4 thin layers.

CREAM CHEESE ICING

1	(8 ounce) package cream cheese, softened	1⅓	cups sugar
4	teaspoons vanilla	4	cups frozen nondairy whipped topping, thawed
⅔	cup chocolate syrup		

Prepare icing by mixing cream cheese, vanilla, chocolate syrup, and sugar. Fold the nondairy whipped topping into mixture. Put one layer of cake on plate. Drizzle remaining coffee mixture over layer and ice. Repeat with every layer. Drizzle chocolate syrup over top of cake and sprinkle the remainder of toffee bits on top.

COCONUT CREAM CHEESE FROSTING

4 tablespoons butter, divided

2 cups sweetened coconut

1 (8 ounce) package cream cheese, softened

2 teaspoons milk

3½ cups powdered sugar

½ teaspoon vanilla

Melt 2 tablespoons butter in skillet. Add coconut; stir constantly over low heat until golden brown. Spread coconut on absorbent paper to cool. Cream 2 tablespoons butter with cream cheese. Add milk and sugar alternately, beating well. Add vanilla; stir in 1¾ cups of coconut. Spread on tops and sides of cake layers. Sprinkle with remaining coconut.

Pumpkin-Praline Cheesecake

45	gingersnap cookies	1	teaspoon vanilla
6	tablespoons of butter or margarine, softened	¾	teaspoon salt
4	(8 ounce) packages cream cheese, softened	4	eggs
		1	(16 ounce) can solid pumpkin (not pumpkin pie mix)
1	cup light brown sugar, packed	⅓	cup sugar
3	tablespoons flour	3	tablespoons water
2	teaspoons ground cinnamon	1	cup chopped pecans
1	teaspoon ground ginger	1	tablespoon light corn syrup
1	teaspoon ground allspice		

Preheat oven to 350°. Place gingersnap cookies, in batches, in closed plastic bag and crush into fine crumbs with rolling pin or place in food processor or blender. Mix crumbs and butter together well. Press mixture onto bottom and up sides of a greased 9x2½ inch springform pan to within 1 inch of the top. Set aside.

Beat cream cheese at medium speed until smooth. Slowly beat in brown sugar. Add flour, cinnamon, ginger, allspice, vanilla, salt, eggs and pumpkin. Beat well 3 minutes, occasionally scraping bowl. Pour cream cheese mixture into crust and bake for 1 hour.

Turn oven off and let cheesecake remain in oven for another hour. Remove and completely cool in pan on wire rack. Cover and refrigerate at least 6 hours.

While cheesecake is chilling, heat sugar and water over low heat until sugar dissolves, stirring occasionally. Increase heat to medium and boil rapidly without stirring until syrup turns a light golden brown, about 5 to 6 minutes. Working quickly, stir in chopped pecans and spread praline mixture onto a cookie sheet in a thin layer. Cool and chop into small pieces. Store in a container until ready to use. When cheesecake is ready, loosen side of pan from cheesecake and remove. Loosen cake from pan bottom and slide onto a plate. Gently spread corn syrup on top of cake and sprinkle with praline crumbs.

"Love each other as I have loved you. Greater love has no one than this,

that He lay down his life for his friends."

John 15:12

Turtle Cheesecake

CHOCOLATE WAFER CRUST

2 cups chocolate wafer crumbs ⅓ cup butter, melted
¼ cup sugar

Preheat oven to 325°. Combine chocolate wafer crumbs, sugar and butter, stir well. Firmly press mixture into bottom and sides of a lightly-greased 9 inch springform pan. Bake 10 minutes. Cool on wire rack.

CHEESECAKE FILLING

3 (8 ounce) packages cream cheese, softened
1¼ cups sugar
4 large eggs
1 (8 ounce) container sour cream
1 tablespoon vanilla extract

Beat cream cheese at medium speed with an electric mixer until creamy. Add sugar, beating well. Add eggs, one at a time, beating after each and scraping the sides and bottom as needed. Stir in sour cream and vanilla. Pour into crust.

CHOCOLATE LAYER

¼ cup butter
1 (6 ounce) package semisweet chocolate morsels

Melt butter in a small heavy saucepan; add chocolate morsels. Stir over low heat just until chocolate melts and mixture blends. Spread chocolate mixture over cheesecake; chill 15 minutes.

CARAMEL TOPPING

1 (12 ounce) jar caramel topping
1 cup chopped pecans

Combine caramel topping and pecans in a small saucepan. Bring to a boil, while stirring constantly over medium heat, boil 2 minutes. Remove from heat and cool 5 minutes. Spread over chocolate layer; cool completely. Serve immediately or cover and let stand at room temperature at least 30 minutes before serving.

"Oh, taste and see that the Lord is good; blessed is the man who trusts in Him!"

Psalm 34:8

Chocolate Pecan Cupcakes

1 cup butter	1½ cups sugar
4 (1 ounce) semi-sweet chocolate baking squares	1 cup all-purpose flour
1½ cups chopped pecans	4 large eggs, lightly beaten
	1 teaspoon vanilla extract

Preheat oven to 325°. Melt together butter and chocolate in a heavy saucepan over medium heat; stir in pecans. Remove from heat.

Combine sugar, flour, eggs and vanilla extract. (Do not beat.) Stir in chocolate mixture. Place baking cups in muffin pans; spoon batter into cups, filling three-fourths full. Bake 35 minutes (Do not overbake.)

These are very good with Chocolate-Marshmallow Frosting.

Makes 16 cupcakes

CHOCOLATE-MARSHMALLOW FROSTING

3 cups miniature marshmallows	6 ounces unsweetened chocolate, chopped
¾ cup butter or margarine, cut into pieces	6 cups powdered sugar
¾ cup evaporated milk	1 tablespoon vanilla extract

Melt marshmallows, butter, evaporated milk, chocolate and sugar in a 2 quart saucepan over medium-low heat, stirring 5 minutes or until mixture is smooth.

Transfer chocolate mixture to a large bowl. Place the bowl into a larger bowl filled with ice and water. Gradually add powdered sugar, beating at low speed with an electric mixer. Increase speed to medium-high, and beat 5 minutes or until frosting is cool, thick and spreadable. Stir in 1 tablespoon vanilla.

Makes 4½ cups

"I have come that they may
have life and have it to the full."

John 10:10

Special Mocha Cupcakes

2 eggs	1½ cups all-purpose flour
½ cup cold brewed coffee	1 cup sugar
½ cup canola oil	⅓ cup baking cocoa
3 teaspoons cider vinegar	1 teaspoon baking soda
3 teaspoons vanilla extract	½ teaspoon salt

Preheat oven to 350°. In a large bowl, beat the eggs, coffee, oil, vinegar and vanilla until well blended. In a small bowl, combine the flour, sugar, cocoa, baking soda and salt; gradually beat into coffee mixture until blended.

Fill paper-lined muffin cups ¾ full. Bake 20 to 25 minutes or until a toothpick comes out clean. Cool 10 minutes before removing from pan to wire rack to cool.

Makes 12 cupcakes

MOCHA FROSTING

3 tablespoons milk chocolate chips

3 tablespoons semi-sweet chocolate chips

⅓ cup butter, softened

2 cups powdered sugar

1-2 tablespoons brewed coffee

½ cup chocolate sprinkles

In a microwave, melt chips and butter; stir until smooth. Transfer chocolate mixture to a large bowl. Gradually beat in powdered sugar and coffee until smooth. Pipe frosting onto cupcakes. Top with sprinkles.

Butter Cream Icing

1 (16 ounce) can solid vegetable shortening	1 tablespoon almond extract
2 pounds powdered sugar	1 tablespoon (clear) vanilla extract
8 tablespoons milk	

Mix shortening and ½ sugar on medium speed with electric mixer. (A stand mixer works well.) Add ½ milk; alternate adding remaining milk and sugar. Stir in extracts. Mix at ¾ power about 10 minutes, until icing gets a cloud-like appearance. Use food coloring if desired.

May also be used for piping decorations.

Caramel Icing

2 cups brown sugar	1 (5 ounce) can evaporated milk
½ teaspoon salt	2½ cups powered sugar
1 stick plus 2 tablespoons salted butter	1 teaspoon vanilla extract

Mix brown sugar, salt and butter in saucepan. Bring to a bubbly boil. Add evaporated milk and bring to a boil. Cook 3 minutes, stirring constantly. Let cool. Add powdered sugar and beat with a mixer. Add vanilla. Spread on cake or cupcakes.

Miss Margaret's Caramel Icing

3 cups sugar (reserve ½ cup for browning)	2½ sticks butter
	¾ cup milk
	2 teaspoons vanilla

Mix sugar, butter and milk in large pot. Stir over medium heat until thoroughly mixed. Remove from heat and set aside until sugar is browned. Spray a frying pan with nonstick cooking spray. Put ½ cup sugar in frying pan and cook on medium heat until all sugar melts and turns brown. Add to mixture in pot. Bring to a boil, stirring well. Boil on medium high for 8 minutes or until soft ball stage (235°F). Add vanilla. Beat until proper consistency to spread. Spread between layers and on top and sides of cake.

Coconut Cream Cheese Frosting

1 (8 ounce) package cream cheese, softened	1 teaspoon vanilla extract
½ cup butter or margarine, softened	1 (16 ounce) package powdered sugar
3 tablespoons milk	1 (7 ounce) package sweetened flaked coconut

Beat cream cheese and butter at medium speed with an electric mixer until creamy. Add milk and vanilla, beating well. Gradually add sugar, beating until smooth. Stir in coconut.

Makes 4 cups

MEMA'S CHOCOLATE ICING

2 cups sugar

½ cup cocoa

2 sticks butter

½ cup milk

1 teaspoon vanilla

Mix sugar and cocoa. Melt butter in heavy saucepan over medium-high heat. Add milk, sugar/cocoa mixture. Stir until mixture comes to a rolling boil. (Bubbles will form on top.) Boil for 60 seconds only! If you overcook, mixture will turn to sugar. Remove from heat and stir until thick enough to spread on cake.

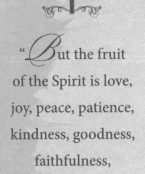

Apple Pie

1	deep-dish pie crust	2	heaping tablespoons sugar
7-8	medium Granny Smith apples, peeled, cored, and sliced thinly	2	tablespoons brown sugar
		⅓	cup light corn syrup
1	tablespoon cornstarch	2	tablespoons cold butter
½	teaspoon salt	1	ready-made pie crust
3	tablespoons butter	2	tablespoons melted butter
1	teaspoon cinnamon	2	tablespoons sugar

Preheat oven to 425°. Place deep-dish pie crust on cookie sheet lined with foil and sprayed. Fill deep crust with apples, piled high. Combine cornstarch, salt, butter, cinnamon, sugar, brown sugar, corn syrup and cold butter in a pot a on the stove and heat on low heat. Stir until sugars melt. Carefully drip this sauce over apples. Slice butter into small pieces and put on top of apples. Place ready-made crust on top of pie and crimp the edges together to seal. Cut 4 small slits in pie crust for steam to escape. Rub melted butter on top of crust. Sprinkle with sugar. Bake 30 to 45 minutes until bubbly and golden. Check during baking to see if it will be necessary to cover crust with foil to prevent overbrowning.

Easy Apple Dumplings

2	Granny Smith apples	1	cup sugar
1	package crescent rolls	½	cup water
½	cup brown sugar		Cinnamon and sugar mixture
1	stick butter		

Preheat oven to 350°. Peel and cut apples into fourths. Wrap crescent rolls around apple pieces and place in 9x13 inch baking dish. Sprinkle brown sugar on and around apples. Melt sugar, butter and water until blended. Pour over crescent rolls. Sprinkle with cinnamon and sugar mixture. Bake approximately 30 minutes.

Blackberry Cobbler

4	cups fresh blackberries	1	cup all-purpose flour
1	large egg	6	tablespoons butter, melted
1	cup sugar		

Preheat oven to 375°. Place fruit in lightly greased small baking dish, (8x8 inch) square or round. Combine egg, sugar and flour in mixing bowl and stir until mixture is like a coarse meal. Sprinkle over fruit. Drizzle with melted butter. Bake 35 minutes until lightly browned and bubbly. Let stand 10 to 15 minutes before serving.

May substitute apples, blueberries and peaches in this recipe. If using canned fruit, drain well first.

Sweet Potato Pie

2	(29 ounce) cans sweet potatoes, mashed	2	eggs
		1	teaspoon vanilla
1	cup sugar	¼	cup margarine
¼	cup milk		

Preheat oven to 350°. Mash sweet potatoes; combine with sugar, milk, eggs, vanilla and margarine.

TOPPING

1	cup crisp rice cereal	½	cup sugar
¼	cup margarine, melted	½	cup chopped pecans

Mix cereal, margarine, sugar and pecans; spread over potato mixture. Bake 30 minutes.

"He makes me lie down in green pastures, he leads me beside quiet waters, he restores my soul. He guides me in paths of righteousness for his name's sake."

Psalm 23: 2-3

Strawberry Crème Pie

½	cup whipping cream	½	teaspoon vanilla
1	tablespoon sugar	1	pie shell, baked
⅓	cup all-purpose flour	1½-2	cups fresh ripe strawberries (better if in season)
¾	cup sugar		
¼	teaspoon salt	3	tablespoons powdered sugar
2½	cups whole milk		
4	egg yolks, beaten		Optional: Frozen whipped topping
1	tablespoon butter		

Whip cream with sugar until very thick. Refrigerate at least 2 hours.

Put flour, sugar and salt in a saucepan. Slowly stir in 1 cup milk, stir until smooth. Add remainder of milk. Stir over direct heat until thick (can be done in a double boiler), stirring constantly about 5 to 6 minutes.

Remove from heat; quickly add ½ of hot mixture to egg yolks, stirring constantly. Pour back into saucepan, stir. Cook about 2 minutes longer. Remove from heat. Add butter and vanilla. Pour into bowl, cover and refrigerate at least 2 hours.

Cook pie shell when ready to assemble pie. Pour ½ of crème mixture into cooled pie shell. Spread on sides. Arrange strawberries on top, sprinkle with powdered sugar. Pour rest of filling on top; covering all of fruit. Spread crème on top of pie.

May use frozen whipped topping instead of whip cream.

"Delight yourself in the Lord and he will give you the desires of your heart."

Psalm 37:4

Harvest Pie

1	large butternut squash, halved and seeded (about 2½ pounds)	¼	cup all-purpose flour
½	cup fat-free evaporated milk	¼	cup dark brown sugar, packed
¾	cup sugar	2	tablespoons butter, chilled and cut into small pieces
½	cup egg substitute	3	tablespoons chopped pecans
1	teaspoon vanilla extract	½	(15 ounce) package refrigerated pie dough
½	teaspoon ground cinnamon	10	tablespoons fat-free whipped topping (optional)
⅛	teaspoon ground allspice		
⅛	teaspoon ground cloves		

Position oven rack to lowest position. Preheat oven to 400°. Place squash; cut sides down, on a foil-lined baking sheet coated with cooking spray. Bake 30 minutes or until squash is tender. Cool slightly, peel. Mash pulp to measure 2 ½ cups. Combine pulp and milk into a food processor, process until smooth. Add sugar, egg substitute, vanilla, cinnamon, allspice and cloves; process until smooth.

Increase oven temperature to 425°. Combine flour and brown sugar in a medium bowl; cut in butter using two knives. Add pecans, toss to combine. Roll dough into a 13 inch circle, place into a (9 inch) deep-dish pie plate coated with cooking spray. Fold edges under, flute. Pour the squash mixture into the prepared crust.

Place the pie plate on the bottom rack, bake 15 minutes. Remove pie from oven. Reduce oven temperature to 350°. Sprinkle flour mixture evenly over filling; shield edges of pie crust with foil. Return pie plate to bottom rack; bake an additional 40 minutes or until center is set. Cool on wire rack. Garnish each serving with 1 tablespoon whipped topping.

For a lower calorie version, you may use fat-free evaporated milk and fat-free whipped topping. May use ½ cup of egg substitute.

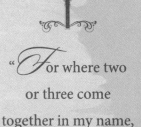

"*For where two or three come together in my name, there am I with them.*"

Matthew 18:20

HOW TO PRE BAKE A PIE CRUST

Preheat oven to 350°. Line the crust with parchment paper, aluminum foil or a large coffee filter. Fill half full with pie weights, rice or beans. Bake 20 minutes. Remove weights. Prick bottom of crust several times with fork; bake an additional 5 to 10 minutes. Cool completely before filling.

PIE CRUST

2 cups plain flour

1 teaspoon salt

½ cup oil

¼ cup cold milk

Stir together ingredients into two balls. Press into 2 glass pie dishes. Make holes in crust with fork. Bake 400° until browned.

Buttermilk Coconut Pie

1	tablespoon flour	1	(3½ ounce) can coconut
1½	cups sugar	½	cup buttermilk
3	eggs, beaten	¾	stick butter, melted
1	teaspoon vanilla	1	deep dish pie crust

Preheat oven to 350°. Mix flour with sugar. Add eggs, vanilla, coconut, buttermilk, and butter and pour into unbaked pie crust. Bake 50 to 60 minutes, until center is set.

Red, White and Blueberry Trifle

¼	cup plus ⅔ cup sugar	2	(8 ounce) packages cream cheese
¼	cup fresh lemon juice		
¼	cup water	2	cups heavy cream, at room temperature
¼	teaspoon almond extract		
1	premade angel food cake, cut into 1 inch slices	2	pints blueberries
		2	pints strawberries, hulled and sliced

Heat ¼ cup sugar, lemon juice and water in a saucepan over medium-high heat, stirring until the sugar dissolves. Remove from heat and stir in the almond extract.

Brush both sides of each slice of cake with the syrup. Cut slices into 1 inch cubes.

Beat the remaining ⅔ cup sugar and the cream cheese with a mixer on medium speed until smooth and light. Add the cream and beat on medium-high speed until smooth and becomes the consistency of whipped cream.

Arrange half of the cake cubes in the bottom of a 13 cup trifle dish. Sprinkle evenly with a layer of blueberries. Dollop half of the cream mixture over the blueberries and gently spread. Top with a layer of strawberries. Layer the remaining cake cubes on top of the strawberries, then sprinkle with more blueberries and top with the remaining cream mixture. Finish with the remaining strawberries and blueberries, arranging in a decorative pattern. Cover and refrigerate 1 hour.

Magic Coconut Pie

4 eggs, beaten
1¾ cups sugar
½ cup self-rising flour
2 cups milk
½ cup butter, melted
1 teaspoon vanilla
1½ cups shredded coconut

Preheat oven to 350°. Combine eggs, sugar, flour, milk, butter, vanilla and coconut in a mixing bowl. Pour into a greased 9 to 10 inch pie plate.

Bake 1 hour. Cool and let settle before cutting. It makes its own crust!

Never Fail Velvety Egg Custard Pie

4 eggs, slightly beaten
⅓ cup sugar
¼ teaspoon salt
1 teaspoon vanilla
2½ cups milk, scalded
Dash of nutmeg
1 (9 inch) deep dish pie crust, thawed

Preheat oven to 475°. Combine eggs, sugar, salt and vanilla; mix well. Slowly stir in hot milk. Pour into pastry crust. (Be sure to fill at the oven in order to keep from spilling.) Sprinkle dash of nutmeg on top of pie. Bake for 5 minutes. Reduce oven temperature to 425°. Bake 10 minutes or until blade of knife inserted in middle comes out clean. Cool on wire rack. Serve cool or thoroughly chilled.

"After this there was a feast of the Jews, and Jesus went up to Jerusalem."

John 5:1

Grandmothers are mothers who are grand.

Restoring the sense that our most precious things

Are those that do not change much over time.

No love of childhood is more sublime,

Demanding little, giving on demand.

More inclined than most to grant the wings

On which we fly off to enchanted lands.

Though grandmothers must serve as second mothers,

Helping out with young and restless hearts,

Each has all the patience wisdom brings,

Remembering our passions more than others,

Soothing us with old and well-honed arts.

~Author Unknown

Len Berg's Macaroon Pie

1 dozen saltine crackers, finely crushed	3 egg whites, stiffly beaten
¾ cup finely chopped dates	½ cup chopped nuts
1 cup sugar	1 teaspoon almond extract

Preheat oven to 350°. Combine cracker crumbs and dates; mix well. Fold sugar into beaten egg whites. Combine date mixture, egg whites, nuts and almond extract; mix. Pour into greased pie or cake pan and bake 30 minutes.

Buttermilk Pecan Pie

3 eggs	2 tablespoons all-purpose flour
1 stick butter, melted	
½ cup buttermilk	1½ cups pecans, broken into small pieces
1½ cups sugar	
1 teaspoon vanilla	1 (9 inch) frozen pie shell

Preheat oven to 350°. Mix eggs, butter, buttermilk, sugar, vanilla, flour and pecans. Pour into pie shell. Bake 45 to 60 minutes.

Cookies in a Crust

2 eggs	1 (6 ounce) package semisweet chocolate chips
⅓ cup all-purpose flour	
⅓ cup sugar	⅔ cup chopped walnuts
⅓ cup packed brown sugar	1 butter-flavored pie crust
½ cup butter or margarine, melted and cooled	

Preheat oven to 325°. In a large bowl, beat eggs until foamy. Add flour and sugars, blend thoroughly. Mix in melted butter. Stir in chips and walnuts, pour into pie crust. Bake 1 hour or until golden brown. Cool on wire rack. If desired, garnish with whipped cream or ice cream.

NO CRUST PIE

1 cup sugar

3 egg whites, stiffly beaten

8 whole graham crackers

1 teaspoon baking powder

½ cup chopped pecans

1 teaspoon vanilla

Preheat oven to 375°. Fold sugar into beaten egg whites. Crush crackers very coarsely in plastic bag. Add baking powder to bag. Fold cracker mixture, pecans, and vanilla into egg white mixture. Pour into buttered pie plate. Bake 15 minutes.

Best served with whipped cream, sweetened with 2 to 3 tablespoons of powdered sugar.

Darling's Easy Fudge Pie

1 stick butter, melted	¼ cup all-purpose flour, sifted
¼ cup cocoa	½ teaspoon vanilla
2 eggs, beaten	1 cup chopped pecans
1 cup sugar	1 pie crust

Preheat oven to 350°. Blend cocoa into melted butter. Add eggs, sugar, flour, vanilla and pecans. Pour into unbaked pie shell. Bake 40 minutes or until knife inserted comes out clean. Do not over bake. Cool and refrigerate overnight. Great cold or heated and served with vanilla ice cream or whipped cream.

May bake in 8x8 inch pan and cut in squares.

Chocolate Cobbler

1 cup all-purpose flour	½ cup milk
2 teaspoons baking powder	⅓ cup butter, melted
¼ teaspoon salt	1 teaspoon vanilla extract
7 tablespoons cocoa powder, divided	1½ cups brown sugar, packed
1¼ cups sugar, divided	1½ cups hot coffee

Preheat oven to 350°. Mix flour, baking powder, salt, 3 tablespoons cocoa powder, and ¾ cup of white sugar. (Batter will be thick.) Reserve remaining cocoa and sugar. Stir milk, butter and vanilla into the flour mixture. Mix until smooth. Pour into an ungreased (8 inch) baking dish. In a separate bowl, mix the remaining white sugar (½ cup), brown sugar and remaining 4 tablespoons of cocoa. Sprinkle this mixture evenly over the batter. Pour the hot coffee over all. Do not stir! Bake 40 minutes or until center is set. Let stand for a few minutes before serving.

Serve with vanilla ice cream using the gooey sauce to spoon on top.

German Chocolate Pie

¼ cup butter, melted
1½ cups sugar
2 eggs, slightly beaten
⅓ cup cocoa

½ cup evaporated milk
½ cup coconut
½ cup chopped pecans
1 (9 inch) deep dish pie crust, thawed

Preheat oven to 400°. Mix butter and sugar with mixer. Add eggs, cocoa, evaporated milk, coconut and pecans; mix well. Prick pie crust with fork. Pour mixture into crust. Bake 35 to 45 minutes until pie is set. Cool and serve with vanilla ice cream or whipped cream.

This is similar to German Chocolate Pie at S & S Cafeteria.

Chocolate Cream Pie

1 (9 inch) pie crust, pre-baked
1¼ cups sugar
¼ cup cornstarch
½ teaspoon salt
3 cups whole milk
4 egg yolks, beaten
3 ounces unsweetened chocolate, chopped

4 tablespoons butter
1 teaspoon pure vanilla extract
1 pint whipping cream
¼ cup sugar
1 ounce semisweet chocolate, shaved

Combine sugar, cornstarch and salt in a large saucepan. Add milk and chocolate and cook over medium-high heat until the chocolate is melted and the mixture is slightly thickened. Reduce heat and continue cooking for 4 minutes. Remove from heat.

Add about ½ cup of the chocolate mixture to the beaten eggs and stir. Add the eggs to the saucepan, bring to a low boil and stir continuously for 4 minutes. Stir in the butter and vanilla. Pour into the baked pie crust, cool, and chill about 2 to 3 hours. Place the whipping cream in a bowl, add the sugar and whip the cream until soft peaks form. Spread the cream over the top of the chilled pie and garnish with chocolate shavings if desired.

Chocolate Eclair Pie

PUDDING MIXTURE

Graham crackers, enough to cover bottom of 9x13 inch pan, twice

2 small packages instant vanilla pudding

3 cups milk

1 (8 ounce) container frozen nondairy whipped topping, thawed

Butter a 9x13 inch dish. Line bottom of dish with graham crackers. Mix pudding with milk, fold in whipped topping. Pour half of pudding mixture over crackers. Add another layer of crackers. Pour remaining pudding mixture over crackers. Top with last layer of crackers.

FROSTING

1 square of unsweetened baking chocolate

3 tablespoons milk

1 tablespoon light corn syrup

1 tablespoon butter, melted

1½ cups powdered sugar

Melt chocolate in double boiler on low heat. Whisk in milk, corn syrup, butter and sugar. Pour over top layer of crackers. Refrigerate 24 hours.

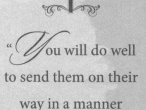

Not Your Everyday Banana Pudding

2 bags Pepperidge Farm Chessmen shortbread cookies

6-8 bananas, sliced

2 cups milk

1 (5 ounce) box instant French vanilla pudding

1 (8 ounce) package cream cheese, softened

1 (14 ounce) can sweetened condensed milk

1 (12 ounce) container frozen nondairy whipped topping, thawed

Line bottom of a 9x13x2 inch dish with 1 bag of cookies. Put bananas on top. Blend milk with pudding, mix well with mixer. In a separate bowl beat cream cheese and condensed milk until smooth, fold in whipped topping. Add to pudding mixture, stirring until well blended. Pour mixture over cookies and bananas, cover with remaining cookies. Refrigerate.

Makes 12 servings

"*You* will do well to send them on their way in a manner worthy of God."

3 John 1:6

Peanut Butter Pie

2   (3 ounce) packages cream cheese, softened
½   cup peanut butter
1   cup powdered sugar, sifted

1   (8 ounce) carton frozen nondairy whipped topping, thawed
1   chocolate pie shell

Combine cream cheese and peanut butter. Add powdered sugar and beat mixture until smooth. Gently fold in whipped topping. Spoon mixture into pie shell. Chill pie in refrigerator for a minimum of 4 hours.

PEANUT BUSTER

1 package chocolate sandwich cookies, crushed

½ cup melted butter

½ gallon vanilla ice cream, softened

1 package salted peanuts

2 jars chocolate sauce

1 (12 ounce) container frozen whipped topping, thawed

Combine chocolate sandwich cookies and butter and press into the bottom of a 9x13 inch glass oven proof baking dish for the crust. Layer vanilla ice cream, peanuts, chocolate sauce and whipped topping. Freeze.

Fluffy Tropical Pie

1   (14 ounce) can sweetened condensed milk
1   (12 ounce) container frozen whipped topping, thawed
1   (20 ounce) can crushed pineapple, drained
2   tablespoons lemon juice
½   cup mashed ripe banana (about 1 large banana)

1   large orange, peeled and sectioned
½   cup sweetened flaked coconut, plus a little extra for garnishing
½   cup chopped walnuts, toasted
½   cup maraschino cherries
2   (9 inch) graham cracker crusts

Stir together condensed milk and whipped topping. Fold in pineapple, lemon juice, banana, orange sections, coconut, walnuts and cherries. Pour evenly into crusts. Cover and freeze 12 hours or until firm. Remove from freezer about 10 minutes before serving.

Garnish if desired with a dollop of whipped topping, toasted sweetened coconut, a cherry and mint sprig.

Classic Key Lime Pie

CRUST

1⅔	cups graham cracker crumbs	¼	cup sugar
		6	tablespoons butter, melted

In a bowl, combine graham cracker crumbs, sugar and butter. Press into the bottom and sides of a 9 inch pie plate. Prebake the crust 8 minutes.

PIE

3	cups sweetened condensed milk	1	tablespoon grated lime zest, plus more for garnishing
½	cup sour cream	1	pint whipping cream
¾	cup Key lime juice	¼	cup sugar

Combine condensed milk, sour cream, Key lime juice and zest in a medium mixing bowl. Pour mixture into the graham cracker crust and bake 8 more minutes. Chill pie in the refrigerator thoroughly, about 2 to 3 hours. Prior to serving, prepare the whipped topping. Place the whipping cream in a bowl, add sugar and whip until soft peaks form. Spread the cream over the top of the pie.

May garnish with grated Key lime zest.

Makes 8 servings

"Every good and perfect gift is from above, coming down from the Father of the heavenly lights, who does not change like shifting shadows."

James 1:17

Ice Cream Sandwich Dessert

1-2	boxes ice cream sandwiches (enough to line 8x12 inch casserole)	1	jar caramel ice cream topping
		1	large container whipped topping, thawed
1	jar hot fudge ice cream topping	2	cups chopped chocolate covered toffee bars

Line an 8x12 inch casserole dish with ice cream sandwiches. Pour desired amount of hot fudge and caramel toppings over sandwiches. Cover with whipped topping. Sprinkle chopped candy bars on top and freeze.

Frozen Key Lime Pie

GRAHAM CRACKER CRUST

1½ cups graham cracker crumbs   ¾   stick butter, melted
¼   cup plus 1 tablespoon sugar

Preheat oven to 350°. Mix graham cracker crumbs, sugar and butter. Press mixture into sprayed pie plate. Go up sides, trying to keep an even thickness. Bake 10 minutes until slightly golden. Cool completely.

KEY LIME FILLING

6   extra large egg yolks
¼   cup sugar
1   (14 ounce) can sweetened condensed milk

2   tablespoons lime zest
¾   cup freshly squeezed lime juice (4 to 5 limes)

Beat egg yolks and sugar with electric mixer on high speed for about 5 minutes, until thick. Add sweetened condensed milk, lime zest and lime juice. Beat on medium speed. Pour into pie shell and freeze.

WHIPPED CREAM TOPPING

1   cup heavy cream
¼   cup sugar
½   teaspoon vanilla extract

Lime wedges, sliced thinly for decoration

Beat cream on high speed with the whisk attachment until soft peaks form. Add sugar and vanilla and beat until firm. Spread topping or pipe onto pie and decorate with lime wedges. Freeze at least 4 hours.

"I will praise you, O Lord, with all my heart; I will tell of all your wonders. I will be glad and rejoice in you; I will sing praise to your name, O Most High."

Psalm 9:1-2

Frozen Margarita Pie

CRUST

½ cup plus 2 tablespoons butter, divided

1¼ cups thin salted pretzels, crushed

½ cup sugar

Grease a 9 inch pie plate. Melt butter in saucepan or microwave on low heat. Stir in pretzel crumbs and sugar. Press firmly over bottom and sides of pie plate. Place in freezer.

FILLING

1 (14 ounce) can sweetened condensed milk

1½ tablespoons freshly squeezed lime juice

1½ tablespoons Tequila

1 tablespoon plus 1 teaspoon Triple Sec

1 drop green food coloring

2½ cups whipping cream

Mix sweetened condensed milk, lime juice, Tequila, Triple Sec and food coloring in a small bowl. In large bowl, beat cream until soft peaks form. Gradually fold in condensed milk mixture. Fold into pie crust and freeze uncovered for 6 hours. Wrap airtight and freeze 2 hours. To serve, set at room temperature for 15 minutes for easier slicing. May decorate with lime slices or more whipped cream.

Great for summertime!

May omit the Triple Sec and Tequila and increase the lime juice to ⅔ cup.

I pray dear God that I might not criticize my brother until I have walked a mile in his moccasins.

~Old Indian Prayer

Strawberry Freeze

CRUST

1	cup flour	½	cup chopped pecans
¼	cup brown sugar	½	cup butter, melted

Preheat oven to 350°. Mix crust ingredients together and crumble evenly into a greased 9x13 inch glass baking dish. Bake 7 to 10 minutes, stirring frequently so the crust will brown evenly. When cool, take out about ⅓ cup of crumbles to save for the topping. Press the rest of the crumbles into the bottom of the pan.

FILLING

2	egg whites	2	tablespoons fresh squeezed lemon juice
1	cup sugar	½	pint whipping cream, whipped or 8 ounces of frozen whipped topping
1	(10 ounce) package frozen strawberries, thawed		

While crust is cooling, mix egg whites, sugar, strawberries and lemon juice on high speed for about 10 minutes, until stiff peaks form. Fold in whipped cream. Spread filling evenly on top of crust, and sprinkle remaining crumbs on top. Cover and freeze overnight. Will keep in the freezer for several weeks if covered tightly.

"Be joyful always; pray continually; give thanks in all circumstances, for this is God's will for you in Christ Jesus."

1 Thessalonians 5:16-18

Peppermint Ice Cream Pie

CREAM FILLED CHOCOLATE SANDWICH COOKIE CRUST

16 cream filled chocolate sandwich cookies

2 tablespoons butter, melted

Preheat oven to 350°. Pulse cookies in food processor until coarsely ground. Add butter and mix until it resembles wet sand. Transfer crumbs to the pie plate. Press crumbs evenly on bottom and bake until the crust is fragrant and set, about 15 minutes.

PEPPERMINT FILLING

½ teaspoon peppermint extract

½ cup crushed hard peppermint candies

1 (½ gallon) vanilla ice cream, softened

Mix flavoring and candy into ice cream, pour into crust. Top with a sprinkle of crushed peppermint and freeze for several hours. Serve frozen.

Grasshopper Pie

Use Cream Filled Chocolate Sandwich Cookie Crust recipe for pie crust (see above).

FILLING

1 (½ gallon) vanilla ice cream, softened

¼ cup crème de menthe

3 tablespoons crème de cacao

½ cup mini chocolate chips

Mix ingredients into ice cream, pour into crust. Top with a sprinkle of mini chocolate chips and freeze for several hours. Serve frozen.

Light ice cream or frozen yogurt will stay frozen longer. If serving outdoors during warm weather, this may help dessert stay frozen.

"May the Lord bless you and keep you; may the Lord shed His light upon you, May the Lord look upon you kindly and give you peace."

Numbers 6: 24-26

PEANUT BUTTER BALLS

1 cup light corn syrup

2 cups sugar

¼ cup honey

2 cups peanut butter

1 (12 ounce) box corn flakes cereal

In a large pot, bring syrup, sugar and honey to a boil. Remove from heat. Add peanut butter, stir well and immediately begin adding corn flakes until too stiff to stir. Butter hands and roll into small balls. Dough will be very warm. Place on wax paper to cool. Store in airtight container.

Cissy's Sugar Cookies

1	cup salted butter	2½	cups all-purpose flour, divided
⅔	cup sugar		Extra flour for rolling dough
1	egg		Cookie cutters
1	teaspoon vanilla		

Preheat oven to 350°. Cream butter and sugar until pale and fluffy. Add egg and vanilla; mix and use spatula to scrape the sides. Add half of flour and stir until combined. Add second half of flour and stir to combine. Refrigerate dough until stiff (4 or more hours).

Roll out dough to ¼ inch on a floured piece of parchment or wax paper. Use cookie cutters to cut cookies and transfer to a clean piece of parchment or waxed paper covered cookie sheet. Cookies hold their shape best when they are cold. Refrigerate between rolling and baking to ensure that they keep their decorative look. Bake 8 to 12 minutes, depending upon size of cookie.

FROSTING

1	tablespoon melted butter	1	tablespoon milk
¼	teaspoon lemon juice	¾	cup powdered sugar
1	teaspoon vanilla		Food coloring

Melt butter and add lemon juice, vanilla and milk. Slowly stir in powdered sugar and color with chosen food coloring. Frosting consistency should be similar to molasses. Dip cookies face down in frosting and place on wire rack to dry.

Grandma's Tea Cookies

½	cup butter or margarine	1	teaspoon vanilla
½	cup sugar	1	cup self-rising flour, sifted
1	egg, beaten		

Preheat oven to 350°. Cream butter and sugar. Add egg and vanilla, beat well. Blend in flour. Drop from teaspoon onto greased baking sheet 2 inches apart. Bake 10 to 12 minutes.

Makes 2 dozen cookies.

Cranberry-Chocolate Chip Biscotti

⅓	cup butter, softened	2	eggs
⅔	cup sugar	2½	cups all-purpose flour
1	teaspoon baking powder	½	cup dried cranberries
½	teaspoon baking soda	½	cup chocolate chips

Preheat oven to 375°. Beat butter with an electric mixer on medium speed 30 seconds. Add sugar, baking powder, baking soda and beat until combined.

Beat in eggs. Reduce speed to medium-low. Gradually add flour. Beat until mixture resembles coarse meal. Stir in cranberries and chocolate chips with a spoon. Shape dough into two 9x2 inch rolls. (It will be a bit dry.)

Place rolls on ungreased cookie sheet, flatten slightly. Bake 20 minutes or until wooden toothpick comes out clean. Cool on baking sheet for 1 hour.

Reduce oven temperature to 325°. Slice each roll crosswise at 40 to 45 degree angle into ½ inch slices. Place slices cut side down on cookie sheet. Bake 8 minutes. Turn and bake an additional 8 minutes, until crisp and light brown. Transfer to a wire rack and cool.

These are great for a snack. They only have 106 calories and 4 grams of fat.

Makes 28 cookies

"*A*sk and it will be given to you; seek, and you will find; knock, and it will be opened to you."

Matthew 7:7

Lace Cookies

1	cup sugar	¼	teaspoon baking powder
1	cup oatmeal	¼	teaspoon salt
1	stick butter, softened	½	teaspoon vanilla
1	tablespoon flour		

Preheat oven to 350°. Mix sugar, oatmeal, butter, flour, baking powder, salt and vanilla. Place ¼ to ½ teaspoon (very small amount, it will spread) of batter on cookie sheet lined with parchment paper. Bake 5 minutes. Let cool on pan, transfer to a wire rack. Store in airtight container.

Crunchy Chewies

1	cup plain flour	¼	cup instant oatmeal
½	teaspoon baking powder	¾	cup coconut
½	teaspoon baking soda	2	sticks butter, softened
½	cup crushed corn flakes cereal	¼	cup sugar
¼	cup golden raisins	¾	cup brown sugar
¼	cup dried cranberries	1	egg
		1	teaspoon vanilla

Preheat oven to 350°. Mix flour, baking powder, baking soda, corn flakes, raisins, cranberries, oatmeal, and coconut in a bowl. In a separate bowl cream the butter, sugars, egg and vanilla. Mix both bowls together to complete the dough.

Spoon dough onto a parchment paper lined cookie sheet. Bake 5 to 6 minutes or until golden brown.

Honey and Pecan Squares

CRUST

⅔	cup powdered sugar	2	sticks butter, room temperature
2	cups unbleached all-purpose flour		

Preheat oven to 350°. Grease 9x12 inch baking pan. Sift sugar and flour together. Cut in butter using 2 knives or a pastry blender until fine crumbs form. Pat crust into the baking pan. Bake 20 minutes; remove from oven leaving oven at 350°.

TOPPING

⅔	cup butter, melted	½	cup brown sugar
½	cup honey	3½	cups coarsely chopped pecans
3	tablespoons heavy cream		

Mix melted butter, honey, cream, and brown sugar together. Stir in pecans, ensuring that they are coated well. Spread over crust. Return to oven and bake 25 minutes. Cool completely before cutting into squares.

It is better to use honey that has the comb in it. It is well worth the effort.

Makes 36 squares

PECAN COOKIES

1 stick margarine

1 stick butter

1 cup light brown sugar

1 cup chopped pecans

1 package whole graham crackers

Preheat oven to 350°. Mix butter, margarine and sugar. Boil 2 minutes, do not stir. Add pecans and cool slightly. Arrange graham crackers on nonstick pan. Pour mixture over graham crackers. Bake 10 minutes. Cool on parchment paper.

Dark Chocolate Chews

1	cup dark chocolate chips	2	cups all-purpose flour
1	teaspoon brewed coffee	¼	teaspoon salt
1	stick unsalted butter, softened	½	teaspoon baking powder
1¼	cups sugar	½	teaspoon baking soda
2	large eggs		

Preheat oven to 350°. Heat chocolate chips in top of double boiler over simmering water until just melted. Add coffee. Using electric mixer, cream butter and one cup of the sugar in large mixing bowl; mix in eggs, melted chocolate chips and coffee. Gradually add flour by half cups on lowest speed, followed by salt, baking powder and baking soda. Blend thoroughly until flour is completely incorporated.

Place remaining ¼ cup sugar in small bowl. Roll dough into 1 inch balls and roll in sugar to coat. (Can chill dough 10 minutes if too sticky to form balls.) Place 2 inches apart on sprayed cookie sheet. Bake 8 to 10 minutes. Cool on cookie sheet 1 to 2 minutes before transferring to cooling rack. Will set up, but should be very chewy. Place in airtight container after completely cooled.

"These cookies are our family's favorite and bring back "sweet" and fun memories. It was always a messy time preparing and baking these with the kids, and my kitchen often testified of that fact. It would have been so much easier for me to have done it all by myself; however, the joy on their faces as they created these yummy delights, and their great satisfaction knowing they helped, was worth every speck of flour in the wrong place afterwards.

It was also a wonderful reminder of God's grace to His children. A wise mother of four reminded me that it would be much easier, and less messy, for God to do everything all by Himself as well. How wonderful that in His grace, He chooses to let us take part in His great work. Our joy, and satisfaction in helping, is worth it all to Him. Amazing!

It's my hope that many will get their hands and kitchens messy making wonderful memories with these delicious cookies, and take time to reflect on the wonder and grace of our great God, as you clean up the mess!"

~Beverly Thompson

Lemon Butter Cookies

2 cups butter, softened	½ teaspoon salt
1 cup powdered sugar	1 teaspoon lemon extract
3 cups all-purpose flour	1 teaspoon grated lemon rind

Preheat oven to 325°. Beat butter until creamy. Gradually add powdered sugar, beating well after each addition.

Combine flour and salt; gradually add to butter mixture, beating until blended. Stir in lemon extract and rind. Form dough into desired shapes using a cookie press and place onto parchment paper-lined baking sheets. Bake 12 to 15 minutes. Cool on wire racks.

Makes 8 dozen (2¼ inch cookies)

Melia's Marvelous Cookies

½ cup butter, softened	4½ cups uncooked regular oats
1 cup sugar	2 teaspoons baking soda
1 cup plus 2 tablespoons firmly packed brown sugar	¼ teaspoon salt
3 large eggs	1 cup tiny candy-coated chocolate pieces
2 cups creamy peanut butter	1 cup semisweet chocolate morsels
¼ teaspoon vanilla extract	

Preheat oven to 350°. Beat butter at medium speed with an electric mixer until creamy; gradually add sugars, beating well. Add eggs, peanut butter and vanilla. Beat until mixture is blended. Stir in oats, baking soda and salt. (Dough will be stiff.) Stir in chocolate pieces and morsels. Pack dough into a ¼ cup. Drop 4 inches apart onto baking sheets covered with parchment paper. Lightly press each cookie into a 3½ inch circle. Bake 12 to 15 minutes. Center of cookie should be soft. Cool slightly on baking sheets; remove to racks to cool completely.

Makes 2½ dozen cookies

MAMA O'S LADYFINGERS

1¼ sticks margarine

5 tablespoons powdered sugar

1 tablespoon ice water

1 teaspoon vanilla

2 cups cake flour

1 cup chopped pecans

Preheat oven to 325°. Cream margarine and sugar together. Add water and vanilla. Cut in flour and pecans. Work into dough. Roll into finger shapes, in palm of hand. Bake on greased cookie sheet 20 to 30 minutes or until light brown. While hot, roll fingers in powdered sugar.

Will keep about 2 weeks

Nanny's Sugar Cookies

1	cup powdered sugar	4	cups plus 4 tablespoons all-purpose flour
1	cup sugar	1	teaspoon salt
1	stick butter, softened	1	teaspoon baking soda
1	stick margarine, softened	1	teaspoon vanilla
2	eggs	1	teaspoon cream of tartar
1	cup vegetable oil		

Preheat oven to 350°. Mix sugars, butter, margarine, eggs, oil, flour, salt, baking soda, vanilla, and cream of tartar. Mix well; roll into small balls. Place on greased cookie sheet.

Using a glass that has a design on the bottom, dip in water, dip in sugar, and press down to make a design. Dip in sugar each time and press each cookie. May sprinkle with a little more sugar. Bake 10 to 15 minutes.

Mother Doll's Ice Box Cookies

1	cup butter	½	teaspoon salt
2	cups brown sugar	½	teaspoon baking soda
2	eggs	1	cup chopped almonds or pecans
1	cup vanilla		
3½	cups plain flour		

Preheat oven to 300°. Cream butter and sugar, add eggs and vanilla. Mix well. Sift flour, salt and baking soda; add nuts. Roll out into a round roll. Refrigerate overnight. Turn out onto a floured board. Slice very thinly. Bake 20 to 25 minutes.

Makes 5 dozen cookies

My Dad loves these Ice Box Cookies! His mother kept some on hand in the "icebox" at all times. What a wonderful treat to enjoy with your mother after a full day of school.

~Susan Floyd Causey

"*Trust* in the Lord with all your heart and lean not on your own understanding, in all your ways acknowledge Him, and He will direct your path."

Proverbs 3:5-6

Mommy Jo's Ice Box Cookies

1	cup solid vegetable shortening	4	cups plain flour
2	cups brown sugar	1	teaspoon baking soda
2	eggs	1	teaspoon cream of tarter
1	teaspoon vanilla	1	teaspoon salt
		1	cup chopped pecans

Preheat oven to 350°. Cream shortening, sugar, eggs and vanilla. Add sifted flour, baking soda, cream of tarter, salt and pecans. Shape into rolls; wrap in waxed paper or foil and refrigerate. Thinly slice and bake 8 minutes.

For red and green Christmas cookies, divide dough and add food coloring.

Chewies

1	(1 pound) box light brown sugar	2	cups self-rising flour
½	cup softened margarine	1	teaspoon vanilla extract
3	eggs	1	cup chopped pecans
			Powdered sugar

Preheat oven to 300°. Cream sugar and margarine. Add eggs and beat well. Blend in flour and then add vanilla extract and nuts. Bake in a well-greased 13x9x2 inch pan 45 minutes. Cookies will fall. When cool, sprinkle with sugar and cut into squares.

Makes 2½ dozen cookies

Chewy Granola Bars

4½	cups rolled oats	½	cup honey
1	cup all-purpose flour	⅓	cup packed brown sugar
1	teaspoon baking soda	2	cups chocolate chips (optional)
1	teaspoon vanilla		
⅔	cup butter, softened		

Preheat oven to 325°. Lightly grease 9x13 inch pan. Combine all ingredients in a large mixing bowl. Lightly press mixture into pan. Bake 18 to 22 minutes or until golden brown. Let cool 10 minutes and cut into squares. Let bars cool completely in pan before removing or serving.

"*Mommy Jo has made these cookies every Christmas for as long as I can remember. All her children and grandchildren look forward to this traditional treat. At Christmas, you know a special package will arrive with Mommy Jo's "red and green" Christmas cookies, among other treats.*

When I lived away, it was like a piece of home arriving in the mail that made me eager to get home to celebrate all of our Christmas traditions. A loving mother nurtures the heart with love and lovingly prepares food that warms the soul."

~Lea Collins Lisenby

Nana's Fruitcake Cookies

½ pound green candied cherries, chopped

½ pound red candied cherries, chopped

1 pound green candied pineapple, chopped

1 pound pecans, chopped

1 pound dates, chopped

1 can coconut (optional)

3 cups all-purpose flour, divided

1 teaspoon baking soda

1 teaspoon ground cinnamon

1 teaspoon ground nutmeg

1 teaspoon ground cloves

½ cup butter or margarine, softened

½ cup firmly packed brown sugar

4 eggs

½ cup bourbon

3 tablespoons milk

Preheat oven to 300°. Combine cherries, pineapple, pecans, dates, and ½ cup flour; toss well to coat. Set aside. Combine remaining flour, baking soda, cinnamon, nutmeg and cloves. Set aside.

Cream butter. Gradually add sugar, beating until light and fluffy. Add eggs and beat well. Add dry ingredients, bourbon, and milk. Mix well. Stir in fruit mixture.

Drop dough by teaspoonfuls on lightly greased cookie sheets. Bake 20 minutes.

Makes 9 dozen

Blueberry Crunch

1 (20 ounce) can crushed pineapple, drained

2-3 cups blueberries

1 cup sugar, divided

1 box yellow cake mix

2 sticks butter, melted

1 cup chopped pecans

Preheat oven to 350°. Butter 9x13 inch baking dish. Spread the pineapple and top with layer of blueberries. Sprinkle ¾ cup sugar evenly over blueberries. Sprinkle cake mix evenly over sugar. Pour melted butter evenly over cake mix. Sprinkle chopped nuts over butter. Sprinkle remaining ¼ cup sugar over nuts. Bake 50 to 60 minutes or until brown on top.

"*This is my favorite cookie. I'm not sure if these are my favorite because they taste so wonderful or because my mama made Fruitcake Cookies every Christmas for as long as I can remember.*

Fruitcake Cookies mean that it's almost Christmas. Fruitcake Cookies mean, I'm home. Fruitcake cookies mean my mama loves me so much. Fruitcake cookies mean I have to hurry and eat them before my daddy eats them all up! I've tried making them myself; however, they never taste like Mama's do, and I expect they never will."

~Jan Barry

Cream Cheese Brownies

4	(1 ounce) unsweetened chocolate baking squares	6	large eggs, divided
4	(1 ounce) semisweet chocolate baking squares	1	teaspoon vanilla extract
⅓	cup butter or margarine	2	tablespoons all-purpose flour
2	(3 ounce) packages cream cheese, softened	1½	cups semisweet chocolate morsels, divided
¼	cup butter or margarine, softened	2	teaspoons vanilla extract
2	cups sugar, divided	1	cup all-purpose flour
		1	teaspoon baking powder
		1	teaspoon salt

Preheat oven to 325°. Microwave unsweetened and semisweet chocolate squares and ⅓ cup butter in a 1 quart glass bowl at high for 2 minutes or until melted, stirring once. Cool and set aside.

Beat cream cheese and ¼ cup butter at medium speed with an electric mixer until creamy. Gradually add ½ cup sugar, beating well. Add 2 eggs, one at a time, beating until blended. Stir in 1 teaspoon vanilla. Fold in 2 tablespoons flour and ½ cup chocolate morsels. Set aside.

Beat remaining 4 eggs in a large bowl at medium speed. Gradually add remaining 1½ cups sugar, beating well. Add melted chocolate mixture and 2 teaspoons vanilla, beat mixture until well blended.

Combine 1 cup flour, baking powder and salt. Fold into chocolate batter until blended, and stir in remaining 1 cup chocolate morsels.

Reserve 3 cups chocolate batter; spread remaining batter evenly in a greased 13x9 inch pan. Pour cream cheese mixture over batter. Top with remaining batter, swirl mixture with a knife.

Bake 40 to 45 minutes. Cool and cut brownies into squares.

Makes 1½ dozen

The Bomb Brownies

1   box Chewy Fudge Brownie Mix

5-6 tablespoons chocolate syrup

2   Cadbury Milk Chocolate Candy Bars

½   cup semisweet chocolate morsels

Preheat oven to 350°. Mix brownies according to package directions for regular brownies using hot water. Add 2 tablespoons of chocolate syrup to the mixture. Pour ½ of the mixture into the pan. Break apart candy bar on the scored areas and place randomly on top of mixture. Sprinkle morsels over candy and drizzle with the remaining syrup. Cover with remaining brownie batter and bake 25 to 30 minutes.

Spicy Zucchini Bars

½   cup firmly packed brown sugar

½   cup sugar

¾   cup margarine, softened

1¾ cups flour

½   teaspoon baking powder

1   teaspoon cinnamon

½   teaspoon nutmeg

2   eggs

1   teaspoon vanilla

2   cups shredded zucchini, patted dry with paper towels

½-1 cup chopped pecans

½   cup coconut

Preheat oven to 350°. Grease a 15x10 inch jellyroll pan. In a large bowl, cream together brown sugar, sugar and margarine. Mix flour, baking powder, cinnamon, nutmeg, eggs and vanilla into creamed mixture. Stir in zucchini, nuts and coconut. Spread evenly in pan. Bake 30 to 35 minutes until light golden brown. Cool.

FROSTING

3   cups powdered sugar

1   teaspoon cinnamon

3   tablespoons milk

3   tablespoons margarine, softened

1   teaspoon vanilla

Blend frosting ingredients until creamy. Spread over baked cake. Refrigerate and cut into bars.

MAGIC COOKIE BARS

½ cup butter

1½ cups graham cracker crumbs

1 (14 ounce) can sweetened condensed milk

½ cup semisweet chocolate chips

½ cup butterscotch chips

½ cup flaked coconut

½ cup pecans or walnuts, chopped

Preheat oven to 350° (325° if glass dish.) Melt butter in 9x13 inch pan. Sprinkle crumbs over butter. Pour condensed milk evenly over crumbs. Top with remaining ingredients. Bake 25 minutes or until lightly browned. Cool and cut into bars.

Lemon Squares

CRUST

2	sticks butter, softened	½	cup powdered sugar
2	cups plain flour		

Preheat oven to 325°. Mix butter, flour and sugar. Press into a 10x14 inch pan. Bake 15 minutes.

LEMON FILLING

4	eggs	1	tablespoon plain flour
2	cups sugar	½	teaspoon baking powder
6	tablespoons fresh lemon juice	1	cup chopped pecans

Preheat oven to 325°. Beat eggs slightly. Add sugar, lemon juice, flour, baking powder and pecans. Mix and pour on top of pastry. Bake 40 to 50 minutes.

"And we know that in all things God works for the good of those who love him, who have been called according to his purpose."

Romans 8:28

Toffee Bars

1	package saltine crackers	1	(12 ounce) package milk chocolate chips
1	cup butter or margarine		
1	cup sugar	1	cup chopped walnuts or pecans

Preheat oven to 400°. Line a 10x17 inch cookie sheet with foil. It must have a raised edge on all sides. Grease foil with butter wrapper. Cover foil completely with layer of saltines. Melt butter in saucepan, add sugar. Bring to a boil 5 minutes, stirring constantly. Spread quickly onto saltines. Bake 4 minutes or until they have a light caramel look. Sprinkle chocolate chips on top. Place back in oven 3 minutes. Spread chocolate out. Sprinkle nuts on top and press down. Refrigerate overnight (or freeze if you need them quicker). Break into small pieces.

May add ½ (10 ounce) bag chocolate-covered toffee bits to top.

Cream Cheese Mints

1	(8 ounce) package cream cheese
¼	cup butter, softened
1	(2 pound) package powdered sugar
½	teaspoon peppermint extract
	Food coloring, optional
	Powdered sugar

Cook cream cheese and butter in a saucepan over low heat, stirring constantly until smooth. Gradually stir in package of powdered sugar; stir in extract. If desired, divide mixture into 2 portions. Stir in different food coloring.

After mixture cools a bit and begins to stiffen, shape mixture into 1 inch balls. Dip a 2 inch round cookie stamp or bottom of a glass into powdered sugar. Press each ball to flatten. Let stand uncovered 4 hours or until firm. May be frozen.

Homemade Snickers

½	cup butter	30	single wrap caramels
⅓	cup cocoa	1	tablespoon water
¼	cup milk	2	cups salted peanuts
¼	cup brown sugar	½	cup semi-sweet chocolate chips
3½	cups powdered sugar	½	cup milk chocolate chips
1	teaspoon vanilla		

Combine butter, cocoa, brown sugar, and milk. Microwave until it boils. Stir in powdered sugar and vanilla. Pour into a greased 8x8 inch pan.

In another bowl, heat caramels and water until melted. Stir in the peanuts and spread over chocolate layer. Microwave the semi-sweet and milk chocolate chips and spread over caramel. Chill until firm. Slice into pieces.

CHOCOLATE COVERED PEANUT BUTTER CUPS

1½ sticks margarine

1 cup creamy peanut butter

1 pound box powdered sugar

Chocolate bark candy coating

Melt margarine over low heat. Add peanut butter and sugar. Remove from heat and mix well. Press into a 9x13 inch pan. Melt chocolate and pour over mixture. Let stand until firm. Cut into small squares.

Toffee Brittle

1½ cups chopped toasted pecans, divided
1 cup sugar
1 cup butter
1 tablespoon light corn syrup
¼ cup water
1 cup semi-sweet chocolate chips

Spread 1 cup pecans into a 9 inch circle on a lightly greased baking sheet. Bring sugar, butter, corn syrup and water to a boil in a heavy saucepan over medium-high heat, stirring constantly. Cook until mixture is golden brown and a candy thermometer registers 290° to 310° (about 15 minutes).

Pour sugar mixture over pecans on baking sheet. Sprinkle with morsels; let stand 30 seconds. Spread melted morsels evenly over top; sprinkle with remaining ½ cup chopped pecans. Chill 1 hour. Break into bite-sized pieces and store in airtight container.

Microwave Peanut Brittle

1¼ cups dry roasted peanuts
1 cup sugar
½ cup white corn syrup
¼ teaspoon salt
1 teaspoon vanilla
1 tablespoon butter
1 teaspoon baking soda

Combine peanuts, sugar, corn syrup and salt in an 8 cup ovenproof glass container (with handle). Stir with wooden spoon and leave spoon in cup during cooking. Cook on high 4 minutes. Stir and cook 3 minutes. Add vanilla and butter. Stir and cook 1½ minutes on high. Stir in baking soda and pour onto a greased (butter) cookie sheet. Spread thin. Cool and break into pieces. Store in sealed bag to prevent getting sticky.

This is so good that you never would believe that it was cooked in a microwave.

MICROWAVE CHOCOLATE FUDGE

3 cups milk chocolate morsels

1 (14 ounce) can sweetened condensed milk

¼ cup butter, cut into pieces

Combine all ingredients in a 2 quart glass bowl. Microwave chocolate mixture at medium (50% power) 5 minutes, stirring at 1½ minute intervals. Pour into a greased 8 inch square dish. Cover and chill 8 hours. Cut into 1½ inch squares. Store in refrigerator.

Microwave Truffles

6 ounces semi-sweet chocolate chips
6 ounces milk chocolate chips
¼ cup finely chopped pecans
¼ cup finely chopped almonds
¼ cup plus 2 tablespoons whipping cream
2 teaspoons almond extract
¼ cup butter

Place 24 small foil candy cups in miniature muffin cups or on a baking sheet. Spoon ½ teaspoon of almonds and pecans into each cup. Set aside cups and remaining almonds and pecans.

In a 2 quart microwave-safe bowl, combine chocolate chips and butter. Microwave at 50% power 1½ minutes or until melted. Stir in cream and extract. Beat with an electric mixer until slightly thickened, scraping sides of bowl occasionally. Pour into prepared cups. Top with remaining nuts. Refrigerate until set.

Pecan Praline Popcorn

6½ quarts popped corn
1 cup pecan halves or pieces
2 sticks butter
½ cup light corn syrup
2 cups packed brown sugar
2 teaspoons salt
1 teaspoon baking soda

Grease large roasting pan. Put popped corn and pecans in roasting pan and set aside. In saucepan, heat butter, syrup, sugar and salt. Bring to a boil. Maintain boil at medium-high heat for 5 minutes, stirring constantly. Remove from heat and stir. Vigorously beat in baking soda. Pour mixture over popped corn. Place in 225° oven 1 hour, stirring every 15 minutes to coat corn. Pour out on foil or waxed paper to cool. Store in airtight container.

For easy clean up use a disposable aluminum roasting pan.

MICROWAVE DIVINITY

4 cups sugar

1 cup corn syrup

¾ cup water

¼ teaspoon salt

3 egg whites

1 teaspoon vanilla extract

1 cup pecans

Mix sugar, syrup, water and salt in 2 quart microwave-safe dish and stir. Microwave 19 minutes. Stir every 5 minutes. Beat egg whites until stiff. Slowly pour syrup mixture over egg whites and beat 12 minutes with electric mixer or by hand until stiff. Add vanilla extract and pecans. Drop by tablespoon on wax paper. May also spread in pan or dish and cut into squares.

Pralines

1½ cups sugar
1½ cups firmly packed brown sugar
1 cup evaporated milk

¼ cup butter
2 cups pecan halves, toasted
1 teaspoon vanilla extract

Bring sugars and milk to a boil in a Dutch oven, stirring often. Cook over medium heat, stirring often, 11 minutes or until a candy thermometer registers 228° (thread stage). Stir in butter and pecans. Cook stirring constantly, until candy thermometer registers 236° (soft ball stage).

Remove from heat, stir in vanilla. Beat with a wooden spoon 1 to 2 minutes or just until mixture begins to thicken. Quickly drop by heaping tablespoons onto buttered parchment paper; let stand until firm.

It is important to let the mixture begin to thicken before dropping it onto the parchment paper.

Pralines can be eaten as a candy, ground and used as a filling or dessert ingredient, or sprinkled atop desserts as a garnish.

Bourbon-Pecan Toffee: Substitute ¼ cup bourbon for ¼ cup water. Proceed as directed.

Almond Toffee: Substitute 1 cup of chopped toasted slivered almonds for 1 cup chopped pecans to sprinkle on baking sheet. Substitute ½ cup toasted sliced almonds for ½ cup chopped pecans to sprinkle over chocolate. Proceed as directed.

Hawaiian Toffee: Substitute 1 cup chopped toasted macadamia nuts for 1 cup chopped pecans to sprinkle on baking sheet. Substitute ½ cup toasted sweetened flaked coconut for ½ cup chopped pecans to sprinkle over chocolate. Proceed as directed.

"I am the vine; you are the branches. If a man remains in me and I in him, he will bear much fruit, apart from me you can do nothing."

John 15:5

"Many, O Lord my God, are the wonders you have done. The things you planned for us no one can recount to you. Were I to speak and tell of them, they would be too many to declare."

Psalm 40:5

Adams Family Peach Ice Cream

2   cups fresh sliced peaches
1½ cups sugar
1   (12 ounce) can evaporated
    milk
1   (14 ounce) can sweetened
    condensed milk

1   pint half-and-half
1   (16 ounce) container frozen
    non-dairy whipped topping
2   teaspoons vanilla

Mash peaches and sugar together in large bowl until sugar dissolves. Stir in evaporated milk, sweetened condensed milk, half-and-half, whipped topping and vanilla. Pour into ice cream freezer and follow manufacturer's directions. Pour into airtight freezer container; freeze 2 hours before serving.

This is a very creamy ice cream.

Makes 4 quarts

CHOCOLATE ICE CREAM

6 chocolate-covered caramel nougat candy bars

1 (14 ounce) can sweetened condensed milk

1 (12 ounce) can evaporated milk

½ gallon milk

3 eggs

2 small packages instant chocolate pudding

Melt candy bars on low heat. Stir in milks, eggs, and pudding; mix well. Pour into ice cream freezer and follow manufacturer's directions.

Banana Split Ice Cream

4   eggs
1¼ cups sugar
6   cups milk
½   teaspoon salt
1   (14 ounce) can sweetened
    condensed milk

2   cups half-and-half
1   tablespoon vanilla flavoring
2   bananas, chopped
1   (10 ounce) jar maraschino
    cherries, drained and
    chopped

Beat eggs at medium speed until frothy. Gradually add sugar; beat until thick. Add milk and salt. Pour into saucepan, stir constantly over low heat until thoroughly heated. Let cool. Add sweetened condensed milk, half-and-half, vanilla, bananas and cherries. Place in refrigerator 30 minutes. Pour into ice cream freezer and follow manufacturer's directions.

Len Berg's HMFPIC – Homemade Fresh Peach Ice Cream

7   cups half-and-half
1   quart puréed peaches
3   cups sugar

3   tablespoons lemon juice
¼   teaspoon salt
1   teaspoon almond flavoring

Mix half-and-half, peaches, sugar, salt, lemon juice and almond flavoring. Pour into ice cream freezer and chill container in freezer for 2 hours before inserting into churn. Churn according to manufacturer's directions.

LEN BERG'S RESTAURANT

The announcement, "HMFPIC – You Know Where" is a familiar reminder of this special summer treat which was served at Len Berg's Restaurant. Len Berg's Restaurant was founded in 1908 by Mr. Leonard Berg and was later owned by Mr. and Mrs. Arthur P. Barry, Sr. In 1968, Mr. Jeff Amerson purchased the restaurant, which was later owned and operated by his son, Jerry. Len Berg's was located in the Old Post Office Alley in downtown Macon since 1950 and was visited by many generations of Maconites for over 55 years.

Orange Sherbet Ice Cream

1   (20 ounce) can crushed pineapple, undrained

1   (14 ounce) can sweetened condensed milk
1   (2 liter) bottle orange soda

Combine pineapple and sweetened condensed milk. Add soda; stir. Place into ice cream freezer and follow manufacturer's directions.

Strawberry Ice Cream

4	cups sliced fresh strawberries	2	(14 ounce) cans sweetened condensed milk
½	cup sugar		
2	cups heavy whipping cream	4	cups half-and-half
		1	vanilla bean, split lengthwise

In a medium bowl, combine strawberries and sugar. Let stand 30 minutes.

In a large bowl, beat cream at medium-high speed with a mixer until soft peaks form. Add condensed milk and beat until stiff peaks form. Add half-and-half, beating until combined. Scrape seeds from vanilla bean into cream mixture. Stir in strawberry mixture.

Pour mixture into the container of an electric ice cream freezer. Freeze according to manufacturer's instructions. Ice cream will be soft. For a firmer ice cream, place in a freezer safe container and freeze.

Peach Sauce

4	medium peaches, peeled and pitted	1	tablespoon cornstarch
¼	cup light corn syrup	1	tablespoon water
¼	cup sugar	2	tablespoons light rum

Simmer the peaches in a heavy saucepan covered in water 10 minutes. Drain peaches and purée in blender or food processor. Discard the water.

Put purée back in pan and add corn syrup and sugar. Stir cornstarch into water in a separate bowl until dissolved. Stir cornstarch mixture into purée and bring to a boil over high heat.

Remove from heat, stir in rum and cool to room temperature.

Serve immediately. Serve over freshly cut peaches, cakes, bread pudding or rice pudding.

BLUEBERRY SAUCE

⅓ cup sugar

½ teaspoon ground cinnamon

2 teaspoons cornstarch

Pinch of salt

1 pint blueberries, washed, stems removed

¼ cup fresh squeezed lemon juice

Stir sugar, cinnamon, cornstarch and salt in a heavy pan. Stir over medium heat until sugar melts. Add in blueberries and stir until they pop and sauce becomes clear. Stir in the lemon juice and serve immediately, while very warm.

Serve over vanilla ice cream, pound cake, pancakes, waffles or French toast.

CUSTARD SAUCE

6 egg yolks

⅔ cup sugar, divided

2 cups milk

1 tablespoon brandy

1 teaspoon vanilla extract

Whisk together egg yolks and ⅓ cup sugar in a large bowl 3 minutes or until blended. Bring milk and remaining ⅓ cup sugar to a boil in a medium saucepan, whisking constantly. Stir about ¼ of hot milk mixture gradually into yolks; add to remaining hot mixture, stirring constantly. Cook over medium-low heat, stirring constantly, 10 minutes or until custard is thick enough to coat back of a wooden spoon. Remove from heat. Pour through a fine wire mesh strainer in a bowl. Stir in brandy and vanilla.

Chocolate Sauce

4	squares unsweetened chocolate	1½	cups sugar
1	stick butter	½	cup cocoa
		½	pint heavy cream

Melt chocolate and butter in top of double boiler, add sugar and cocoa. Cook 45 minutes, stirring often. Mixture will look curdled. Do not be alarmed. Add cream and cook 10 additional minutes, continuing to stir. Serve hot.

Store sauce in a jar in the refrigerator where it will keep about a month.

Delicious on vanilla ice cream with toasted pecans, on a cake, or for dipping fruit.

Ultimate Fudge Sauce

1	cup heavy whipping cream	⅓	cup corn syrup
¾	cup sugar	¼	cup unsalted butter
8	ounces unsweetened chocolate, firmly chopped	1½	teaspoons vanilla extract
		¼	teaspoon salt

Combine whipping cream and sugar in a heavy saucepan. Place over medium heat and cook, stirring constantly, until sugar dissolves. Stir in chocolate, corn syrup and butter. Cook over medium-low heat, stirring constantly, until chocolate melts and all ingredients are blended.

Remove from heat; stir in vanilla and salt. Let cool to room temperature. Transfer sauce to jars with tight-fitting lids. Store in refrigerator.

To serve, spoon sauce into a microwave-safe bowl and microwave at high for 20 second intervals or until able to pour.

"*I* will bless her with abundant provisions;
Her poor will I satisfy with food."

Psalm 132:15

Index

242